Personalized Learning in Gifted Education

Gifted students can exhibit extreme variance in both their abilities and their interests, yet they are often treated within schools as one homogeneous, specialized population. *Personalized Learning in Gifted Education* helps educators strengthen their differentiation of both instruction and services for advanced students.

This book:

- helps educators develop the specific gifts and talents of the gifted students they serve
- demonstrates how educators can utilize the wealth of data they have at their disposal
- provides a rationale and blueprint for a stronger, more personalized approach to gifted education
- offers suggestions for both elementary and secondary schools.

Recommendations center around five features of personalized learning: personalized learning plans, project- or problem-based learning, competency-based progression through the curriculum, criterion-referenced assessments, and multi-year mentoring.

Todd Kettler is Associate Professor of Educational Psychology at Baylor University, USA. He is Co-Editor of the *Journal of Advanced Academics*, and his research and teaching focus on gifted education models and learning designs to support exceptional achievement.

Cheryl Taliaferro has worked as a teacher and administrator in gifted education for more than 25 years. She currently serves as District Liaison for ASPIRE Academy for Highly Gifted Students in Grapevine, Texas, and teaches graduate courses in Curriculum and Instruction at Texas A&M-Commerce.

Personalized Learning in Gifted Education

Differentiated Instruction That Maximizes Students' Potential

Todd Kettler and Cheryl Taliaferro

NEW YORK AND LONDON

Cover image: Shutterstock

First published 2022
by Routledge
605 Third Avenue, New York, NY 10158

and by Routledge
2 Park Square, Milton Park, Abingdon, Oxon, OX14 4RN

Routledge is an imprint of the Taylor & Francis Group, an informa business

© 2022 Taylor & Francis

The right of Todd Kettler and Cheryl Taliaferro to be identified as authors of this work has been asserted in accordance with sections 77 and 78 of the Copyright, Designs and Patents Act 1988.

All rights reserved. No part of this book may be reprinted or reproduced or utilised in any form or by any electronic, mechanical, or other means, now known or hereafter invented, including photocopying and recording, or in any information storage or retrieval system, without permission in writing from the publishers.

Trademark notice: Product or corporate names may be trademarks or registered trademarks, and are used only for identification and explanation without intent to infringe.

Library of Congress Cataloging-in-Publication Data
Names: Kettler, Todd, author. | Taliaferro, Cheryl, author.
Title: Personalized learning in gifted education: differentiated
instruction that maximizes students' potential / Todd Kettler and Cheryl Taliaferro.
Description: New York, NY : Routledge, 2022. |
Includes bibliographical references.
Identifiers: LCCN 2021044831 (print) | LCCN 2021044832 (ebook) |
ISBN 9781032145006 (hardback) | ISBN 9781646322022 (paperback) |
ISBN 9781003237136 (ebook)
Subjects: LCSH: Gifted children–Education. | Individualized instruction.
Classification: LCC LC3993 .K47 2022 (print) |
LCC LC3993 (ebook) | DDC 371.95–dc23/eng/20211012
LC record available at https://lccn.loc.gov/2021044831
LC ebook record available at https://lccn.loc.gov/2021044832

ISBN: 978-1-032-14500-6 (hbk)
ISBN: 978-1-646-32202-2 (pbk)
ISBN: 978-1-003-23713-6 (ebk)

DOI: 10.4324/9781003237136

Typeset in Optima
by Newgen Publishing UK

Access the Support Material: www.routledge.com/9781646322022

Contents

List of Figures — vii
List of Tables — viii

PART I: FOUNDATIONS OF PERSONALIZED LEARNING — 1

1. The Theory and History of Personalized Learning — 3
2. Gifted Education, Talent Development, and Personalized Learning — 28
3. Personalized Learning and Student Achievement — 53

PART II: CORE STRATEGIES OF PERSONALIZED LEARNING IN GIFTED EDUCATION — 75

4. Personalized Talent Development Plans — 77
5. Competency-Based Progressions and Acceleration — 102
6. Inquiry Models of Learning — 125
7. Criterion-Referenced Assessment of Student Progress — 147
8. Multi-Year Mentoring for Talent Development — 170

Contents

PART III: APPLYING PERSONALIZED LEARNING IN GIFTED EDUCATION   195

9. Personalized Learning Examples in Gifted Education   197

10. The Role of Technology in Personalized Learning   216

11. Implementation of and Teacher Support for Personalized Learning   243

Figures

2.1	Foundations of Gifted Education	33
2.2	Social, Emotional, and Cognitive Development in Gifted Education Learning Environments	40
4.1	Self-Assessment for the Implementation of Personalized Learning Plans	84
4.2	Assessment Rubric for Gifted Students' Personalized Talent Development Plans	87
4.3	Worksheet for Developing an Advanced Learning Plan	92
4.4	Skills Self-Assessed and Developed by Middle School Students in ASPIRE Academy's Personalized Learning Plan	96
6.1	Design-Based Inquiry Learning Cycle	138
6.2	Creative Problem-Solving Inquiry Model	141
7.1	Template for English Language Arts Depth and Complexity Text Analysis	161
7.2	English Language Arts Depth and Complexity Text Analysis: *Harrison Bergeron*	162
8.1	Seven Facets of Mentoring for Talent Development	174
9.1	ASPIRE Academy Supplemental Report Card	207
10.1	Four Functions of Technology in Personalized Learning	222
11.1	Applying Kotter's (1996) Model of Change to Implement Personalized Learning	260

Tables

2.1	Skills Associated with Advanced Cognitive Development	34
2.2	Comparing Personalized Learning and Differentiation	38
2.3	Recommended Program Elements in Gifted Education	42
3.1	Elements of Effective Schools or Programs	66
5.1	States Utilizing Competency-Based Progressions in 2017	107
5.2	State Policies for Acceleration	109
5.3	Types of Acceleration	111
6.1	Principles of Inquiry Learning	126
6.2	Teacher Role Using the Problem-Based Learning Inquiry Model	131
7.1	Modified Depth and Complexity Frame	160
7.2	Stakeholder Meeting Chart	163
7.3	Intended and Unintended Consequences	165
7.4	Elements Assessed in Middle School Texas Performance Standards Project	167
8.1	Mentorship Typology	173
10.1	Transformative Technology Is Changing the Role of Teachers	217
10.2	Average Effects of 1:1 Technology Programs on Student Achievement	218
10.3	Student Use of Technology in Personalized Learning Education	224
10.4	Examples of Technology Tools to Support Personalized Learning	238
11.1	Bray and McClaskey's (2013) Stages of Personalized Learning Environments	249

PART

I

Foundations of Personalized Learning

# The Theory and History of Personalized Learning

If you read reports or news stories about the current state of the American K–12 education system, you are likely to get somewhat depressed. In addition to facing very real challenges regarding how to maintain the physical and emotional safety of students while they attend school, schools also appear to be floundering to meet their most essential purpose – educational achievement. At the end of each school year, standardized test scores in various forms are reported to parents and community members, and each new reporting cycle is typically accompanied by a slew of meetings on school campuses as administrators and teachers seek to target their students' deficiencies and develop plans for raising scores in specific areas during the upcoming school year. Of almost singular concern are scores that fall below basic levels of proficiency.

However, this *quasi*-obsession with test scores that has overtaken much of modern schooling's mission and purpose over the past several decades does not seem to be producing much in the way of significant improvement. For the past decade, results from the National Assessment of Educational Progress, which determines achievement levels in core subjects for American students in grades 4, 8, and 12, have remained lackluster, with a mixture of some modest gains as well as some modest losses reported each year. Perhaps more concerningly, though, the percentage of American students scoring at advanced levels in various subject areas remains fairly small, typically in the single digits, with obvious gaps persisting among different subgroups (The Nation's Report Card, 2020). Similarly, results from international tests indicate that elementary and secondary schools

DOI: 10.4324/9781003237136-2

in the United States are simply not producing enough students who have achieved academic excellence (Plucker & Peters, 2016).

As so many schools focus their time, energy, and monetary resources seemingly spinning their wheels over the problem of how to raise achievement levels from below basic or basic to proficient, it is no wonder that parents of gifted and advanced students feel like their children are being left behind. Visit any online forum or attend a conference devoted to gifted students, and it won't take long to find the parents searching for recommendations and assistance on how to meet their children's educational needs. Many of their children seem trapped in a system that is either unsympathetic or unable to help them. However, while most educators will readily admit that our educational system's hyper-focus on test scores and academic proficiency in core content areas is both inappropriate and ineffective, too few seem to be able to break free of the system that has been created.

It doesn't mean breaking free is impossible, though. What is required is a paradigm shift. The current paradigm under which our educational system exists has created a host of problems for individual students and for society at large, which needs a large talent pool of well-educated individuals to solve its most pressing problems and to help it continue to advance. To change the current paradigm, we need to return to an understanding that education, at its best, is not about group averages or group proficiency. Education is about identifying and fostering the passions, interests, and talents of individual students in ways that will benefit both the students and society. Education is not about the group. Education is personal.

Hoping to achieve this type of paradigm shift, some schools over the past decade have turned to personalized learning. Spurred by promises offered through recent advances in educational technology and funded by federal, state, and local governments, as well as private foundations that understand the current system is simply failing too many students in too many ways, these schools have sought to reconceptualize education. They have envisioned and implemented personalized learning in a variety of ways and, while the research base on its effectiveness is not yet robust, it does indicate that personalized learning holds promise for providing an alternative to traditional schooling that takes into account the needs of individual students rather than groups. It may, therefore, be one of the best ways to ensure that gifted and advanced students receive the appropriate level of education that has eluded too many them for far too long.

Theories and Practices That Inform Personalized Learning

Personalized learning is not a theory or an established pedagogy in itself. Rather, it is an approach to teaching – perhaps a pedagogical approach whose current form is still in its infancy – with many existing variations. If you ask ten educators what they believe personalized learning looks like in schools, you are likely to receive ten different responses. Although a common definition of personalized learning is still being developed, it is generally understood to be a student-centered approach that takes into account individual students' skill levels, interests, and talents in order to create learning experiences that are meaningful for them. Several common elements exist among the variations in the ways it is practiced. Additionally, it does draw in its various implementations from a rich history of educational theories and well-established, research-based practices. The next subsection of this chapter will trace some of the theories and practices that inform our current understandings of personalized learning.

Earliest Forms of Personalized Learning

Education is the means by which cultural capital (Bourdieu, 1990) is transferred from one generation to the next. This cultural capital includes the knowledge, behavior, and skills that a person needs in order to be a well-regarded member of society. Passing on cultural capital from one generation to the next ensures both the practical survival of each new generation and the survival of the culture or society itself. From the earliest of times, human beings have sought to pass on to their progeny the knowledge, skills, values, and social norms most prized by their social groups through informal educational processes that were highly personalized.

In its earliest forms, education was a type of informal apprenticeship, as mothers, fathers, and elder family members taught each child how to fulfill the expected duties of their role within the society. Hunting, farming, defense methods, domestic skills, and religious practices were taught individually or in small groups. Lessons typically continued until they were adequately learned because oftentimes survival depended on it. Traditionally, mothers taught their daughters how to cook and care for

Foundations

children, and fathers taught their sons to farm, hunt, and fight. During quiet family times and during communal gatherings, stories were passed down, often orally and religious in nature, in order to teach lessons and to serve as guides for behavior.

Historically, as technological capabilities continued to advance, work became more specialized, and education expanded to include formal apprenticeships in trades and crafts, such as blacksmithing, masonry, and baking. These formal apprenticeships were also personalized in the sense that the apprentices learned a specialized skill, either individually or in small groups, until they mastered it. Whether the apprenticeship was voluntary or forced, the lessons did have an immediate relevance to the learner's own life, and learning necessarily progressed at the apprentice's personal rate of skill development. The educational value of these informal and formal apprenticeships is comparable in purpose to modern internships and mentorships.

Education broadly conceived as a pursuit of deeper knowledge of language, science, history, philosophy, and the arts was often reserved for members of the upper class and religious leaders, and it was oftentimes provided by private tutors, whose teaching skills and methods varied considerably. However, at least one student-centered teaching practice has been highlighted as a centerpiece of effective instruction since the days of ancient Greece, when Socrates spent days at the agora, an Athenian marketplace, surrounded by aristocratic youth desiring to be educated by him. It was in this environment that Socrates refined a radical, new educational method that would eventually come to bear his name. His open-ended questioning strategy allowed students to ask questions about topics of importance to them. Rather than providing answers to the students' questions, Socrates responded with additional questions that encouraged the students to engage in deeper thinking about the topic.

Known today as the Socratic method, this style of teaching is dependent on dialogue and requires students to actively participate in their own learning and, thusly, in the construction of meaning. Socratic discussions provide an opportunity for students to think deeply and critically, and to explore a variety of viewpoints concerning what is true, what is good, and what is just. They are currently utilized in a range of secondary classrooms around the country. Socratic seminars are frequently recommended in professional development sessions for Gifted and Talented teachers, Advanced Placement (AP) teachers, and Advancement Via Individual

Determination (AVID) teachers. This student-centered instructional method represents an early, more formally structured form of personalized learning.

Industrialized Schooling in the United States

As it was first instituted, formal schooling in the United States varied according to geographic location and social class. Some members of society – especially women, non-Anglos, and lower-class Whites living in sparsely populated areas – may have received no formal education in literacy, math, history, or science at all in their lifetimes. In contrast, members of the middle and upper classes, particularly those living in established communities in the Northeast, may have employed private tutors or attended either public or private schools for as many years as feasible for their family's social and economic situation. Middle- and upper-class boys, especially those who intended to obtain leadership roles in society, often attended a Latin grammar school, whose purpose was to prepare them for university admissions.

As the United States continued to expand, and as having a literate population came to be more widely viewed as a necessary condition for the success of the country as a whole, formal education began to become more commonplace. In its earliest forms, this education may have lasted for only a few years and was meant to impart basic literacy, math, and civics skills to students. Especially in small, rural communities, early public education consisted of all of the community's children learning together in a one-room schoolhouse with a single teacher. In this model, differentiation had to be practiced as the students were of a wide variety of different ages; however, in accordance with generally-accepted religious and social norms that reinforced the belief that children should be quiet and obedient, rules and procedures tended to be rigid, allowing scant regard for the children's ability to be autonomous learners. It would be difficult to conceive of this type of environment as anything other than teacher-centered.

As the Industrial Revolution changed the landscape of the United States, education also changed. The rapid increase in the number of available jobs in factories led to greater urbanization, as people left their farms and moved to cities in order to work. Child labor laws were instituted in order to protect children from dangerous work conditions, and the expectation spread that all children needed to receive at least a basic, formal education. Coupled with greater concern for children's rights were industrialists' growing needs for educated workers. In the mid-1800s, individual state governments began making education compulsory, with the final state passing a compulsory education law in 1917. Although a common agreement had been reached within the United States that all of its citizens should be educated, disagreements arose about what content should be taught and what teaching practices should be utilized.

A common criticism leveraged against American schooling as it is traditionally practiced is that it has relied for too long on a factory model of education. Drawing a comparison to the factories that spurred economic and social growth during the Industrial Revolution, critics complain that public schools – like urbanization – remove children too far from their natural learning environments. Something important to the act of education has been lost as a result.

Instead of treating children like human beings with unique talents and interests, the American education system treats students like products that can be moved along a metaphorical assembly line of schooling. At each new stage of the assembly line, the children receive a few new parts, which equate to the knowledge or skills that schools impart to them at each new grade level. Students are expected to emerge at the end of this assembly line, typically at age 18, as some sort of completed product. Quality-checks and controls are put into place to ensure that each part of the assembly line works efficiently to complete its role. Organized in groups according to age, students are expected to progress through a similar curriculum at a similar rate, in a manner that fails to account for individual variations in the students themselves.

The student's role in this system necessarily is passive, and obedience and conformity are expected. When the educational assembly line doesn't work as intended and people become disillusioned with the overall product, as occurred during the 1950s when Russia launched *Sputnik* and beat the United States to outer space, and again in the 1980s when *A Nation at Risk: The Imperative for Educational Reform* (US National Commission on Excellence in Education, 1983) reported that American schools were failing, additional quality checks and controls are put in place. In recent decades, standardized testing has become ubiquitous in public schools as state and federal governments try to hold schools and teachers accountable for students learning in a system that was never designed to meet all of their needs.

Theory and History of Personalized Learning

At best, criticism against the way that traditional schooling has developed lays bare the reality that many modern schools are designed to advance a whole group of same-aged students to a predetermined level of basic competency and to reward them for complacency and obedience – skills that industrialists often value in their workers. It is not designed to create opportunities for individual students to develop their capacities to the highest extent possible. At worst, critics claim that schools are intentionally designed to withhold an advanced education from the general population in order to maintain the *status quo* within society, with the power of the elite held firmly in place through the additional opportunities they can access outside of the traditional school setting. Students who do not have regular opportunities to question, critique, or develop advanced skills will surely not become adults who make any kind of meaningful advances within society. Personalized learning can only be fully understood in contrast to this system, a system to which it offers a more meaningful alternative.

Progressive Education

As a reaction against industrialized and depersonalized methods of education, several educational reformers have sought alternate solutions, all of which returned the child to the center of the learning process. Elements of all of these solutions can be seen in modern conceptualizations of personalized learning.

Perhaps one of the earliest contributors to child-centered education and a harbinger of Progressive education, French philosopher Jean-Jacques Rousseau (1969, originally published 1750–1755) sought to discover the laws of nature and hoped to offer a way to align society with those natural laws. Believing that human beings are born naturally good but that society and humankind's actions corrupt individuals, Rousseau (1979, originally published 1762) considered nature to be the great educator, as it bestows knowledge to human beings directly through their senses, without the artificial, human practices that can make formal schooling tedious and ineffectual. Accordingly, he advocated that education should follow children through their natural stages of development and that instruction should be active and experience-based.

Another strong advocate of child-centered education, Italian physician and educator Maria Montessori (1995, originally published 1967; 2002,

9

originally published 1912) believed that an educator's work should be centered around recognizing and respecting each child's unique personality. Like Rousseau, she developed a system of education that followed the phases of children's natural development, with early lessons designed around practical activities, such as setting a table, folding cloth, and learning how to tie laces and fasten buttons. These early practical activities increase a child's sense of independence and self-reliance, while also developing the fine motor skills needed for writing and work. Writing, reading, and math lessons likewise leverage students' senses in the early years and develop their concrete thinking with specialized manipulatives, such as sandpaper letters, golden beads strung together to represent different quantities, and rods and blocks of all shapes and sizes. The teacher carefully structures the learning environment for the children, yet the children move through it at their own pace under the direction of the teacher. Since children learn and develop at different rates, they are grouped into multi-age classrooms, typically with three traditional grade levels in each class. This structure facilitates children engaging in collaborative activities with intellectual peers. Students typically receive an individual or small group lesson when they are ready to be introduced to a new concept or skill, and then they practice on their own, receiving regular feedback from the teacher. Rather than offering traditional grades, teachers utilize standards-based grading in which they track their students' progress on learning specific skills and concepts by indicating degrees of mastery for each one.

In the United States, one of the foremost educational reformers was Progressive educator John Dewey. Believing that the purpose of education is human growth and that education should be social and truly democratic in nature, Dewey (2009, originally published 1916) maintained that educational goals cannot be predetermined. Rather, Dewey's educational methods, which he practiced as founder of the University of Chicago Laboratory Schools, relied on experimentalism and problem-based learning. Supplied with an environment rich in tools and guided by teachers, students of all ages engaged in the authentic work of investigating problems in non-traditional classroom spaces, including gardens, kitchens, workshops and labs. Academic skills and knowledge were developed in these authentic contexts, with students learning new material as they needed it to solve an existing problem. Students and teachers therefore shared responsibility for the curriculum.

Constructivism

Building on the work of Progressive educators, Constructivists also posit that knowledge is socially constructed and that education should be student-centered. Constructivist theories are heavily rooted in Jean Piaget's theories of cognitive development (Ginsburg & Opper, 1969). Piaget (1959) described knowledge as being actively constructed by the child; whenever a new idea is encountered, the child must reconcile it with their own prior knowledge during a process described as either *assimilation* or *accommodation*. The child either assimilates the new knowledge into ideas that are already known, or the child adjusts what was previously understood to make sense of the new information.

Piaget's ideas heavily influenced other theorists whose ideas can also be seen in the conceptualizations of personalized learning that focus on students actively participating in their own learning while being guided by teachers who create the optimal conditions for that learning. Lev Vygotsky (1978) described the ideal point of instruction as being in the child's *zone of proximal development*, a place where learning is neither too easy nor too hard but can be accomplished with some assistance. Jerome Bruner (Ratner & Bruner, 1978) referred to the assistance that children need as *scaffolding* (Wood et al., 1976). Scaffolding should not be construed as occurring in a dyadic relationship, in which one expert or authority figure constructs all of the scaffolding deemed necessary for the student to learn. Rather, it implies an activity that is dialogic in nature and in which several players may work together to construct the scaffolding that helps another learn. Similarly, Louise Rosenblatt's reader-response theory asserts that understanding is actively constructed by readers each time they transact with a text, either for informational purposes or for pleasure (Rosenblatt, 1994, originally published 1978; Rosenblatt, 1995, originally published 1938). A reader's interpretation of a text is heavily influenced by the reader's past experiences, both personally and academically, and can change upon rereading. One aspect of the teacher's role is to help facilitate the student's thinking about the text and thus help the student develop a deeper understanding of how their own experiences are shaping the interpretation in appropriate or inappropriate ways.

Critical Pedagogy

In more recent decades, as civil rights issues have come to the forefront of society and education, critical theories in education have expanded on the work of Progressives and Constructivists in order to advocate directly for social justice and social change. As an instructional approach, critical pedagogy grew out of the work of Paulo Freire, a Brazilian educator whose family was thrust into poverty when he was young. During this experience, it became apparent to him that students cannot learn when they are hungry, and he dedicated his life to helping others leverage education and literacy to overcome social injustices. Freire (2000, originally published 1968) rejected what he described as the banking model of education, a metaphor which compares students to empty piggy banks waiting to be filled with knowledge by a teacher. This description is similar to the factory metaphor used to criticize American education. Instead, Freire advocated for a re-envisioning of education in which students have a place as co-creators of knowledge. Viewing education as inherently political, critical pedagogy is designed to help students question and challenge oppression. Similar to the preceding theories, critical pedagogy is student-centered and seeks to help students use education to solve real problems in life. Critical theorists maintain that student-centered dialogic discussions are the key to learning and they describe these dialogic processes as liberatory, as students have a voice in their own learning and thus actively participate in the formation of their education and their selves. Critical theories also inform personalized learning insofar as they both attempt to address issues of equity, and center education around the empowerment of students.

Applications

Many common teaching and learning practices that are appropriate for personalized learning environments have their roots in Progressive, Constructivist, and critical theories. Reading and writing workshops give students voice in developing and constructing their own literacy identities. Harkness discussions and Socratic seminars provide students with opportunities to discuss advanced concepts and ideas with others in order to test and refine their own understandings of content. Project-based learning and problem-based learning encourage students to apply their knowledge in authentic ways. And the ever-ubiquitous differentiation, when considered in its best sense of "consistently using a variety of instructional approaches to modify content, process, and/or products in response to learning readiness and interest of academically diverse students" (Tomlinson, 1995, p. 80), lies at the heart of all of these theories. Additionally, standards-based grading and competency-based progressions provide the reporting structures needed to advance students appropriately and ensure they truly are receiving what they need in the classroom.

A Recent History of Personalized Learning in the United States

As industrialization defined much of the shape and character of American education throughout the 19th and 20th centuries, globalization is defining education in the new millennium. Advances in technology, communications, and travel, and the worldwide spread of capitalism have brought about vast increases in the flow of trade, finance, culture, ideas, and people, which in turn has resulted in new demands in the workplace. While earlier industrialists needed workers with basic levels of education, leaders of international corporations now need workers with an advanced education and highly sophisticated critical- and creative-thinking skills in order to keep their businesses competitive. As they have had to rely heavily on importing this level of talent from outside of the United States, business leaders have been perhaps among the most vocal sounding the alarm that our current educational system is inadequate. In order to help fix this serious problem, they have invested a portion of their time and their fortunes to innovating American education. Federal, state, and local governments have also heeded their warnings and invested in innovations as well. Some of those innovations have come in the form of personalized learning.

Research into Personalized Learning

For over a decade, the Bill & Melinda Gates Foundation has used its vast resources and influence to support research into and promote the growth of personalized learning through several of its partner groups,

Foundations

as well as its own initiatives. Since it was set up in 2005, the Charter School Growth Fund, funded in part by the Bill & Melinda Gates Foundation and the Chan Zuckerberg Initiative, had provided resources and support to more than 1,075 charter schools by 2020 (Charter School Growth Fund, 2020), many of which utilize elements of personalized learning in their programs (RAND Corporation & Bill & Melinda Gates Foundation, 2014). In 2010, the Foundation partnered again with the Chan Zuckerberg Initiative, foundations with ties to tech companies Hewlett-Packard and Dell, and others to fund the Next Generation Learning Challenges (NGLC). As of 2020, NGLC had invested over $40 million in more than 100 schools that implemented some form of personalized learning (NGLC, 2020). In 2012, the Foundation launched a three-year pilot study of personalized learning via the Bill & Melinda Gates Foundation's Personalized Learning Pilots, with the goal of eventually expanding the most effective pieces of personalized learning to other schools. As part of a competitive application process to receive funding from the Personalized Learning Pilots, schools were asked to describe their vision for integration of personalized learning into reading and math courses, to utilize competency-based learning progressions, and to demonstrate their use of innovative practices (Pane et al., 2015).

The RAND Corporation was then commissioned by the Foundation from 2012 to 2015 to study the various ways schools were implementing personalized learning on their campuses and the impact of those efforts on student achievement. As part of this work, RAND researchers sought to identify both the challenges that schools faced with implementation and the factors that helped to facilitate implementation. The study was conducted in stages, and the results were released in a series of reports. All of the schools studied received funding from the Bill & Melinda Gates Foundation through one of the three programs described above. The first phase of research focused on 23 charter schools (RAND Corporation & Bill & Melinda Gates Foundation, 2014), the second on 62 charter and public district schools (Pane et al., 2015), and the third on 40 NGLC schools, more than three quarters of which were charter schools (Pane et al., 2017).

While the number of schools that were selected to participate in the RAND study varied throughout the different stages, they all shared some similar characteristics. Primarily located in urban areas, most of the schools served a large proportion of students from low-income, minority backgrounds. Additionally, all of the schools were in the early stages of implementing personalized learning, with most having been involved with personalized learning between one and three years.

Results

Personalized learning was envisioned and implemented differently among the schools. For example, some schools set aside time for teachers to work with students individually, some relied on project-based learning, and a few disbanded grade levels entirely so students could truly progress through the curriculum at their own rate. However, several commonalities did exist among the schools. Many of the schools included four distinct elements in their visions, all of which were interrelated:

1. The schools maintained learner profiles for each student.
2. Learner profiles were used to create each child's personal learning path.
3. Progression through the curriculum was competency-based.
4. Flexible learning environments allowed for personalization.

Achievement results for students overall were positive; however, several limitations within the studies mean that the results need to be interpreted cautiously. On average, students did demonstrate modest positive gains in reading and math. Furthermore, students who had been engaged with personalized learning for at least two years showed even greater gains. Students who began the first year below national averages showed improvement in the first year, and by the end of the second year they had risen above national averages. Compared to students from a national sample, the students in these personalized learning schools demonstrated more growth throughout one year than similar students from the national sample. However, there is no way of knowing if students from the national sample also attended schools that utilized some elements of personalized learning.

These results were complicated by the fact that they were not seen evenly across all schools. The specific factors that led some schools to have greater achievement results than others remain unknown. Furthermore,

Foundations

it cannot be stated with certainty that personalized learning was the factor that caused gains in some students' scores; some other element of their learning experience may have been responsible. Finally, even if personalized learning was responsible for the gains, it is impossible to know from existing data which elements of personalized learning were the most effective, especially since all of the schools practiced and implemented it differently. More empirical research is needed.

Government-Funded Support

Race to the Top Grants
In 2009, President Obama signed into law the American Recovery and Reinvestment Act, which sought to stimulate the economy, create jobs, and invest in critical sectors of American life, including education. The Act allocated $4.35 billion for the Race to the Top Fund, a competitive grant program which sought an overhaul of the entire American public education system. States could apply for funding by demonstrating their commitment to a variety of educational reforms and outlining a plan for implementation; these reforms included significant efforts to improve educational data systems and student achievement. Forty-six states and the District of Columbia applied for grants through this fund and committed to significant reforms in their educational systems.

Building on this initial work at the state level, in 2012, a district-level Race to the Top program was implemented (US Department of Education, n.d.; US Department of Education, 2017). The Race to the Top-District program committed $300 million to school districts who applied for the funding through a competitive grant process. These grants were meant to support schools in providing personalized learning to increase student achievement and prepare students to meet standards for college and career readiness. Applicants needed to certify that their proposed programs would serve a minimum of 2,000 students, at least 40% of whom were from low-income families. In addition, robust data collection programs and evaluation systems needed to be in place to monitor implementation and success. A total of 15–25 grants were expected to be awarded, which would last for four years and range from $5 million to $40 million. Funding was based on the number of students who would participate in the program. Within a month of announcing this initiative, the US Department of Education (2012) revealed that almost 900 applicants had submitted an

16

Theory and History of Personalized Learning

intent to apply for these grants. These applicants represented 48 states and the District of Columbia.

A total of 16 grants were awarded in 2012, and in 2013, the program was reopened to a second round of applications. Throughout 2012 and 2013, grants totaling $500 million were awarded to 21 school districts, charter school districts, and educational cooperatives. While that number may seem fairly small, a later report from the District Reform Support Network (2016) found that many of the applicants who did not receive federal funding were able to proceed with at least some of their plans anyway:

> Personalized learning has been embraced by non-RTT-D [Race to the Top-District] schools and districts across the country and is gaining momentum and interest from additional education agencies. On a national level, over 550 school districts or consortia of districts competed in the two Race to the Top-District funding cycles. Many districts that did not receive funding continued on to implement one or more aspects of personalized learning.
> (District Reform Support Network, 2016, p. 6)

While we do not have concrete data on how prolific different elements of personalized learning have become, we do know that schools across the country have been able to allocate funding to provide some version of it to their students.

Results

Two years after the last grants were awarded, in 2015, the District Reform Support Network released the results of a two-part study funded by the US Department of Education to analyze the implementation and outcomes of personalized learning by four grant awardees: Iredell-Statesville Schools in North Carolina, which focused their efforts on improving English language arts in middle school and high school; Miami-Dade County Public Schools in Florida, which focused on improving middle school math; and New Haven Unified School District in California, and Metropolitan School District of Warren Township in Indiana, both of which utilized personalized learning in all subjects for grades K–12.

Several positive commonalities were found across the schools studied. Classrooms had become more student-centered as the role of teacher had shifted to that of facilitator and guide. Positive changes in student engagement were noted as students were given more choice and control over their learning. The teachers also evidenced a shift in mindset as they became more willing to try new things and began to collaborate more regularly with their colleagues.

Technology was effectively used as a tool to support learning, and the teachers helped make decisions in selecting the resources to use. Assessments had been restructured in several important ways. Technology enabled students to receive real-time feedback on their work, and teachers were able to use that data to group students more effectively according to what they needed at any given time. Students tracked their own progress by documenting and graphing their personal scores on spreadsheets. Assessments also expanded to include evaluative conferences centered on work portfolios and performance tasks that required students to apply what they had learned to a real-world task that often required collaboration with peers.

College- and career-based learning and readiness were also addressed in multiple ways. Project-based learning that focused on real-world applications and collaborative work helped foster these skills. In addition, the high schools focused on expanding students' opportunities to learn beyond the traditional school setting. Some students were able to complete off-campus internships with local businesses for academic credit. Schools also worked to expand their online course offerings so students could earn academic credits in coursework that could not be offered in-person at their schools.

OTHER STATE AND DISTRICT ADOPTERS

Several additional states and districts have been adopters of personalized learning and will be profiled throughout this book. At the state level, Vermont, New Hampshire, Kentucky, Michigan, and Ohio all made large-scale policy changes that impacted how their students could progress through the curriculum. At the district-level, personalized learning reforms were implemented in Fulton County, GA; Piedmont, AL; Horry County, SC; Chugach, AL; and Adams County, CO. In addition, a pilot program called LEAP introduced personalized learning to several traditional, charter, and private schools throughout Chicago.

Common Implementation Challenges

Whether the schools received their funding from a Race to the Top-District grant, an initiative supported by the Bill & Melinda Gates Foundation, or state or local support, some common challenges with implementation have emerged. The first involves school leaders effectively communicating their vision for personalized learning. Given that personalized learning currently lacks a common definition, clearly articulating to the teachers, students, and parents how and why it will be operationalized in a particular way in their school is of paramount importance. People cannot meet a goal when the goal is not clear. To facilitate the clear communication of this vision, school leaders should also be careful about embracing too many new initiatives at one time. When the principal, the superintendent, and the math department all introduce a new program at the start of the school year, teachers can quickly become overloaded, and the result may be that none of the programs are done well.

Second, as part of offering a clear vision for personalized learning, school leaders should articulate how much choice and autonomy students will receive, and how students will be prepared and supported in making effective choices. Students, especially those not accustomed to making educational decisions for themselves, may have difficulty when offered too many choices. They may not have a clear understanding of how to recognize when they are learning within their own zone of proximal development and, therefore, may gravitate towards activities and experiences that are either too easy to promote any kind of real learning or too difficult for them to successfully complete. Furthermore, they may misguidedly choose to complete a long list of activities that they enjoy but don't result in growth. Confounding these difficulties, some students may not yet have developed the self-regulation strategies needed to keep themselves on task and learning. An important distinction that can be made in this regard lies in the difference between flexible pacing and self-pacing (Pane, 2018). Unlike self-pacing, flexible pacing – which allows students options but within certain parameters – preserves choice and autonomy for students, while also ensuring that appropriate academic standards and expectations are met.

Third, personalized learning requires a great deal of flexibility on the part of schools and teachers. Traditional school structures simply do not support it. School leaders need to be willing and able to rethink the structures that they can control, such as bell schedules, course enrollment, how credit is awarded, and what they ask teachers to prioritize. Even then, some structures that are beyond local control may still inhibit the use of personalized learning. State and federal guidelines regarding standardized testing remain a reality, so students who are learning at a different pace or in a different sequence may be required to test over material that they have not seen in some time. In Texas, for example, middle school students enrolled in Geometry or a higher level math subject must still take a state math test that corresponds to their enrolled grade level every spring; in a particularly ridiculous instance, we have known an eighth-grade student who scored a 5 on an AP Calculus exam who was expected to spend half of a school day in testing to prove his proficiency with eighth-grade math standards. As teachers from some of the Race to the Top-District schools noted, "state accountability requirements inhibit risk-taking approaches in the classroom… there is a disconnect between what we are doing in the classroom [to personalize learning for each student] and the standardized test" (District Reform Support Network, 2016, p.15).

Graduation requirements are also set at the state level, and college admissions still heavily influences what risks schools and students may be willing to take. For example, it is not yet clear how a system that falls too far outside of the existing norms for grades and transcripts will be perceived when its students begin applying to college. Some notable work is being undertaken in that regard by the Mastery Transcript Consortium, which counts over 330 high schools among its members (Mastery Transcript Consortium, 2020). This Consortium, working in advisory with several prominent US universities, has designed a new type of high school transcript that reports students' interests, and mastery of skills and content rather than grades and GPAs. While this work is undoubtedly exciting and promising, it remains in the early stages of development and use.

Fourth, ensuring that teachers have the support and resources that they need to implement personalized learning is of paramount importance. Unfortunately, many of the materials being used to implement personalized learning are still fairly immature in their development, and technologies do not always integrate with each other in ways that make for ease of use by educators and students. Additionally, digital resources used with students need careful vetting by instructional technology experts who have a deep understanding of the mechanics of system requirements and the implications of what is written in privacy and data sharing agreements. They also need to be vetted by the teachers who will be expected to use these resources. Their classroom experience gives them deep understanding of how students might best interact with the resources and what potential problems they may face.

Schools that allow teachers a voice in selecting these resources have fared better than schools in which teachers were given all of the resources in advance and told that they had to use them and nothing else. Prescriptive educational programs and top-down directives are antithetical to the purpose and practice of personalized learning.

Lastly, personalized learning as it has been enacted in most schools has relied heavily on the use of technology. Managing a large number of new devices that are used by students with varying degrees of concern for them can, in and of itself, be a large task, and the management of those devices is just one part of what is needed when large-scale technology changes occur in schools. Infrastructure – such as charging stations, networks with well-functioning and adaptable filters, and appropriate internet access – must be in place to support the use of the devices. Furthermore, students and teachers alike must be provided with ongoing training to ensure that they can effectively use their devices and all applications and programs that become part of the curriculum. Too often educators assume that today's generation of students will be able to quickly navigate all new technologies because they are digital natives. That is not the case and expecting them to do so is the equivalent of expecting anyone who can read to be able to pick up and understand Dante's *Divine Comedy* in its original Italian. Yes, it is a written text, but even the best readers may not be comfortable with the nuances of poetry, much less an allegorical epic poem that was shaped by medieval Roman Catholic culture and written in another language.

In a case study of one urban charter school attempting to implement technology-based personalized learning, Bingham (2017) describes a disastrous first-year outcome, brought about by a combination of many of the factors previously mentioned. The school experienced a severe disconnect between vision and practice, with the teachers lacking a clear vision of what was expected. The teachers and students also lacked many of the resources and structures that they needed to be successful. Teachers initially had no input into materials and resources, and students were given far too many choices, which inadvertently included the option of not completing work at all. When Bingham observed classes, she often

Foundations

saw students off-task on their devices. A faculty meeting in December was marked by tension and frustration as teachers reported that some of their students had not accessed content in months. Not unpredictably, "teachers responded to constant challenges – including difficulties managing students' use of technology, problems with digital resources, and overwhelming workloads – by reverting to instructional practices that were more comfortable. In most cases, this meant a return to more traditional forms of instruction, including whole-group instruction and 'low-tech' practices" (Bingham, 2017, p. 532). To its credit, the school used year two to completely regroup, which meant putting personalized learning on the sideline in order to focus on creating structures within the school that would help students and teachers be successful. In year three, they were able to return to trying to implement a new version of personalized learning that utilized more structures and resources (including software that allowed teachers to monitor what students were doing online) and that gave teachers more autonomy with the curriculum.

Additional Critiques

Because the recent explosion of personalized learning in schools has been tied closely with new advances in technology that make obtaining and organizing data both relatively simple and quick, it is also worth noting that some of the shortcomings within personalized learning have also been a result of technology. As schools have increasingly infused classrooms with devices, concerns have been raised by teachers, psychologists, and parents alike in a number of forums – from school board meetings to educational and psychological journal articles to parenting blogs – about the appropriate limitations of student technology use. The irony that many medical professionals have been encouraging parents to limit their children's screen time for health and psychological reasons, while, at the same time, schools have been dramatically increasing it, has certainly not been lost on many.

One outspoken critic of the way personalized learning has been practiced in many schools is Paul France, whose book *Reclaiming Personalized Learning: A Pedagogy for Restoring Equity and Humanity in our Classrooms* (2020) details his experiences as he helped found three personalized learning microschools in Silicon Valley from 2014 to 2017.

22

Theory and History of Personalized Learning

In these schools, each student had an individualized personal playlist for learning. This high level of individualization created a teacher workload that he describes as "immense and unsustainable" (p. 2). It also seemed to be without actual benefit, as France observed no increase in test scores and no differences in students' writing, critical thinking, problem-solving, or empathy towards others when compared to students whom he had previously taught.

What France came to see as the biggest problem, though, was the dehumanizing element of this instructional approach, as students worked largely in isolation from their peers. He describes his concern thusly:

> The stark differentiation between *humanized* personalization and *dehumanized* personalization is what lies at the center of my criticism of technology-powered personalized learning. Technology-powered individualization is just as industrialized as the standardized practices of the late 20th and early 21st centuries. It still encompasses a one-size-fits-all approach to teaching and learning; the only difference is that it's delivered digitally... This isn't learning that's inherently meaningful and personal; it's learning that *dehumanizes*.
>
> (France, 2020, p. 3)

France does believe, however, that personalization can be humanized and advocates for a type of pedagogy that prioritizes the human experience over the technological. Progressive, Constructivist, and critical pedagogy theorists certainly provide strong pathways for achieving that level of humanized personalization.

France's vision of personalized learning relies on creating a collective school culture, equity, and sustainable pedagogical practices. Unfortunately, in discussing equity, he misses a very important point about what equity and personalization should really mean. While he advocates for an outstanding educational environment in which differentiation is practiced and learning is a social process, he – like many others currently – insists that limits should be placed on that learning by conceding, "I'm often asked, But what about the high achievers? Is it fair for them to be in classes where they're forced to 'go more slowly' than they are able to go? In short, the answer is yes" (France, 2020, p. 34). And therein lies the problem of most of the personalized learning programs studied and described thus far.

Like France, schools that have been supported in implementing personalized learning through Race to the Top-District grants and the Bill &

Melinda Gates Foundation, as well as a host of others, have all intentionally focused their efforts on closing achievement gaps rather than excellence gaps. And they therefore fall into the same trap that industrialized schooling did – they set the bar too low and do not create a way for advanced and gifted students to truly excel in the ways that could be most meaningful to them.

Personalized Learning for Gifted and Talented Students

At the beginning of this chapter, we defined education as the means by which cultural capital is transferred from one generation to the next. In embracing a vision of personalized learning for advanced and gifted students, what is the cultural capital that we wish to transmit? It is the advanced knowledge and advanced skills that students need to develop in order to rise to eminence in their chosen fields of study. Our current educational system has proven to be woefully inadequate in this regard, and it certainly cannot be faulted because that is not what it was designed to accomplish. Do some students move through the system successfully and achieve great successes anyways? Of course, they do. But these students do so in spite of the system rather than because of it. Learning not just how to apply to college but how to *choose* a college, and then a graduate or professional school, and then a particular profession, and then excel in that profession, requires specific subsets of knowledge that most teachers, counselors, and school administrators are not trained to provide. Instead, students who navigate this pathway successfully often do so by relying on advice from their family members, family friends, and mentors. And in our modern, globalized world in which information can be found and organized at our fingertips, and conversations and meetings with professional mentors can be held so easily in a virtual environment, there is no longer any excuse for this to continue to be the case.

Throughout this book, we will outline our vision of personalized learning for gifted and advanced learners, a vision that, thus far, has been missing from far too many professional conversations. It relies on the best understandings that educational theorists have developed to explain how students learn and construct meaning, and it consists of five key features, supported by research in gifted education: (1) personalized talent development plans; (2) competency-based progressions and acceleration; (3) inquiry models of learning; (4) criterion-referenced assessment of student progress, and (5) multi-year mentoring for talent development.

Summary

Forms of personalized learning have long existed and have a rich track record of successfully educating students in both formal and informal structures. However, personalization was largely lost as schools adopted industrial methods to educate large numbers of students. Modern efforts to revive personalized learning via technological advancements, especially as promoted through private philanthropic and government grants and programs, have resulted in some improvements for some students. However, gifted students have been largely unaddressed as a subpopulation for the modern personalized learning movement. While personalized learning remains an ambiguous term, key features of it will support the development of gifted learners.

References

Bingham, A. J. (2017). Personalized learning in high-technology charter schools. *Journal of Educational Change, 18*(4), 521–549. https://doi.org/10.1007/s10833-017-9305-0

Bourdieu, P. (1990). Symbolic capital. In *The logic of practice* (pp. 112–121). Stanford University Press.

Charter School Growth Fund. (2020). *Our approach.* https://chartergrowthfund.org/about/

Dewey, J. (2009 [1916]). *Democracy and education: An introduction to the philosophy of education.* Feather Train Press.

District Reform Support Network. (2016). *Transforming the culture of teaching and learning: Four Race to the Top district grantees' implementation of personalized learning.* https://rttd.grads360.org/#communities/pdc/documents/12121

France, P. E. (2020). *Reclaiming personalized learning: A pedagogy for restoring equity and humanity in our classrooms*. Corwin.

Freire, P. (2000 [1968]). *Pedagogy of the oppressed*. Continuum.

Ginsburg, H., & Opper, S. (1969). *Piaget's theory of intellectual development: An introduction*. Prentice Hall.

Mastery Transcript Consortium. (2020). *Mastery Transcript Consortium*. https://mastery.org/

Montessori, M. (1995 [1967]). *The absorbent mind: A classic in education and child development for educators and parents*. Holt Paperbacks.

Montessori, M. (2002 [1912]). *The Montessori method*. Dover.

NGLC. (2020). *About Next Gen learning*. Next Generation Learning Challenges. www.nextgenlearning.org/about

Pane, J. F. (2018). *Strategies for implementing personalized learning while evidence and resources are underdeveloped*. RAND Corporation. www.rand.org/pubs/perspectives/PE314.html

Pane, J. F., Steiner, E. D., Baird, M. D., & Hamilton, L. S. (2015). *Continued progress: Promising evidence on personalized learning*. RAND Corporation. www.rand.org/pubs/research_reports/RR1365.html

Pane, J. F., Steiner, E. D., Baird, M. D., Hamilton, L. S., & Pane, J. D. (2017). *Informing progress: Insights on personalized learning implementation and effects*. RAND Corporation. www.rand.org/pubs/research_reports/RR2042.html

Piaget, J. (1959). *The language and thought of the child* (Vol. 5). Psychology Press.

Plucker, J. A., & Peters, S. J. (2016). *Excellence gaps in education: Expanding opportunities for talented students*. Harvard Education Press.

RAND Corporation & Bill & Melinda Gates Foundation. (2014). *Early progress: Interim research on personalized learning*. Bill & Melinda Gates Foundation. https://usprogram.gatesfoundation.org/news-and-insights/usp-resource-center/resources/early-progress-interim-research-on-personalized-learning--report

Ratner, N., Bruner, J., & Bruner, J. (1978). Games, social exchange, and the acquisition of language. *Journal of Child Language, 5*(3), 391–401.

Rosenblatt, L. M. (1994 [1978]). *The reader, the text, the poem: The transactional theory of the literary work*. Southern Illinois University Press.

Theory and History of Personalized Learning

Rosenblatt, L. M. (1995 [1938]). *Literature as exploration* (5th ed.). Modern Language Association.

Rousseau, J. J. (1969 [1750–1755]). *The first and second discourses.* (R. D. Masters, Ed.) (R. D. Masters & J. R. Masters, Trans.) St. Martin's.

Rousseau, J. J. (1979 [1762]). *Emile: Or on education.* (A. Bloom, Trans.) Basic Books.

The Nation's Report Card. (2020). *Report library.* www.nationsreportcard.gov/report_archive.aspx

Tomlinson, C. A. (1995). Deciding to differentiate instruction in middle school: One school's journey. *Gifted Child Quarterly, 39*(2), 77–87. https://doi.org/10.1177/001698629503900204

US Department of Education. (2012). *Nearly 900 intents to apply submitted for $400 million Race to the Top-District competition to implement local reforms.* www.ed.gov/news/press-releases/nearly-900-intents-apply-submitted-400-million-race-top-district-competition-implement-local-reforms

US Department of Education. (2017). *Race to the Top District.* www2.ed.gov/programs/racetothetop-district/index.html

US Department of Education. (n.d.). *Background. Race to the Top District competition draft.* www.ed.gov/race-top/district-competition/background

US National Commission on Excellence in Education. (1983). *A nation at risk: The imperative for educational reform. A report to the nation and the Secretary of Education, United States Department of Education.* https://edreform.com/wp-content/uploads/2013/02/A_Nation_At_Risk_1983.pdf

Vygotsky, L. S. (1978). *Mind in society: The development of higher psychological processes.* Harvard University Press.

Wood, D., Bruner, J., & Ross, G. (1976). The role of tutoring in problem solving. *Journal of Child Psychiatry and Psychology, 17*(2), 89–100.

# Gifted Education, Talent Development, and Personalized Learning

Personalized learning has been implemented in schools with students at all levels. It has been applied to struggling students, average students, and above-average students. Gifted and talented students have been included in school-wide personalized learning initiatives as well. Examining the funding and reports allocated to personalized learning in the last decade, it would seem that personalized learning is mostly a targeted intervention for average performing or slightly below-average performing students, and much of the reported research on personalized learning has included school-wide models where all students in the school are involved in the initiative (Pane et al., 2017). Since the US Department of Education defined personalized learning in 2010 (US Department of Education, 2010), there has been very little specific scholarship in the field of gifted education on the topic of personalized learning. This chapter explores the theoretical similarities of personalized learning and gifted education and concludes that (a) there is substantial congruence between gifted education and personalized learning; (b) gifted students could benefit from well implemented models of personalized learning; and (c) adoption of personalized learning approaches could benefit all students, but especially gifted and talented students.

Similarities Between Personalized Learning and Gifted Education

In 2010, the US Department of Education defined personalized learning and reiterated that definition again with further clarification in 2016.

According to that definition, personalized learning is "instruction in which the pace of learning and the instructional approach are optimized for the needs of each learner. Learning objectives, instructional approaches, and instructional content (and its sequencing) all may vary based on learner needs. In addition, learning activities are meaningful and relevant to learners, driven by their interests, and often self-initiated" (US Department of Education, 2016, p. 7). Personalized learning was further clarified through definitions of some key terms. Individualization should include pacing adjustments to align with the learning needs of the student, and differentiation is the act of modifying instruction based on student preferences. Comparing the federal definition to theory and practice, Walkington and Bernacki (2020) contend that for an educational program to truly be considered personalized learning it should distinctly include the following characteristics: meaningfulness, relevance, interest-driven instruction, and self-initiated work by the students.

A state initiative for personalized learning in Rhode Island (Eduvate Rhode Island, 2017) characterized personalized learning according to eight facets: (1) individualization, (2) differentiation, (3) aligned to standards, (4) student ownership, (5) interest-driven, (6) socially embedded, (7) flexible learning environments, and (8) continuous formative assessment. Personalized learning programs may include all eight elements, or they may include a combination of some, but not all elements.

Some states and school districts are approaching personalized learning through the guidance of the Every Student Succeeds Act (ESSA) (Zhang et al., 2020). While ESSA does not specifically call for personalized learning, the ESSA guidance encourages schools to customize learning for students and use individualized pathways, competency-based progressions, and technology to leverage customized learning opportunities. In other words, even when personalized learning is not specifically mandated in policy, aspects of personalized learning are proliferating as educational systems are responding to educational policy guidelines.

Strength-based approaches are also a facet of personalized learning. Personalized learning should systematically identify students' areas of strength and then tailor learning opportunities to build on and expand those strengths. Strength-based approaches can also be linked to career education and career interest exploration. This learner-centered approach to personalized learning seeks to make the day-to-day educational

Foundations

experience meaningful, as the development of knowledge and skills is intentionally connected to students' strengths, interests, and career targets.

Giftedness and Talent Development

Conceptions of giftedness have been debated for decades. Some definitions emphasized native abilities, while others emphasized developed knowledge and skills. The National Association for Gifted Children (NAGC) organized a task force to clarify the definition of giftedness in a way that reflects both scholarship and practice. The group concluded that gifted students are those who "perform – or have the capability to perform – at higher levels compared to others of the same age, experience, and environment in one or more domains" (NAGC, 2019a, p. 1). Two facets of this definition stand out. First, giftedness is performance-based. Students who are gifted perform at higher levels than other students in one or more domains such as mathematics, language arts, science, or social studies. There may be cases where performance is not consistently observed; therefore, giftedness also includes evidence of potential performance at higher levels than other students.

Second, giftedness is comparative. Students who are gifted are recognized based on how they perform compared to other students with certain similarities. The three categories of comparative similarity are age, experience, and environment. Gifted performance derives from comparison to students of similar age. Even if a student were accelerated, the metric of when they are performing at gifted levels is based on comparison to students of the same age. Experience is the second category of comparative similarity. Experience is similar to educational opportunity. To make fair comparisons, recognition of gifted levels of performance should only compare students to other students who have had the same or very nearly the same experiences or opportunities to learn. The third comparative similarity is environment. Not all learning environments are equal, and over time, the inequalities of those environments result in inequalities of performance. To make the fairest judgments about gifted levels of performance, students should only be compared to other students who live and learn in very similar environments.

In recent years, talent development theory and research has influenced views on giftedness and gifted education (Olszewski-Kubilius et al., 2018; Subotnik et al., 2011). Talent development theorists define giftedness as performance at the upper-end of a domain, which is similar to other definitions (e.g. NAGC). Consistent with other developmental theories, giftedness is considered dynamic. Giftedness in individuals develops through interactions with the environment and specific learning opportunities. The early stages of giftedness are characterized by potential. As abilities are developed, giftedness manifests as achievement in one or more domains. Similarly, as giftedness matures in adulthood, it is documented by exceptional performance and achievements in a career field. The peak development of giftedness is characterized as eminence, or domain-changing work in a field of study (Subotnik et al., 2011). Whereas policy definitions of giftedness are restricted to school-age manifestations, talent development theory defines giftedness across the lifespan as a complex developmental phenomenon.

Gifted Education

Gifted education includes a broad range of practices and procedures implemented to address the learning and development needs of high performing students. The primary goal of gifted education is exceptional student performance in one or more domains of talent. In pursuit of this goal, typical practices in gifted education begin with recognition of a group of students who perform beyond the scope of the typical curriculum in a domain (mathematics, science, language, etc.). The hallmark feature of gifted education is advanced content matched to students' areas of academic strength and interest. The gifted education theory of differentiation (Brody, 2020; Dai, 2020; Kettler, 2016) may be summarized by the following:

- Advanced content substantially differentiated from the typical curriculum develops knowledge, skills, and expertise that exceed the typical performance targets of a school curriculum.
- Acceleration and enrichment are two mechanisms for transforming typical content into advanced content that is developmentally appropriate for high performing students.
- As students develop through grade levels, advanced content to match their domain-specific performance levels continues to deviate further from the content of the typical school curriculum.

Foundations

- In many cases the learning environment must be altered to accommodate the matching of advanced content to the developmental needs of high performing students.

Perhaps the way to conceive of the practices and procedures of gifted education involves the programming standards developed to guide school systems in the use of evidence-based practices (NAGC, 2019b). Those standards make explicit how to design and implement gifted education based on the theory of differentiation and the goal of exceptional student performance in one or more domains. The standards are presented across six components that we might characterize as the foundations of gifted education (see Figure 2.1).

Aligning Gifted Education and Personalized Learning

Personalized learning initiatives have largely involved general education. Gifted students may have been involved in school-wide initiatives, but most advocates of the personalized learning movement have maintained a distance with gifted education. Even so, personalized learning aligns well with the foundations of gifted education (Johnsen, 2016).

Advanced Learning and Development

Students selected for participation in gifted education are those who perform at remarkably high academic levels or show the potential for remarkably high academic performance. These students generally have cognitive abilities ranging from above average to exceptional. Cognitive ability, or intelligence, is a human trait often explained by individual differences theory. In other words, having a high level of the trait (e.g. cognitive ability) corresponds to differential performances and skills in specific areas. The differential performances and skills often present a mismatch between the student and the typical school curriculum and instruction. Thus, a foundational component of gifted education is acknowledging and understanding how students' advanced learning abilities and development

32

Talent Development

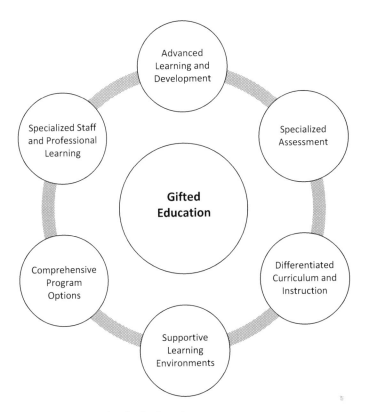

Figure 2.1 Foundations of Gifted Education
Note: These six components form the foundation of gifted education. While there may be variance in implementation, quality gifted education should address all six foundational components. These foundational components are articulated in the national standards (NAGC, 2019b) and some state policies and standards

require differentiated education. Personalized learning is a systematic way of responding to advanced learning and development for the students in gifted education.

High cognitive ability has been found to correspond to 10 advanced cognitive abilities (see Table 2.1) that impact how students respond to typical and differentiated curriculum. Educators should seek evidence of these advanced learning skills and engage students in developmentally appropriate curriculum and instruction. By matching each student's developmental level to appropriately challenging activities, educators make the learning personal and targeted to the student.

Foundations

Table 2.1 Skills Associated with Advanced Cognitive Development

Skill	*Description*
Processing Speed	Students with high ability typically process new information faster than average ability peers on both simple and complex tasks.
Thorough Problem Solvers	Students with high ability typically use a wider variety of problem-solving strategies and generate more elaborate solutions than average ability peers.
Metacognitive Strategies	Students with high ability typically employ more metacognitive strategies to monitor and adjust their learning than average ability peers.
Sustained Attention	Students with high ability typically demonstrate longer and more thorough attention to learning tasks than average ability peers.
Superior Memory	Students with high ability typically demonstrate superior memory and more efficient recall than average ability peers.
Abstract Thinking and Generalization	Students with high ability typically think more abstractly and make more generalizations and connections within and across content than average ability peers.
Curtailed Learning	Students with high ability typically learn new content with fewer repetitions and minimal or even no formal instruction compared to average ability peers.
Critical Thinking	Students with high ability typically demonstrate more sophisticated critical and analytical thinking skills than their average ability peers.
Creative Thinking	Students with high ability typically demonstrate more creativity skills such as divergent thinking, problem finding, conceptual combination, and remote associations than their average ability peers.
Executive Functioning	Students with high ability typically exhibit superior executive functioning, including cognitive flexibility, inhibitory control, and strategic planning than their average ability peers.

Source: Adapted from Kettler (2017) and Kettler & Payne (2021)

Personalization goes beyond matching curriculum to developmental levels. High cognitive ability and domain-specific talents are precursors to personalized college and career exploration. Personalized learning includes self-understanding of interests and abilities. Educators can provide guidance to students as they navigate college and career possibilities aligned with their ability, talents, and interests. Additionally, personalized learning with high ability students involves attending to the psychosocial and affective growth necessary to support talent development and exceptional achievement. Student-centered and personalized gifted education occurs in the day-to-day differentiation of learning, as well as in social and emotional support systems and transition planning.

Specialized Assessment

Gifted education involves specialized assessments that provide information about identification and selection to participate in gifted and talented programs. Additionally, it should include assessments to provide detailed information about students' strengths, growth trajectories, and personalized talent exploration and development. State and school district policies often specify guidelines and procedures for the identification process in gifted education. Too often this process simply yields dichotomous information – the student either qualified or did not qualify for gifted education programming. Personalized learning with gifted students seeks descriptive and diagnostic assessment information from which responsive learning interventions can be built based on specific data about the student. The more comprehensive and detailed the assessment information, the greater the potential for personalization becomes.

Merging specialized assessment with personalized learning begins with an assessment process that identifies gifted students in ways that align with programs and services. For instance, the assessments should measure abilities that match the gifted and talented curriculum. Talent development theory calls for increasingly domain-specific approaches to gifted education (Subotnik et al., 2011). Thus, the most sophisticated gifted education programs may be organized based on the domains in which services are provided. Perhaps those domains are the core curriculum of mathematics, science, language arts, and social studies. Identification for services would be aligned to each of those domain areas yielding a

Foundations

tight alignment between assessment and services. For instance, to qualify for the mathematics gifted education program, specific math abilities, achievement, and interests would be assessed. Similarly for language arts, language abilities, achievement, and interests would be assessed. As gifted education programs move toward domain-specificity in assessment and services, the learning becomes more personalized from the beginning. Moreover, the process for identification in gifted education yields more than a yes/no decision; instead, it provides a battery of assessment data that allows the school to provide gifted education that matches the students' profile of ability, achievement, and interest.

Using specialized assessment to personalize gifted education extends beyond domains of talent and potential. Students with high cognitive ability may have coexisting exceptionalities (Barnard-Brak et al., 2015; Reis et al., 2014). The evidence of twice exceptional students' ability profiles, has been widely documented, and most recommendations for serving twice exceptional students call for personalized and strength-based approaches (Fugate et al., 2020). The identification of twice exceptional students for gifted education requires broad and inclusive knowledge of exceptionalities, specialized assessments to document ability profiles, and an understanding of the cognitive impact of the inhibiting exceptionalities (e.g. ADHD, specific learning disability). This assessment data becomes the foundation for developing personalized plans. A personalized learning approach to gifted education is a strong foundation for the identification and services for twice exceptional learners.

Gifted education and talent development should include assessment processes to document students' growth trajectories commensurate with their abilities. Educators should develop and use formative assessments as foundational tools to personalize learning in each domain. Just as students in the gifted education program may vary in their educational needs from general education students, variance will also be present among the students in each domain of the gifted education program. Some students in gifted mathematics may be one or two grade levels ahead; others may be three or four grade levels ahead. Even within a grade level in the gifted mathematics program, one student may excel at geometry and proofs, while another excels in mathematical modeling. Personalized gifted education should routinely account for both macro and micro differences in students. The most successful gifted education programs use frequent and ongoing assessments to make decisions about curriculum and instruction.

36

Documenting these results and making corresponding differentiation decisions is the essence of personalized learning in gifted education.

Differentiated Curriculum and Instruction

Differentiated curriculum and instruction that is responsive to the advanced academic needs of students is the foundation of gifted and talented education. Curriculum in gifted education should be demarcated from the typical curriculum in three primary areas: (1) use of advanced content, (2) emphasis on complex thinking, and (3) focus on conceptual understanding (Kettler, 2017). Teachers should routinely design learning that incorporates conceptually complex learning demands and performances authentic to expertise in the domain (VanTassel-Baska & Baska, 2019). Differentiated curriculum and instruction often requires modifications of content standards. Teachers may accelerate student learning through progressively aligned above-level standards. In addition to acceleration of standards, differentiation may involve modifying standards with techniques of depth and complexity.

Personalizing learning based on student readiness and academic needs is fundamentally an act of differentiation. One way to think of this relationship is that all personalization is differentiation, but not all differentiation is personalization. In other words, personalized learning techniques are a more nuanced or sophisticated variation of differentiation. Personalized learning is differentiation at a finer grain; it takes account of a broad range of variables that represent each student's unique learning trajectories, strengths, and interests. Students become participants in personalized learning as they develop and become increasingly self-aware and metacognitive (Tomlinson, 2014). Students' career interests may serve as a personalized filter through which differentiated curriculum and instruction becomes more personalized for each student.

Personalized learning and differentiation are generally similar but there are some subtle differences between the two approaches (see Table 2.2). These similarities verify why personalized learning and gifted education are a theoretical fit (Bingham et al., 2018; Bray & McClaskey, 2013). For instance, personalized learning is a more individually focused and nuanced approach to modifying curriculum and instruction for advanced or accelerated learners. As technologies improve and teachers become adept

Foundations

Table 2.2 Comparing Personalized Learning and Differentiation

Facet	Personalization	Differentiation
Typical Similarities		
Relation to General Curriculum	Modifies the general curriculum based on student characteristics	Modifies the general curriculum based on student characteristics
Broad Goal	Enhance engagement and student learning	Enhance engagement and student learning
Assessment	Formative assessment used to adjust curriculum and instruction	Formative assessment used to adjust curriculum and instruction
Teacher Training	Requires specialized training	Requires specialized training
Subtle Differences		
Orientation	Focus on one student	Focus on groups of students
Role of Learner	Active participant in learning trajectories	Passive participant in learning trajectories
Learning Pathways	Competency-based progressions	Uses acceleration and enrichment
Technology	Technology is intentionally used to document and guide learning	Technology may or may not be used as part of learning activities
Self-Direction	Routine use of self-assessment, metacognition, and student-directed learning decisions	Occasional use of self-assessment and metacognition

Source: Adapted from Bray & McClaskey (2013)

at using data to make personalized modifications, students, especially gifted or advanced students, could experience an ever more sophisticated fit between learning needs and learning design.

Supportive Learning Environments

Each learning environment ought to be welcoming and safe for all students. In gifted education the learning environment should also reflect the cognitive, social–emotional, and psychosocial characteristics of high ability students. Learning environments should maintain high expectations

Talent Development

while fostering curiosity and an intrinsic love of learning. Students should encounter challenging learning activities that provide opportunities for self-exploration, and the development of students' academic interests. Teachers should play the role of intellectual role models, helping students form their identities as learners and thinkers. The learning environment in gifted education should celebrate and embrace diversity of persons and ideas, and it should be an intellectual safe-haven where students feel free to try out ideas in a community of supportive peers.

The gifted education learning environment intentionally addresses social, emotional, and academic development of high ability students. Social and emotional learning environments address needs in three skill areas: (1) social and interpersonal skills (e.g. teamwork, conflict resolution), (2) emotional regulation skills (e.g. managing stress, coping with frustration, showing empathy), and (3) cognitive success skills (e.g. setting goals, perseverance, grit, focusing attention) (Aspen Institute, 2019). In a supportive learning environment, students see the purpose in their learning experiences, and they develop agency as they become active participants. In strong gifted education programs, students find a sense of community where they are challenged and supported. This community becomes a safe harbor in which they learn social and interpersonal skills, emotional regulation skills, and cognitive success skills.

As school systems apply personalized learning to the supportive learning environments in gifted education, it is critical to maintain an interpersonal experience even as the learning becomes increasingly personal. Students' personalized learning plans may include specific focus areas devoted to the three areas of development shown in Figure 2.2. Personalized interventions and learning opportunities can be tailored to the unique needs and profiles of each student. For example, the following examples of skills and competencies (Aspen Institute, 2019) could be specified, taught, and monitored for students in the gifted and talented program:

Social and Interpersonal Skills

- resolving conflicts with individuals or groups
- navigating social situations
- demonstrating respect toward other students and adults
- working cooperatively as part of a team
- advocating for oneself

Foundations

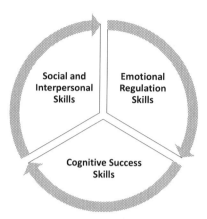

Figure 2.2 Social, Emotional, and Cognitive Development in Gifted Education Learning Environments

Note: Schools actively facilitate social, emotional, and cognitive development in these three areas of skill acquisition (Aspen Institute, 2019). These three skill areas should permeate the learning environment and integrate into curriculum and instruction

- demonstrating agency to accomplish social goals.

Emotional Regulation Skills

- defining and recognizing emotions
- managing your own emotions
- recognizing the emotions of others
- demonstrating empathy
- coping with unpredictable situations
- recognizing and managing stress.

Cognitive Success Skills

- focusing attention for sustained time
- setting personal goals
- planning and organizing toward goal attainment
- recognizing root causes of problems
- solving problems

- perseverance

- failing forward.

These are examples of skills and competencies in each area, and schools can modify and extend these lists of skills. When merging personalized learning approaches into gifted education environments, it is important to understand the characteristics of high ability students, including their need for social, emotional, and psychological development. Intentional approaches with clearly defined outcomes and processes are the most effective way to implement social and emotional learning, and consistent work toward development of these skills can have a significant positive impact on the environment of the gifted education program.

Comprehensive Program Options

Gifted education programs offer a continuum of services that are aligned to provide appropriate learning opportunities based on students' cognitive and affective needs. Gifted programs address the broad goal of developing academic potential into demonstrated exceptional performances. Programs also address social and emotional development, career pathway and interest development, and goals to foster positive identity development and self-actualization, and to help students flourish. While these are goals for all students, the essence of gifted education programming is to account for ways that exceptional cognitive ability demands specialized or modified services and interventions.

Evidence-based practices should be the hallmark features of gifted education. The NAGC Programming Standards (2019b) represent a comprehensive statement of evidence-based practices recommended for school districts. One measurable goal demanding broad use of evidence-based practices is annual growth commensurate with students' abilities, and students with high cognitive ability typically begin a school year above grade level and should continue to grow by more than what is typically expected for general education students. In essence, while they begin at achievement levels above typical grade level peers, they should end each year even further ahead because annual growth for high ability reflects a steeper achievement slope. Table 2.3 presents a description of

Foundations

Table 2.3 Recommended Program Elements in Gifted Education

Program Element	Description
Grouping Arrangements	Schools group students intentionally for instructional purposes to facilitate the delivery of modified curriculum and instruction. Grouping arrangements may include cluster grouping, ability-grouped classes, enrichment labs, school-within-a-school models, and specialized schools.
Acceleration	Schools provide and encourage students to take multiple opportunities for acceleration both inside and outside of schools. These may include grade-skipping, early entrance, curriculum telescoping, tiered objectives, and accelerated summer programs.
Enrichment	Schools provide students advanced learning opportunities that go beyond the typical school curriculum. The enriched curriculum is modified to increase depth, breadth, and complexity. Enrichment may occur at the individual lesson level and at broader levels like specialized courses or summer programs.
Mentorship and Internships	Schools actively arrange and support mentorships and internships for high school students in the gifted education program. Through these apprenticeship learning models, students gain unique tacit knowledge and expertise in career fields of interest.
Online Learning	Schools arrange and support online learning opportunities to enhance student learning in gifted education. Online learning may provide advanced courses that are not typically offered in schools, and they may also provide opportunities to accelerate through standard courses to access more advanced learning.
Independent Study	Schools facilitate independent studies at all grade levels so that students can learn at advanced levels in areas of interest. Through independent studies, students gain skills of self-directed learning, self-regulation, executive functioning, and self-efficacy.

Talent Development

Table 2.3 Cont.

Program Element	Description
Authentic Research	Schools teach students authentic research processes aligned to the work of experts in fields of study. Students actively engage in doing scientific research, historical research, literary criticism, social science survey research, or design-based research.
Career Education	Schools incorporate career education for high ability students into the gifted education program. Students learn the vast landscape of career fields, as well as the educational trajectories required to work in those fields. Career education may also involve self-awareness learning so that students match their profiles accurately to career fields of interest.

eight recommended practices consistently employed in gifted education programs. These practices include intentional and systematic grouping practices that accommodate the delivery of curriculum that is modified in depth, breadth, and pacing (Gentry & Owen, 1999; Kulik, 1992; Reis & Renzulli, 2010). Delivering such a modified curriculum is difficult if not impossible without the intentional use of academic grouping that is flexible and equitable.

Personalized learning models used in gifted education should emphasize the evidence-based practices mentioned in Table 2.3 blended with personalized learning components. The personalized approaches should include intentional and flexible grouping, broad use of acceleration, and continuous progress learning trajectories. Learning experiences should be challenging and engaging in response to students' interests and ability profiles. One way that personalized learning particularly enhances gifted education programming is in the area of guidance and career education (Puffer, 2015). Detailed student profiles and resulting personalized talent development plans support specialized career education and guidance counseling to prepare students for advanced and technical career fields commensurate with their interests and high abilities. Career education for gifted students is further supported by well-organized internship and mentorship programs and summer enrichment experiences.

Foundations

Specialized Staff and Professional Learning

Gifted education is a specialized field with professional standards defining teachers' knowledge and skills expectations. The standards are presented in the Teacher Preparation Standards in Gifted Education and Advanced Standards in Gifted Education Teacher Training of the National Association for Gifted Children Council for Exceptional Children (NAGC-CEC) (NAGC, 2013). Teachers working in gifted education programs are expected to know foundational knowledge about giftedness and gifted education. They are expected to be knowledgeable in the theory of differentiated learning and have the skills to fluently execute differentiation practices in their areas of teaching expertise. Expert teachers in gifted education understand advanced trajectories of cognitive development, as well as foundations of social and emotional development, and also the trajectories of students with multiple exceptionalities.

The success of gifted education programs requires a specialized staff with meaningful professional expertise, as well as ongoing professional learning. Blending gifted education and personalized learning requires similar but even more specialized training. Teachers working in a personalized learning gifted education program will need significant training to adapt their practices to the model of personalized learning (Bingham et al., 2018). Training needs for personalized learning typically involves training in the required technologies used in the program, assessment practices, and tools, and developing and using personalized learning plans. Specialized training is needed ahead of program implementation, and ongoing training and support is necessary well beyond initial implementation. Schools should use evidence-based training models such as coaching, peer-mentoring, and professional learning teams.

Gifted Education Models and Personalized Learning

Over decades of gifted education scholarship, several common models for gifted education programs and services have been developed and widely used (Sternberg & Ambrose, 2020). School systems do not have to abandon the use of these common models to apply personalized learning approaches in gifted education. In what follows, several common models of gifted education are briefly described as viable frameworks to incorporate personalized learning principles and practices (Cross & Olszewski-Kubilius, 2020; Plucker et al., 2017).

Schoolwide Enrichment Model

The schoolwide enrichment model (SEM) is a multi-component approach to gifted education that has been widely used for more than four decades (Renzulli & Reis, 2014). The SEM applies three levels of enrichment learning in response to students' strengths and interests. A first step of the SEM is compiling a strength-based profile for each student that includes ability strengths, interests, and prior achievement. This profile is quite similar to the personalized plans central to personalized learning. Learning trajectories for each student can be personalized by blending facets of personalized learning with the pedagogy of the SEM. Students' interests are significant drivers of enrichment experiences, which include inquiry models, as well as acceleration techniques (Renzulli & Reis, 2020). While some personalized learning can be integrated with Type 1 (general exploratory activities) and Type 2 (individual and group skill and process training activities) enrichment in the SEM, the Type 3 (individual and small group investigations of real problems) enrichment phase is an exact match with personalized learning approaches.

Talent Search Model

The talent search model of gifted education dates back to the 1970s when Julian Stanley developed the model and started the Study for Mathematically Precocious Youth (Stanley, 2005). The model includes some hallmark features that have influenced gifted education broadly through the years. First, schools use above level, domain-specific testing to identify exceptional talent. Those identified are placed in accelerated learning programs where they progress through domain-specific content at a pace commensurate with their ability (Brody, 2017). The curriculum is modified according to the needs of these students, and this process is very much a personalized process. Personalized learning plans would become the

Foundations

primary way to document students' strengths, achievements, and interests as they progress through advanced coursework in their area of strength. The model also emphasizes students' participation in extracurricular events such as contests and competitions in their area of strength, as well as summer enrichment programs, mentorships, and internships (Brody, 2020). The talent search model merges seamlessly with personalized learning in school systems.

Talent Development Model

The talent development model is primarily represented by the talent development megamodel (Olszewski-Kubilus et al., 2018) at present, though other models have been presented over the previous 40 years (Gagné, 2018; Wai et al., 2010). This model views giftedness as a developmental process, and the role of educators is to identify early potential and provide advanced learning opportunities in domain-specific areas of talent development (e.g. math; science, technology, engineering, and mathematics (STEM); humanities; arts). The model develops talent in accord with students' interests and proclivities using high-dose interventions that allow the students to develop significant content expertise at a pace consistent with the students' commitment and typical talent trajectories of the domain. Developing psychosocial skills supportive of student success and achievement are also critical features that are consistent with personalized learning approaches. Talent development requires personalized attention and opportunity, making this model a great fit with personalized learning theory.

Autonomous Learner Model

Similar to the previous models, the autonomous learner model (ALM) began in the 1970s to provide an organizational framework for gifted education, emphasizing development of personal autonomy. The model includes five dimensions that define approaches to developing self-directed high ability students (Betts et al., 2017). In the orientation dimension, students learn about themselves, their abilities, interests, and self-beliefs (self-esteem, self-efficacy, confidence). The individual development dimension provides programs and services through which students develop cognitive skills, social and emotional competencies, and psychosocial skills that facilitate success. The enrichment dimension further develops cognitive and social–emotional skills as students explore deeper and more engaging work in the interest or passion areas. Seminars are the fourth dimension of the ALM in which students work in small groups to study a topic or solve a problem. The most personalized of the five dimensions is the in-depth study dimension in which students pursue an authentic research project in their primary area of interest and ability development. All five dimensions align with the theory of personalized learning and can be enhanced through use of personalized learning plans, ongoing assessments, and mastery learning progressions.

Advanced Academics Model

In contrast to the previous models that have been used for decades, the advanced academics model is a recent development that applies a data-driven, differentiation approach to developing the skills and talents of students (Peters & Borland, 2020). The fundamental purpose of the model is to identify students who are not being challenged by the typical school curriculum in an area of study offered by the school. Using data to make these determinations, those students are then systematically provided extra challenge through the application of advanced interventions. The model is based on the response to intervention theoretical framework, which is less focused on labeling students and more focused on responding to immediate and documented needs for more personalized instruction. In some cases, the interventions may be mild to moderate to provide appropriate challenge, and in other cases the interventions are intense. This model represents a great gifted education framework capable of merging with personalized learning theory to respond to students' academic needs, as well as interests and personalized long-term goals.

Summary

Gifted education was established in the middle of the 20th century and has been evolving for decades based on research, theory, and practice. The principles, standards, and models of gifted education are well-established and effective when implemented with fidelity. Contemporary, 21st-century personalized learning approaches are congruent with the theories, models, and practices of gifted education. More importantly, personalized learning designs could push gifted education toward more sophisticated, data-driven models that allow educators to respond to students' needs with greater precision and accuracy. Similarly, the development of talented students who demonstrate self-direction, self-regulation, and strong, positive self-beliefs may be enhanced through the merging of existing gifted education models with the tenants of personalized learning theory.

Merging gifted education models with personalized learning theory may provide a framework that enhances the ability of gifted education professionals to address diverse gifted students more effectively. For instance, personalized learning approaches to gifted education allow us to individually address the needs of high ability English language learners, students with multiple exceptionalities, and students with high potential yet limited educational opportunities. Too often gifted education feels like a system that closes doors when students do not fit classic profiles of giftedness. Personalized learning theory has the potential to open those doors – to make gifted education accessible for students with high potential and atypical profiles. Personalized learning approaches to gifted education expand what is possible so that more students find themselves engaged, challenged, and pursuing advanced achievement, and career-focused outcomes.

References

Aspen Institute. (2019). Integrating social, emotional, and academic development: An action guide for school leadership teams. www.aspeninstitute.org/publications/integrating-social-emotional-and-academic-development-sead-an-action-guide-for-school-leadership-teams/

Barnard-Brak, L., Johnsen, S. K., Pond Hannig, A., & Wei, T. (2015). The incidence of potentially gifted students within a special education population. *Roeper Review, 37*(2), 74–83.

Betts, G. T., Carey, R. J., & Kapushion, B. M. (2017). *Autonomous Learner Model resource book*. Prufrock Press.

Bingham, A. J., Pane, J. F., Steiner, E. D., & Hamilton, L. S. (2018). Ahead of the curve: Implementation challenges of personalized learning school models. *Educational Policy, 32*(3), 454–489.

Bray, B., & McClaskey, K. (2013). *A step-by-step guide to personalized learning*. International Society for Technology in Education.

Brody, L. E. (2017). Meeting the individual educational needs of students by applying talent search principles to school settings. In J. A. Plucker, A. N. Rinn, & M. Makel (Eds.), *From giftedness to gifted education: Reflecting theory in practice* (pp. 43–63). Prufrock Press.

Brody, L. E. (2020). The talent search model for identifying and developing academic talent. In T. L. Cross & P. Olszewski-Kubilius (Eds.), *Conceptual frameworks for giftedness and talent development: Enduring theories and comprehensive models in gifted education* (pp. 235–264). Prufrock Press.

Cross, T. L., & Olszewski-Kubilius, P. (Eds.). (2020). *Conceptual frameworks for giftedness and talent development: Enduring theories and comprehensive models in gifted education*. Prufrock Press.

Dai, D. Y. (2020). Evolving complexity theory of talent development: A developmental systems approach. In T. L. Cross & P. Olszewski-Kubilius (Eds.), *Conceptual frameworks for giftedness and talent development: Enduring theories and comprehensive models in gifted education* (pp. 1–28). Prufrock Press.

Eduvate Rhode Island. (2017). Creating a shared understanding of personalized learning for Rhode Island. https://eduvateri.org/wp-content/uploads/2016/09/Personalized_Learning_Paper_Final.pdf

Fugate, C. M., Behrens, W. A., & Boswell, C. (Eds.). (2020). *Understanding twice-exceptional learners: Connecting research to practice*. Prufrock Press.

Gagné, F. (2018). Academic talent development: Theory and best practices. In S. I. Pfeiffer, E. Shaunessy-Dedrick, & M. Foley-Nicpon (Eds.), *APA handbook of giftedness and talent* (pp. 163–183). American Psychological Association. https://doi.org/10.1037/0000038-011

Gentry, M. L., & Owen, S. V. (1999). An investigation of the effects of total school flexible cluster grouping on identification, achievement, and classroom practices. *Gifted Child Quarterly, 43*(4), 224–243.

Johnsen, S. K. (2016). Implementing personalized learning. *Gifted Child Today, 39*(2), 73. https://doi.org/10.1177/1076217516663073

Kettler, T. (Ed.). (2016). *Modern curriculum for gifted and advanced academic students*. Prufrock Press.

Kettler, T. (2017). Curriculum for gifted students: Developing talent and intellectual character. In J. L. Roberts, T. F. Inman, & J. H. Robins (Eds.) *Introduction to gifted education* (pp. 145–164). Prufrock Press.

Kettler, T., & Payne, A. M. (2021). *Cognitive characteristics of high ability students: Theoretical foundations of talent development and differentiated learning provisions*. Department of Educational Psychology, Baylor University.

Kulik, J. A. (1992). *An analysis of the research on ability groupings: Historical and contemporary perspectives*. National Research Center on the Gifted and Talented, University of Connecticut.

NAGC. (2013). *Teacher preparation standards in gifted education*. The National Association for Gifted Children. www.nagc.org/sites/default/files/standards/NAGC-%20CEC%20CAEP%20standards%20%282013%20final%29.pdf

NAGC. (2019a). A definition of giftedness that guides best practice. The National Association for Gifted Children. www.nagc.org/sites/default/files/Position%20Statement/Definition%20of%20Giftedness%20%282019%29.pdf

NAGC. (2019b). Pre-K to grade 12 gifted programming standards. The National Association for Gifted Children. www.nagc.org/resources-publications/resources/national-standards-gifted-and-talented-education/pre-k-grade-12

Olszewski-Kubilius, P., Subotnik, R. F., & Worrell, F. C. (Eds.). (2018). *Talent development as a framework for gifted education: Implications for best practices and applications in schools*. Prufrock Press.

Pane, J. F., Steiner, E. D., Baird, M. D., Hamilton, L. S., & Pane, J. D. (2017). *Informing progress: Insights on personalized learning implementation and effects*. RAND Corporation. www.rand.org/pubs/research_reports/RR2042.html

Peters, S. J., & J. H. Borland. (2020). Advanced academics: A model for gifted education without gifted students. In T. L. Cross & P. Olszewski-Kubilius (Eds.), *Conceptual frameworks for giftedness and talent development: Enduring theories and comprehensive models in gifted education* (pp. 289–316). Prufrock Press.

Plucker, J. A., Rinn, A. N., & Makel, M. (2017). *From giftedness to gifted education: Reflecting theory in practice*. Prufrock Press.

Puffer, K. A. (2015). Facilitating emotional awareness in a career counseling context. *Journal of Career Assessment, 23*(2), 256–280.

Reis, S. M., Baum, S. M., & Burke, E. (2014). An operational definition of twice-exceptional learners: Implications and applications. *Gifted Child Quarterly, 58*(3), 217–230.

Reis, S. M., & Renzulli, J. S. (2010). Is there still a need for gifted education? An examination of current research. *Learning and Individual Differences, 20*(4), 308–317. https://doi.org/10.1016/j.lindif.2009.10.012

Renzulli, J. S., & Reis, S. M. (2014). *The schoolwide enrichment model: A how-to-guide for talent development* (3rd ed.). Prufrock Press.

Renzulli, J. S., & Reis, S. M. (2020). The three-ring conception of giftedness and the schoolwide enrichment model: A talent development approach for all students. In T. L. Cross & P. Olszewski-Kubilius (Eds.), *Conceptual frameworks for giftedness and talent development: Enduring theories and comprehensive models in gifted education* (pp. 145–180). Prufrock Press.

Stanley, J. C. (2005). A quiet revolution: Finding boys and girls who reason exceptionally well mathematically and/or verbally and helping them get the supplemental educational opportunities they need. *High Ability Studies, 16*(1), 5–14.

Sternberg, R. J., & Ambrose, D. (Eds). (2020). *Conceptions of giftedness and talent* (1st ed.). Palgrave McMillan.

Subotnik, R. Г., Olszewski-Kubilius, P., & Worrell, F. C. (2011). Rethinking giftedness and gifted education: A proposed direction forward based on psychological science. *Psychological Science in the Public Interest, 12*(1), 3–54. https://doi.org/10.1177/1529100611418056

Tomlinson, C. A. (2014). *The differentiated classroom: Responding to the needs of all learners* (2nd ed.). Association for Supervision and Curriculum Development.

US Department of Education. (2010). *Transforming American education: Learning powered by technology*. Office of Educational Technology, US Department of Education. www.ed.gov/sites/default/files/netp2010.pdf

Foundations

US Department of Education. (2016). *Future ready learning: Reimaging the role of technology in education.* Office of Educational Technology. https://tech.ed.gov/files/2015/12/NETP16.pdf

VanTassel-Baska, J., & Baska, A. (2019). *Curriculum planning & instructional design for gifted learners* (3rd ed.). Prufrock Press.

Wai, J., Lubinski, D., Benbow, C. P., & Steiger, J. H. (2010). Accomplishment in science, technology, engineering, and mathematics (STEM) and its relation to STEM educational dose: A 25-year longitudinal study. *Journal of Educational Psychology, 102*(4), 860–871. https://doi.org/10.1037/a0019454

Walkington, C., & Bernacki, M. L. (2020). Appraising research on personalized learning: Definitions, theoretical alignment, advancement, and future directions. *Journal of Research on Technology in Education, 52*(3), 235–252. https://doi.org/10.1080/15391523.2020.1747757

Zhang. L., Yang, S., & Carter, R. A. (2020). Personalized learning and ESSA: What we know and where we go. *Journal of Research on Technology in Education, 52*(3), 253–274. https://doi.org/10.1080/15391523.2020.1728448

Personalized Learning and Student Achievement

While personalized learning is multi-faceted and includes several beneficial outcomes, like all other educational approaches, personalized learning must prioritize achievement outcomes. The essence of personalized learning is meeting students' learning needs with individual precision. Those learning needs may include achievement, social and emotional learning, identity development, career interests, and moral and ethical development. While each of these learning needs is important, educational policies and accountability structures certainly direct emphasis to achievement outcomes.

Estimating the achievement effects of personalized learning is complex. Personalized learning achievement effects have been measured across entire school populations at schools implementing personalized learning. However, there are a number of confounding variables that impact those studies including: fidelity of implementation, availability of training and resources, duration of personalized learning implementation, and variance in personalized learning emphases. For instance, a personalized learning school that places the most emphasis on personal interests with identity and career profile development may have several positive effects in the long run but yield minimal impact on immediate math and reading achievement. This type of research study is important and informative, but these studies cannot be the sole body of research on which to judge the merits of personalized learning.

Another way we can look at the achievement effects associated with personalized learning is to examine the research on individual components of personalized learning. For instance, the following components of

DOI: 10.4324/9781003237136-4

Foundations

personalized learning have their own research bases associated with student achievement: (a) personalized plans, (b) mastery learning (competency-based progressions), (c) acceleration, (d) inquiry learning, (e) formative criterion-referenced assessment, and (f) mentoring. Most personalized learning research has not distinguished gifted or high ability learners from the general population of learners, so we generally make assumptions that the impact was similar on all students. Some of the research related to the components of personalized learning have specifically distinguished achievement outcomes for gifted or high ability students. However, we see no theoretical reason to believe that the achievement effects observed for personalized learning affect gifted students differently than they affect the general population of students.

One of the most systematic studies of school-level personalized learning achievement was conducted by the RAND Corporation (Pane et al., 2017). The RAND Corporation was a third-party evaluator for the group of schools ($n = 40$) that received funding from the Next Generation Learning Challenges (NGLC) initiative from 2012 to 2015. For the research design, RAND partnered with the Northwest Evaluation Association (NWEA) and used the Measures of Academic Progress (MAP) assessment as the achievement measure for mathematics and reading. Additionally, NWEA used statistical matching to identify schools with matching demographics (race/ethnicity/socioeconomics) also using the MAP testing to document student achievement. The comparison group of schools also had MAP scores similar to the NGLC schools at the beginning of the study. The schools in the study were diverse and had an average free/reduced lunch participation rate of about 75%. Matching comparison groups of schools were the same locale (rural, urban, suburban), and matching students were the same gender and grade as the treatment group students. Student achievement change was compared over a one-year period with students ($n = 5,500$) in kindergarten to grade 11. Results were aggregated for elementary, middle school, and high school in both mathematics and reading. The outcome variables of interest were changes in mathematics and reading MAP scores. A continuation of the study involved 16 of the original schools ($n = 1,800$ students) and reported achievement change over a two-year period.

The RAND study (Pane et al., 2017) found small but positive achievement effects for the personalized learning schools relative to the matched comparison groups. The personalized learning treatment effect in mathematics was .09 effect size (ES)[1], and the treatment effect in reading was ES = .07. Both of these effect sizes represent an approximate gain over the comparison group of about 3 percentile points in both subjects. For the 16 NGLC schools in the two-year study, gains in the second year were similar but slightly larger than in the first year, suggesting that schools may improve their efficiency by using personalized learning approaches with experience.

While the aggregate achievement effects were small, there were a range of outcomes across the personalized learning schools. Some had quite robust gains, while others actually performed significantly worse than the comparison schools. For instance, in the one-year comparison, one personalized learning middle school saw gains in mathematics of ES = .35 and gains in reading of ES = .22. Another personalized learning high school saw gains in mathematics of ES = .31 and gains in reading of ES = .24. One high school saw reading gains of ES = .42. These are robust treatment effects for a one-year intervention. Six personalized learning elementary schools had mathematics gains of more than ES = .15 with the largest at ES = .29. Four personalized learning elementary schools had reading gains of more than ES = .15 with the largest at ES = .36.

In the two-year achievement study, the same high school that reported gains of ES = .31 and ES = .22 extended those effect sizes to ES = .54 in mathematics and ES = .36 in reading after two years. There were three middle schools reporting effect sizes of greater than ES = .24 across both subjects over two years. In both the one- and two-year comparisons, the overall effects reported for personalized learning were very small for the NGLC schools despite the impressive gains for some schools. The average gains were small because some personalized learning schools saw lower achievement than the comparison groups over both one and two years of implementation. One personalized learning elementary school saw relatively lower scores in mathematics ES = −.44 and reading ES = −.51) after one year. In other words, the comparison groups showed more growth than the personalized learning groups. Similarly, one of the high schools saw significant lower scores in mathematics ES = −.52) and in reading ES = −.25 over two years of implementation. One of the lessons learned, according to the evaluators, is that schools that invested in training and resources for teachers were successful and schools that did not invest or implement with fidelity declined in achievement (Pane et al., 2017).

When comparing elementary (K–5), middle school (6–8), and high school (9–12), the average effects were largest in middle school for both mathematics and reading. The second highest average effect was elementary mathematics, but on average, there were no effects for elementary reading. That does not mean students did not grow in reading achievement; it just means that there were no differences in the growth between personalized learning schools and the comparison group schools. High schools in the personalized learning group overall showed small positive effects for both mathematics and reading achievement.

One analysis of the 2017 RAND study (Pane et al., 2017) examined how the effects of personalized learning compared across students assigned to five ability groups (quintiles). Approximately 18% of the students in the NGLC schools were in the top 20% of national norms in reading and mathematics. The study revealed that personalized learning had positive effects for students of all ability levels. Even though the effects were relatively stronger in the lower quintiles, more than 50% of the personalized learning students in the top 20% grew more than students in the top 20% in the comparison schools. This lends a little evidence that personalized learning works as well for high ability students as it does for average and low ability students as measured by MAP testing. Of course, some gifted education program goals go beyond standardized MAP testing, and those authentic production goals may be supported more robustly by personalized learning approaches.

In a subsequent 2018 report (Pane, 2018), RAND indicated in schoolwide models of personalized learning ($n = 32$ schools), the average achievement gain was approximately 3 percentile points in both mathematics and reading. While on average there was a slight achievement gain, some schools gained more than 3 percentile points and other schools reported negative achievement effects. Each of the 32 schools approached personalized learning using their own version of the model, and some models worked better than others. Below are some potential lessons learned for using personalized learning effectively:

- Mastery learning approaches work best when content is closely matched to students' zone of proximal development.

- High ability learners will see more achievement gains when the personalized learning system allows them to move through content at an accelerated pace.

- The blend of technology-driven mastery learning and teacher-led mastery learning is important. In settings where the teachers lose teaching time attending to the technology, student achievement is lower than settings allowing teachers and technology to work in harmony.
- Schools providing high quality training and support for teachers found more achievement success for students.

Achievement Effects of Personalized Learning Components

While the RAND study evaluated the achievement effects of personalized learning holistically, another way to understand the relationship between personalized learning and achievement is to examine individual components of personalized learning. Personalized learning itself is an umbrella term to describe more discrete educational interventions that tend to influence achievement outcomes for gifted or high ability students, as well as general education students.

Personalized Plans

Personalized or individualized plans have been a part of exceptional student education for decades, but, while they are widely used in special education, they are less likely to be used in gifted education (Swanson & Lord, 2013). Twelve states in the United States have policy requiring some form of individualized plan for students participating in gifted education. Rogers (2007) advocated individualized plans for gifted students as a way to increase the specificity of how teachers plan differentiated learning for gifted students. While there is little research to associate personalized plans for gifted students with achievement, there is research to support the use of specific, measurable goals (DeMink-Carthew et al., 2017). Specific goal-setting for students has demonstrated an aggregate medium effect size of $ES = .56$ (Hattie, 2009). The function of the personalized plan is to connect learning designs to students' specific goals. In a related research approach, the alignment of instruction to specific goals for gifted students tends to

Foundations

decrease or prevent underachievement (Mofield & Parker Peters, 2019; Siegle et al., 2017).

Personalized learning plans are a feature of personalized learning with gifted students. In order to leverage the plan for achievement effects, the plans should include specific goals that are developed collaboratively with the student and the educators, and in many cases also with parents/guardians. The personalized plan should also describe instructional interventions, modifications, and resources that will be used to move the gifted student toward achieving that goal.

Mastery Learning (Competency-Based Progressions)

Bloom (1984) demonstrated the power of individualized tutors to produce large achievement gains compared to whole class instruction. While Bloom's tutors were humans, the expanse of educational technology has introduced computer-based tutoring systems that have demonstrated similar effects (VanLehn, 2011). One of the fundamental theories of mastery learning approaches that distinguish them from traditional approaches is the inverse view of time and achievement. In standard approaches to teaching and learning, time is relatively constant and student achievement varies. In mastery learning approaches, achievement is constant and the time it takes to demonstrate mastery varies. The variability of time in mastery learning allows gifted and high ability students to master content at a faster pace and move on to more advanced content. It is not uncommon to hear gifted students describe their experiences in schools as a continual process of waiting on the teacher or waiting on other students (Peine & Coleman, 2010). Mastery learning approaches allow gifted students to demonstrate competency and to progress to the next set of content objectives without waiting.

More recent studies have found positive achievement effects for mastery learning approaches. Wambugu & Changeiywo (2008) found that high school physics students in a mastery learning setting achieved at higher levels than similar students in a traditional learning physics class. Similarly, Wanchanga & Gamba (2004) found that high school students in a mastery learning chemistry program achieved higher than similar students in a traditional chemistry class. Some research indicates that mastery learning goes beyond achievement effects and also yields improvement in

58

students' confidence in learning situations and attitudes toward learning (Guskey, 2007). Essential features of mastery learning and competency-based progressions are (a) specific feedback from teachers; (b) correctives – learning tasks that allow students to solve learning challenges or gaps; (c) enriched or advanced learning opportunities to complete when students demonstrate mastery of the typical curriculum; and (d) intentional alignment of those enrichment tasks to designated learning progressions that move students toward higher levels of expertise and domain-specific talent (Guskey, 1997; Stiggins, 2008).

Acceleration

The concept of progressing through education at a pace faster than typical has existed for about as long as educational programs have existed. An often cited definition of acceleration is "progress through an educational programme at rates faster or ages younger than conventional" (Pressey, 1949, p. 2). Acceleration may most commonly be thought of as grade-skipping, but contemporary scholarship on acceleration points to multiple forms of progressing through learning at a faster rate (Southern & Jones, 2015). Acceleration includes typical promotion techniques such as early entrance to school and grade-skipping, but it also includes curriculum and instruction techniques such as continuous progress, curriculum compacting, telescoping, self-paced instruction, and multi-grade classrooms. A third category of acceleration techniques is special program options such as Advanced Placement (AP) and International Baccalaureate (IB) programs, dual enrollment programs, mentorship programs, online learning options, and credit by examination opportunities (Southern & Jones, 2015).

These broad conceptions of acceleration techniques are a good fit with the theories and approaches to personalized learning. More importantly, acceleration has yielded substantial research on academic achievement benefits (Kulik & Kulik, 1984; Rogers, 2007). Acceleration overall has an estimated small achievement effect size of .18 on student achievement. The achievement effects for acceleration are greater when students are in college, ES = .31. It is also worth noting that the size of the achievement effect associated with acceleration tends to vary depending on the comparison group. When accelerated students are compared with older students also taking the same curriculum (though not earlier than expected), the effect

Foundations

sizes average about ES = .22. However, when the accelerated students are compared to similar students of their same age, the effects tend to be even greater, ES = .40 (Steenbergen-Hu & Moon, 2011).

When personalized learning includes opportunities to accelerate, student achievement in the domain of acceleration will likely following these same patterns of achievement effects. Whereas most personalized learning research has focused on average or even below average students, those students were likely not engaged in acceleration through their personalized learning. However, personalized learning in gifted education should include accelerated learning opportunities much more often, and this acceleration emphasis will likely lead to more robust achievement effects for students.

Inquiry Learning

Inquiry-based learning models have been increasingly touted as a means of increasing student interest and engagement. While there are multiple variations of the inquiry-based model, there are some classic features for all approaches that fall in the category of inquiry learning. Inquiry learning includes the following steps:

- Students begin the learning process with an introduction to engage their interest.
- Students gather data (research process) as part of the learning cycle.
- Students engage in problem-solving using data they have gathered.
- Students continue into further study to develop more elaborate solution designs.
- Students use communication tools to explain and justify their solution designs (von Secker, 2002).

Discovery-based learning is a type of inquiry learning used primarily in science education under the influence of Bruner's (1960, 1966) cognitive constructivism. Discovery-based learning came under scrutiny at the same time it was rising in popularity. Some studies have found that open-ended inquiry, where students engage in unassisted discovery, are less effective than explicit instruction (Alfieri et al., 2011). However, the same study found that enhanced discovery yielded favorable effect sizes (ES = .30) on average. Enhanced discovery in the inquiry model includes focused feedback during discovery, examples, skill-based scaffolding, and elicited explanation. Thus, data generally indicate that inquiry-based learning within personalized learning can yield positive achievement effects when used as enhanced discovery rather than unassisted discovery.

Common inquiry-based learning models include problem-based learning, project-based learning, design-based learning, creative problem-solving, five-e and seven-e models, and independent study/investigation models. These models have been used in gifted education (Kettler et al., 2018) and general education. While the research indicates that with general education students the enhanced discovery approach is superior to the unassisted discovery, high ability students may be able to successfully achieve learning outcomes working with greater independence in the inquiry models.

While much of the inquiry-based learning has focused on disciplines related to science, technology, engineering, and mathematics (STEM), a few studies have also examined the effectiveness of inquiry-based learning in literacy and social studies. For instance, Chen et al. (2017) tested the achievement impact of inquiry-based learning on information literacy with multiple comparisons across grades 1–6. They consistently found medium to large achievement effects for inquiry-based learning models over time. In the literacy studies demonstrating positive effects for inquiry-based learning, the following learning components were stressed as critical to student achievement in the model: (a) students posing questions in an inquiry space, (b) students seeking evidence to respond to those questions, (c) students developing explanations as responses to the questions, (d) students evaluating those explanations (critical thinking), and (e) students communicating their conclusions (Soares & Wood, 2010).

Several studies of inquiry-based learning within literacy and information science have found that students develop deeper and more conceptual understanding of content when they learn through inquiry (Chen et al., 2014; Eisenberg & Robinson, 2007). The evidence supports the potential achievement effects for inquiry-based learning models used with the personalized learning framework. The critical element of achievement effectiveness is clear adherence to the model features and providing guided support and direction (enhanced model). In some cases, students engaged in inquiry-based learning not only learn content at deeper, conceptual levels, but they also build success skills in information science and self-regulated learning. In other words, the positive effects of inquiry learning go beyond content achievement and also include critical skill areas needed for future success in information-rich work environments.

Formative Criterion-Referenced Assessment

Educators and policy makers have consistently supported the power of formative assessment to enhance student achievement. Several US states, as well as some countries, have included expectations for formative assessment in education policy. Some of the world's highest achieving educational systems such as Sweden, Finland, and Singapore include continuous and formative assessment in their policies and practices. In the formative assessment process, both teachers and students (self-assessment) provide specific feedback so that students can improve their performances (McManus, 2008). Most experts agree on four chief components of the formative assessment process: (1) explaining the learning objectives and criteria for success, (2) effective use of and quality of dialogue about student work, (3) targeted marking and feedback, as well as keeping records of the improvement in student work, and (4) routine use of self- and peer-assessment (Black, 2005; Ozan & Kıncal, 2018; Wiliam & Thompson, 2008).

Criterion-referenced assessment simply means that a student's performance is measured against a predefined standard of performance and not against the student's peer group. When formative assessment is used within a criterion-referenced assessment process, the target skills, dialogue and feedback all specifically focus on how much the student's work is congruent with or deviates from the predefined standards of performance. Whether the feedback is self-assessment, peer-assessment, or teacher-assessment, the focus is comparing and evaluating the student work against the clearly defined standard.

Formative assessment may affect student achievement directly, as well as indirectly. For instance, some studies have found that formative assessment improves students' self-regulation skills (Meusen-Beekman et al., 2016) and improved self-regulation is associated with higher levels of student achievement (Brookhart et al., 2010). The latter study found consistent formative assessment practices increased student motivation, which indirectly supports improved student achievement. The connection between formative assessment, criterion-referenced assessment tools, self-regulation and peer/self-assessment can lead to meaningful achievement gains at both primary and secondary levels of schooling. Meusen-Beekman et al. (2016) identified the key strategies of formative assessment as the following: (a) clarifying and understanding the learning success criteria, (b) developing high quality classroom discussions about success criteria and student work, (c) providing clear feedback based on the success criteria, (d) supporting peer-assessment and feedback as a learning resource, and (e) building motivation and self-regulation through students' ownership of the learning and assessment process.

Personalized learning that includes formative, criterion-referenced assessment implemented with fidelity should support increases in student achievement. These increases may be driven by students' developing self-regulation, motivation, and clear understandings of quality performance criteria. When these learning systems are correctly implemented in the personalized learning framework, student achievement gains should follow.

Mentoring

Mentoring is one of the advocated components of personalized learning. The research on mentoring is diverse in terms of outcomes. Sometimes mentoring seems to be related to non-achievement outcomes, but those non-achievement outcomes may in turn be related to academic achievement. For instance, students with mentors generally have better school attendance than similar students without mentors (Tierney & Branch, 1992). Students with mentors have more positive self-beliefs (self-esteem, self-efficacy, confidence) related to schoolwork than similar students without mentors (Tierney et al., 1995). Students with mentors tend to show improved relationships with others, including parents and peers (Rhodes et al., 1994). More recent research supports the indirect effects of mentoring on achievement. Elementary students who had high school student mentors did improve their relationships with others; that improvement also was related to increased language arts achievement (Karcher et al., 2002).

One of the most thorough studies of the effects of mentoring was a meta-analytic study that reviewed a total of 55 mentoring program

Foundations

evaluations (DuBois et al., 2002). The study found an overall effect size[2] of ES = .14. This overall, meta-analytic effect size supports a small but positive effect for mentoring among school-age youth. There were some moderating variables, meaning that under certain conditions the average effects were smaller or greater. When the goal of the mentoring program was primarily academic (rather than psychosocial), the effects were slightly higher ES = .21; however, mentoring programs that sought a combination of academic and psychosocial outcomes found smaller effects (ES = .08). Mentoring programs that were closely monitored yielded larger effects (ES = .18) than those that were loosely monitored (ES = .06). The gender of the mentor seemed to matter, as female mentors (ES = .24) were more effective than male mentors (ES = .13). Effects were somewhat higher when mentors were matched to the race of the student (ES = .26) or to the interests of the student (ES = .21). How the mentorship program was implemented and sustained seemed to matter as well. When the mentors were more closely supervised, the effects were greater (ES = .18) than when they were not (ES = .11). When mentors had ongoing training for their mentoring role, the effects were greater (ES = .22) than when training was limited to initial training (ES = .11). When the mentors participated in support groups with other mentors, the effects were greater (ES = .21) than when they did not (ES = .13). Similarly, when there were structured supporting activities for mentors to use during mentoring, the effects were greater (ES = .22) than when there were no structured supporting activities (ES = .11).

A more recent study (Henry et al., 2017) examining the academic effects of mentoring on elementary students found positive effects for mentoring on academic achievement in language arts. In the study, the students were high poverty students in grades 3–5. The mentoring was part of a school–family–community partnership. The mentored student group in the longitudinal 3-year study began performing significantly lower than the non-mentored group. Each measurement period, the mentored students improved reading achievement more than the non-mentored students and by the end of the third year, there was no difference between the two groups. In this mentoring study, the mentorship was arranged by the school counselors within the context of a larger school–community partnership.

When implemented within a personalized learning framework, mentoring can yield small positive effects on achievement. The existing research suggests that schools that include mentoring in the personalized learning framework with gifted students will improve effectiveness with training, structure, and ongoing supports for the mentors who work with the students.

Personalized Learning at Effective Schools

One of the most recent studies of personalized learning was a year-long comparative case study exploring the characteristics of two high performing and two low performing high schools located in the same county (Rutledge et al., 2015). All four of the high schools were demographically similar. The students were similar in race, ethnicity, and socioeconomic status. The research team described the higher performing schools as having "strong and deliberate structures, programs, and practices that attended to students' academic and social emotional learning needs" (Rutledge et al., 2015, p. 1061). This distinction was termed "personalization" for academic and social emotional learning. The comparative case study was a thorough exploration of the most critical elements of personalization.

The theoretical foundation for this in-depth examination of personalized learning was school effectiveness theory (Goldring et al., 2009). Goldring and colleagues identified six key factors associated with effective schools. In addition to those six elements, the personalized learning research team added two additional elements (see Table 3.1). These eight elements of effective schools (or programs) are recommended for building and maintaining a gifted and talented education program. Among the eight elements is personalized learning connections; thus, theoretically we should make the connection that personalized learning is a component of effective gifted and talented education, but at the same time personalized learning alone will not be the foundation of effective gifted education. All eight of the descriptors in Table 3.1 should deeply and accurately characterize effective schools and effective gifted education programs.

The Rutledge and colleagues (2015) study attempted to characterize the critical practices in a high school associated with personalization in an effective school or program. Specifically, the four practices identified were related to personalization and student achievement. First, the effective schools/program practiced looping. Looping involves sustained formal relationships between faculty and students over multiple years of schooling. It is through the practice of looping that information and

Foundations

Table 3.1 Elements of Effective Schools or Programs

Element	Description
Quality Instruction	• instruction focuses on higher-order or complex thinking about rigorous and challenging content • instruction leads to active learning, higher-order thinking, and extended writing, argumentation, and explanation • instructional activities are authentic and relevant to students' lives, culture, and lived experiences
Rigorous and Aligned Curriculum	• all courses in the curriculum include ambitious content designed to foster high achievement • the curriculum is aligned to clearly designated outcome standards • the curriculum is implemented with fidelity and integrity to the content and standards
Personalized Learning Connections	• students have meaningful connections with adults in the school, and these connections promote belonging and motivation • faculty and leadership know the students well and routinely express care and concern for the students' educational success • the school exudes a motivational climate that invites students to engage
Culture of Learning and Professional Behavior	• the school/program shares a focus on high expectations for students, faculty, and leadership • students are encouraged and expected to assume personal responsibility for learning, growth, and achievement • the school/program shares a collaborative culture around academic success and the general efficacy of the staff and the students to attain success
Connections to External Communities	• effective schools/programs establish and sustain connections between the school/program and parents and the community • the school/program has high parental involvement at all levels (K–12) • parental involvement is guided by the socioeconomic, cultural, and language needs of the parents/families served by the school/program

Student Achievement

Table 3.1 Cont.

Element	Description
Learning Centered Leadership	• school/program leaders hold and enact a vision of learning, continuous improvement, and high expectations for students and faculty • leaders actively commit to quality instruction, curricular coherence and a culture of professional practice • leaders set a vision for the school/program that reflects high standards of learning and organizational performance for all students
Systematic Use of Data	• effective schools/programs establish a culture of using data to improve the learning experiences of all students • data come from multiple sources and all leadership and faculty are trained to use the data management systems • data are routinely used in program and student-level decisions
Systemic Performance Accountability	• internal and external structures of responsibility for student learning • individual accountability is established within the school/program among leadership, faculty, and students • external accountability are those benchmarked expectations established by the state or external governing agency

Source: Based on Goldring et al. (2009) and Rutledge et al. (2015)

educational resources are used to personalize students' experiences in the school/program.

Second, effective personalization employs coherent behavior management systems. These behavior management systems support students' feelings of safety and trust within the school or program. The behavior management systems promote student engagement, social and emotional support, high expectations for learning and behavior, and an overall positive climate. Most importantly, the coherent behavior management system provides an infrastructure that supports student need and effective personalization of learning.

Third, personalization practices include extensive collection and use of data. Data are a fundamental element that precedes and continues personalized learning. School leaders, counselors, and faculty routinely

Foundations

gather, store, and use data to make decisions about students' learning opportunities. The data include course performance, as well as external testing (e.g. PSAT, ACT). Data also include surveys about personality, preferences, career interests, or academic interests. Effective schools/programs establish and manage systems where data is collected and curated for easy access and use. These data inform faculty conversations about student needs, and they also inform faculty conversations with students.

The final element of effective personalization (Rutledge et al., 2015) was using data to encourage and place students into advanced learning options. Less effective school cultures foster a climate of taking it easy, but effective schools/programs actively develop a climate where students challenge themselves and take ownership of their advanced learning pathways. The data collection process (element three above) leads to matching students to courses that will challenge them academically and move them toward achievement and career goals.

Summary

Personalized learning has been widely discussed and advocated, and it maintains broad interpretations and variation in implementation. The existing research suggests that when implemented with integrity and strong support structures, personalization will lead to achievement, social and emotional balance, and greater engagement in the learning process. In some ways, personalized learning is a conceptual framework for implementing several educational techniques (e.g. mastery learning, mentoring, acceleration). Thus, research on effectiveness must be narrowed to the use of those specific techniques within the personalization framework. The Rutledge and colleagues (2015) study provides a broad and meaningful understanding of how gifted education programs can be organized for exceptional effectiveness wherein personalized learning is an important component, but certainly not the only component. In fact, the most effective use of personalized learning likely involves directing focus and resources to each of the components and practices associated with personalization.

Notes

1 Effect sizes (ES) reported here were calculated as the mean difference (learning growth of the personalized learning (PL) students *minus* learning growth of the comparison group non-PL students) divided by the pooled standard deviation. This is a common technique to compare effects of educational interventions. Typically we consider .20 as a small effect, .50 as a medium effect, and .80 as a large effect. Note that in most cases both PL students *and* comparison groups had learning growth, so the ES indicates how much more the PL groups grew compared to the non-PL group. Thus, even a very small ($< .10$) ES can still be meaningful to support the effectiveness of PL.
2 These effect sizes reflect mean differences divided by pooled variance. An ES of .20 is small, an ES of .50 is medium, and an ES of .80 is large.

References

Alfieri, L., Brooks, P. J., Aldrich, N. J., & Tenenbaum, H. R. (2011). Does discovery-based instruction enhance learning? *Journal of Educational Psychology, 103*(1), 1–18. https://doi.org/10.1037/a0021017

Black, P. (2005). Formative assessment: Views through different lenses. *The Curriculum Journal, 16*(2), 133–135. http://dx.doi.org/10.1080/09585170500135889

Bloom, B. S. (1984). The 2 sigma problem: The search for methods of group instruction as effective as one-to-one tutoring. *Educational Researcher, 13*(6), 4–16.

Brookhart, S. M., Moss, C. M., & Long, B. A. (2010). Teacher inquiry into formative assessment practices in remedial reading classrooms. *Assessment in Education: Principles Policy & Practice, 17*(1), 41–58.

Bruner, J. (1960). The process of education: A landmark in educational theory. Harvard University Press.

Bruner, J. (1966). Toward a theory of instruction. Harvard University Press.

Chen, L. C., Chen, Y. H., & Ma, W. I. (2014). Effects of integrated information literacy on science learning and problem-solving among seventh-grade students. *Malaysian Journal of Library & Information Science, 19*(2), 35–51.

Chen, L. C., Huang, T.-W., & Chen, Y.-H. (2017). The effects of inquiry-based information literacy instruction on memory and comprehension: A longitudinal study. *Library & Information Science Research, 39*(4), 256–266. https://doi.org/10.1016/j.lisr.2017.11.003

DeMink-Carthew, J., Olofson, M. W., LeGeros, L., Netcoh, S., & Hennessey, S. (2017). An analysis of approaches to goal setting in middle grades personalized learning environments. *Research in Middle Level Education, 40*(10), 1–11. https://doi.org/10.1080/19404476.2017.1392689

DuBois, D. L., Holloway, B. E., Valentine, J. C., & Cooper, H. (2002). Effectiveness of mentoring programs for youth: A meta-analytic review. *American Journal of Community Psychology, 30*(2), 157–197. https://doi.org/10.1023/A:1014628810714

Eisenberg, M. B., & Robinson, L. E. (2007). *The super3: Information skills for young learners.* Linworth.

Goldring, E. B., Porter, A. C., Murphy, J., Elliott, S. N., & Cravens, X. (2009). Assessing learning-centered leadership: Connections to research, professional standards, and current practices. *Leadership and Policy in Schools, 8*(1), 1–36.

Guskey, T. R. (1997). *Implementing mastery learning* (2nd ed.). Wadsworth.

Guskey, T. R. (2007). Closing achievement gaps: Revisiting Benjamin S. Bloom's "learning for mastery." *Journal of Advanced Academics, 19*(1), 8–31.

Hattie, J. (2009). *Visible learning: A synthesis of over 800 meta-analyses relating to achievement.* Routledge.

Henry, L. M., Bryan, J., Zalaquett, C. P. (2017). The effects of a counselor-led, faith-based, school–family–community partnership on student achievement in a high-poverty urban elementary school. *Journal of Multicultural Counseling and Development, 45*(3), 162–182. https://doi.org/10.1002/jmcd.12072

Karcher, M. J., Davis III, C., & Powell, B. (2002). The effects of developmental mentoring on connectedness and academic achievement. *The School Community Journal, 12*(2), 35–50.

Kettler, T., Lamb, K. N., & Mullet, D. R. (2018). Developing creativity in the classroom: Learning and innovation for 21st-century schools. Prufrock Press.

Kulik, J. A., & Kulik, C. C. (1984). Effects of accelerated instruction on students. *Review of Educational Research, 54*(3), 409–425.

McManus, S. (Ed.) (2008). *Attributes of effective formative assessment*. Council of Chief State School Officers.

Meusen-Beekman, K. D., Brinke, D. J., Boshuizen, H. P. A. (2016). Effects of formative assessments to develop self-regulation among sixth grade students: Results from a randomized controlled intervention. *Studies in Educational Evaluation, 51*, 126–136. https://doi.org/10.1016/j.stueduc.2016.10.008

Mofield, E., & Parker Peters, M. (2019). Understanding under achievement: Mindset, perfectionism, and achievement attitudes among gifted students. *Journal for the Education of the Gifted, 42*(2), 107–134. https://doi.org/10.1177/0162353219836737

Ozan, C., & Kıncal, R. Y. (2018). The effects of formative assessment on academic achievement, attitudes toward the lesson, and self-regulation skills. *Educational Sciences: Theory & Practice, 18*(1), 85–118. http://dx.doi.org/10.12738/estp.2018.1.0216

Pane, J. F. (2018). Strategies for implementing personalized learning while evidence and resources are underdeveloped. RAND Corporation. www.rand.org/pubs/perspectives/PE314.html

Pane, J. F., Steiner, E. D., Baird, M. D., Hamilton, L. S., & Pane, J. D. (2017). Informing progress: Insights on personalized learning implementation and effects. RAND Corporation. www.rand.org/pubs/research_reports/RR2042.html

Peine, M. E., & Coleman, L. J. (2010). The phenomenon of waiting in class. *Journal for the Education of the Gifted, 34*(2), 220–224.

Pressey, S. L. (1949). *Educational acceleration; Appraisals and basic problems*. Bureau of Educational Research Monographs, No.31. Ohio State University.

Rogers, K. B. (2007). Lessons learned about educating the gifted and talented: A synthesis of the research on educational practice. *Gifted Child Quarterly, 51*(4), 382–396.

Rhodes, J. E., Contreras, J. M., & Mangelsdorf, S. C. (1994). Natural mentor relationships among Latina adolescent mothers: Psychological adjustment, moderating processes, and the role of early parental acceptance. American Journal of Community Psychology, 22(2), 211–227. https://doi.org/10.1007/BF02506863

Rutledge, S. A., Cohen-Vogel, L., Osborne-Lampkin, L., & Roberts, R. L. (2015). Understanding effective high schools: Evidence for personalization for academic and social emotional learning. *American Educational Research Journal, 52*(6), 1060–1092. https://doi.org/10.3102/0002831215602328

Siegle, D., McCoach, D. B., & Roberts, A. (2017). Why I believe I achieve determines whether I achieve. *High Ability Studies, 28*(1), 59–72. https://doi.org/10.1080/13598139.2017.1302873

Soares, L. B., & Wood, K. (2010). A critical literacy perspective for teaching and learning social studies. *The Reading Teacher, 63*(1), 486–494.

Southern, W. T., & Jones, E. D. (2015). Types of acceleration: Dimensions and issues. In S. G. Assouline, N. Colangelo, J. VanTassel-Baska, & A. Lupkowski-Shoplik (Eds.), *A nation empowered: Evidence trumps the excuses holding back America's brightest students* (Vol. 2, pp. 9–18). Belin-Blank Center, College of Education, University of Iowa.

Steenbergen-Hu, S., & Moon, S. M. (2011). The effects of acceleration on high-ability learners: A meta-analysis. *Gifted Child Quarterly, 55*(1), 39–53. https://doi.org/10.1177/0016986210383155

Stiggins, R. (2008). Introduction to student-involved assessment for learning (5th ed.). Prentice Hall.

Swanson, J. D., & Lord, E. W. (2013). Harnessing and guiding the power of policy: Examples from one state's experiences. *Journal for the Education of the Gifted, 36*(2), 198–219. https://doi.org/10.1177/0162353213480434

Tierney, J., & Branch, A. (1992). *College students as mentors for at-risk youth: A study of six campus partners in learning programs.* Public/Private Ventures.

Tierney, J., Grossman, J., & Resch, N. (1995). *Making a difference: An impact of Big Brothers/Big Sisters.* Public/Private Ventures.

VanLehn, K. (2011). The relative effectiveness of human tutoring, intelligent tutoring systems, and other tutoring systems. *Educational Psychologist, 46*(4), 197–221.

von Secker, C. (2002). Effects of inquiry-based teacher practices on science excellence and equity. *The Journal of Educational Research, 95*(3), 151–160. https://doi.org/10.1080/00220670209596585

Wachanga, S. W., & Gamba, P. P. (2004). Effects of mastery learning approach on secondary school students' achievement in chemistry in

Nakuru District Kenya: Egerton Journal. *Humanities Social Sciences and Education*, 5(2), 221–235.

Wambugu, P. W., & Changeiywo, J. M. (2008). Effects of mastery learning approach on secondary students' physics achievement. *Eurasia Journal of Mathematics, Science & Technology Education*, 4(3), 293–302.

Wiliam, D., & Thompson, M. (2008). Integrating assessment with instruction: What will it take to make it work? In C. A. Dwyer (Ed.), *The future of assessment: Shaping teaching and learning* (pp. 53–82). Lawrence Erlbaum Associates.

PART

II

Core Strategies of Personalized Learning in Gifted Education

Personalized Talent Development Plans

Vignette 1

"Hi, Louisa," I say as I pull a chair up to the eighth grader's desk. "Are you ready to discuss your PLP [personalized learning plan]?"

"Yes, I have it open on my laptop."

"Great! When I looked at it yesterday, one of the things that stood out to me that I'd like to spend some time discussing with you today is your list of colleges that you are most interested in attending."

"Yeah, I don't know a lot about different colleges so that would be helpful."

"Good. I see that you have listed MIT as your top choice. Can you tell me a little bit about what interests you about it?"

"Well, my parents have always told me that I need to go to MIT."

"Okay. Did your parents or someone in your family go there?"

"No. My parents went to another college and said that they want me to go somewhere better. They said that MIT is one of the best schools, and that if I go there, I'll be really successful."

"Your parents are right. MIT is an excellent school. You know, one of the things that I remember about working with you last year is that you really disliked math. I remember lots of our conversations focused on your frustrations with that. I'm wondering now if something has changed – did you take a math or science class this summer that you really enjoyed or are you starting to feel better about the things you are doing in math class this year?"

DOI: 10.4324/9781003237136-6

Core Strategies

"Oh my gosh, no! I hate math! I still hate math. I will always hate math. I really just want to finish my math requirements and never have to take another math class again!"

"Okay," I laugh, "so what did you do this summer?"

"I worked on my book some more, the dystopian one I started last year about the colony of cats in outer space, remember?"

"Of course I remember! So how is that going?"

"Really good! I finished the whole first draft, but it needs editing and revising – lots of editing and revising. Jack and Lila are helping me with that when we don't have other homework to do. I also have an idea for a historical fiction novel set in Colonial America that I've started outlining, and I really want to start on that writing soon."

"I'm glad to hear that! Do you know where you are going to submit your novel when you have finished revising it?"

"I'm still looking into that, but I have a few ideas. I'm going over to Elaine's house next week so she can show me how she published hers through Amazon."

"Good! Keep me updated about that, and let me know how I can help you. So here is what I think we should do for the remainder of our conversation. Let's get on MIT's website together so you can get a better feel for what the school is like. I can show you how to find a profile of the students they admit each year and ways you can learn more about the culture of the school. We can talk through what we see there together. I think that this will help you determine whether or not it is a school that could be a good fit for you. Then I'm going to give you the names of a couple of other universities not on your list that I'd like you to explore in the same way before we meet again."

Vignette 2

"So, as I was thinking about my work from earlier this year and what I want to focus on in these last few weeks, one of the things that I kept circling back to was group work," seventh grader Gina tells me, talking hurriedly as she impatiently pushes a wisp of hair

Personalized Talent Development Plans

behind her ear. "At the beginning of the year, I know I was really bossy. Like on the geography project we did in your social studies class, I knew what I wanted our product to look like and refused to compromise on it, and my group members got really mad at me. You saw all the drama around that. That kept happening on other assignments, and it was really frustrating. So, I set a goal of stepping back and listening to others more when we had group work, but I ended up overcompensating, I think. When we did our biomes project in science, I didn't want to say anything because of my goal. So I let everyone else decide what our project would look like, even when I knew that some of their ideas weren't going to work. I really only took the lead on my own section, and it was great, but when we presented the whole thing to the class, the project overall didn't work and it was really embarrassing. But it didn't just embarrass me – it embarrassed my group members too, and that made me feel bad for them and bad about myself because I didn't speak up more. That's why I'm continuing to assess myself pretty low on my collaboration skills," she says as she points to her personalized learning plan on her laptop screen. "In the fall, I started off high on some of the sub-scores here – like 'seeks opportunities to lead' and 'contributes ideas' – but low on 'willingness to compromise' and 'sees value in others' opinions.' At this point, I've just flipped those sub-scores. So now, I want to find that balance and be able to assess myself high in all of those areas. I need to practice compromising more, and figure out how to speak up when I see that there's going to be a problem in a way that lets people know that I value their ideas but want to help all of us produce a good product that doesn't embarrass any of us."

The conversations above are composites of some that we have experienced as we have conferenced individually with gifted students about their educational goals and progress, especially as captured in personalized learning plans (PLPs). Designed to help students consider their personal strengths and areas for improvement, these plans are also a place where students are required to set individual goals, create action plans to meet those goals, and track their progress. Utilizing a personalized talent development approach within a gifted program necessitates helping students along this particular path of self-understanding and improvement.

While the field of gifted education has varied approaches to the way it identifies and serves gifted students, most experts agree that giftedness should not be conceptualized as solely an IQ or aptitude score that reveals inherent, static abilities in students (Callahan, 2018). Additionally, researchers and practitioners alike understand that students' gifts and talents typically do not manifest evenly across all domains. To put it quite simply, even geniuses have things that they aren't good at.

Rather than viewing IQ and aptitude as inherent and static, a talent development approach views giftedness as manifesting within a system that involves both the student and the student's environment (Subotnik et al., 2017). It recognizes that giftedness needs nurturing, and students need both opportunities and resources in order to develop their gifts into something more than potential. In the case of K–12 education, this means that knowledgeable teachers and advisors need to actively assist gifted students in recognizing and further developing their own particular strengths. As described more fully in Chapter 2, a talent development approach helps students develop their gifts along a life-long continuum, moving from potential to competency to expertise to eminence (Dixson et al., 2020). A primary tool that K–12 educators can use to assist students along this journey is a PLP that focuses on talent development.

A Recent History of Personalized Learning Plans

PLPs emerged as one of the key elements utilized in the personalized learning schools funded through the Next Generation Learning Challenges (NGLC) initiative (Pane et al., 2015; Pane et al., 2017; RAND Corporation & Bill & Melinda Gates Foundation, 2014). Called "learner profiles" by NGLC schools and researchers, these documents contain "a record of each student's individual strengths, needs, motivations, progress, and goals based on data from all available sources. Learner profiles are available not only to teachers, but also to students and their families, and are frequently reviewed, discussed, and updated to inform the student's educational plan" (Pane et al., 2017, p. 6). In this regard, they are similar to the Individualized

Education Plans (IEPs) utilized by schools to support students who receive special education services.

A set of comprehensive studies of personalized learning at NGLC schools undertaken by the RAND Corporation analyzed the use of learner profiles in both NGLC schools and a national sample of schools that served as a comparison group. While both groups of schools included similar attributes in their learner profiles and they implemented these plans in similar ways (Pane et al., 2015; Pane et al., 2017), NGLC schools received new data and utilized it more frequently in order to better personalize learning for their students (Pane et al., 2017). In general, NGLC schools updated learner profiles a few times each month as opposed to roughly once per month in the national sample.

However, no differences were reported by students in NGLC schools and students in the national sample related to the frequency with which they discussed their learning progress with their teachers or reset their personal goals for learning, with the researchers concluding that these practices were not widespread in either group (Pane et al., 2015; Pane et al., 2017). It is in this area that we propose a significant difference lies in the learner profiles as typically used by schools and the personalized talent development plans that are most appropriate for personalizing education for gifted students. The conversations that are needed around these documents are a vital and necessary component of their effectiveness, and without those conversations, these documents can easily become one more administrative task that teachers are required to perform with no real benefit to students. A further discussion of how schools and programs can be better structured to ensure that these conversations occur can be found in Chapter 8, in which we discuss multi-year mentoring for gifted students.

Another difficulty that NGLC schools faced, which remains a broader challenge across educational institutions, involves the logistical integration of data systems and school officials' ability to effectively utilize data. To guide students toward successful educational outcomes, educators, students, and students' families need to attend to more than the quantifiable achievement data that is frequently reported for specific academic skills and content knowledge. Psychosocial skills are also great determiners of students' success in schools and adults' success in their careers. While all the NGLC schools collected nonachievement data in areas such as collaboration skills, critical thinking, and resiliency, much of this data collection occurred informally, and it was not integrated cohesively with achievement data into one system (Pane et al., 2017). In fact, it is not uncommon for achievement data to be housed within multiple programs that become functionally difficult to manage, and for achievement data to be housed separately from attendance, grades, and behavioral data. As a result, many of today's schools are "data rich but information poor" (Bailey et al., 2012, p. 5), with educators struggling to find ways to look at the complete picture of each student and to use all available data to inform instructional decisions about individual students. This situation became evident in the RAND study, as teachers from both the NGLC schools and the national sample indicated that they had plenty of data but needed help converting that data into actionable steps (Pane et al., 2015; Pane et al., 2017).

Two educational consultants who have done extensive work in helping schools move along the continuum from developing learner profiles to creating PLPs are Barbara Bray (2019) and Kathleen McClaskey (2020). Using a Universal Design Framework as a lens, they suggest having students begin by creating a learner profile that identifies their personal strengths, challenges, preferences and needs, talents, interests, passions, and aspirations, along with adjectives that describe themselves. Students may be assisted with this using a number of widely available personality profiles and checklists. The learner profile is then used to create a *Personal Learning Backpack* that contains the tools, resources, learning goals, and skills needed for students to overcome their personal challenges and build their strengths. This step also becomes an active way of developing a stronger sense of student agency, as students learn to identify and clearly communicate what they need to be successful. Finally, the learner profile and Personal Learning Backpack are used to create a personal learning plan, which clearly identifies goals, the actions that the student needs to take to achieve the goals, and the evidence that will be provided to demonstrate attainment. Teachers and students collaborate during each step of this process.

Today, several districts and states require the use of PLPs for all students. In fact, according to the US Department of Labor (2016), all but seven states (California, Wyoming, Oklahoma, Arkansas, Tennessee, North Carolina, and New Hampshire) either mandate some type of individualized learning plan for middle and high school students or utilize them without a state mandate. While the requirements for content and implementation vary considerably, with some of them appearing to be merely documentation of a four-year pathway to high school graduation and some kind of post-secondary plan, some of them do rise to the level of goal-setting and personalization that characterize PLPs as described above.

Examples of Personalized Learning Plans

Vermont is one state that requires that all students attending a public school for grades 7–12 have a PLP. This requirement was codified in Act 77 of 2013, which requires that students be given flexible pathways to graduation that are documented in their PLPs. Recognizing some of the inherent problems that can come with the implementation of PLPs, the state asserts that PLPs should be living documents and that emphasis should be placed on the process over the product:

> The actual documentation of the PLP – in whatever form it takes – is only as good as the process that supports the development and use of the document. Fundamental to the successful implementation of PLPs is a meaningful process much more so than a product, even though a clear and thoughtful product is key to ultimate success.
>
> (Vermont Agency of Education, 2019, p. 5)

The discussions and counseling that students and educators can have around the content of these plans is where the power of these documents truly lies.

While Vermont's local school districts are given the flexibility to develop their own format for the personalized learning plans, the state does offer recommendations for what to include. A student profile section is recommended, which would include the student's strengths/abilities/skills, core values, and baseline assessment results, which include academic, career, and interest assessments. Both short-term and long-term secondary and post-secondary goals should be identified, and these goals should be accompanied by action steps and a timeline for achieving them. The type of evidence that can be provided as proof of achievement should be clearly identified and then provided when the goal has been met. The state also emphasizes that this process should be iterative and recommends a place for students, families, and educators involved in the PLP process to provide their reflections.

Because learning how to effectively implement PLPs is a rather involved process for educators and school administrators as well as students – as opposed to a reform that can simply be mandated and implemented (for

Core Strategies

better or worse) in a relatively short amount of time, like administering a new standardized test – Vermont has also created a rubric for the implementation process. The rubric recognizes that teachers may initially see PLPs as one more job requirement, and students may initially see them as pointless. Teachers and students will, with support, move across the rubric's continuum to the ultimate point in which the PLPs are being utilized effectively. Consulting the rubric at various points in the implementation process may provide clarity to educators as they start to use these plans with students and families. If used as part of an honest self-assessment of the process, it can also spark important conversations on campuses about where implementation stands and what needs to be done to improve. Figure 4.1 contains Vermont's

Goals

- Each gifted student should regularly participate in creating and updating documents that identify their individual strengths, needs, interests, and goals. These documents should be accessible at all times by the student, parent/guardian, and school personnel.
- The creation of PLPs should be a collaborative process in which students work with their parents/guardians and school personnel to identify pathways for continued talent development.
- Each gifted student's progress towards reaching their talent development goals should be documented in their PLP. Functioning as dynamic, meaningful artifacts to and for the gifted student, the PLPs should change and progress as students do. PLPs should capture a gifted student's authentic learning and growth.

Stage of Implementation	Description of Stage
Initiating	Gifted students complete a PLP, but many of them resist doing the work because they think it's a "waste of time" or they don't see how it impacts their development. Teachers of gifted students feel that the PLP is an additional job requirement that they have to force students to complete rather than a meaningful guide to personalized talent development opportunities. As a result, the PLP tends to create frustration for both staff and students.

Figure 4.1 Self-Assessment for the Implementation of Personalized Learning Plans

Note: PLP, personalized learning plan

Source: Adapted from Vermont Agency of Education (2019)

Stage of Implementation	Description of Stage
Developing	PLPs are collaboratively created for students at least annually. Parents/guardians are given clear information about the opportunity to engage in this process. Some engage with the process, while some do not. Many students use their PLPs to make some decisions about how they will move through school, engage in extracurricular activities, and plan for post-secondary opportunities. Some students are engaged in customizing their PLPs in interesting ways and report that their PLPs are helpful tools that facilitate their growth. Goals and evidence on PLPs may or may not be aligned clearly with student talent development. School personnel have access to students' PLPs and some of them use the PLPs to build relationships with gifted students.
Performing	Gifted students largely engage in creating their PLPs because they recognize that the process results in a positive impact on their growth and development. The PLPs are personal and engaging, and many gifted students use them for purposes outside of school, like college, scholarship, and job applications. School personnel feel equipped to guide students to use their PLPs to facilitate the students' talent development.

Figure 4.1 Continued

descriptors of three stages of the implementation process, adapted to align with a talent development model for gifted students.

Henry County Schools in Georgia also include learner profiles as one of its five pillars of personalized learning. Six criteria are identified that describe the learner profiles (Henry County Schools, 2018). According to these criteria, learner profiles should include a variety of short- and long-term academic, social, and career goals. They should also identify various characteristics of each student, including strengths, interests, and learning preferences. Student work portfolios should provide evidence of student progress. Finally, advisory structures and conferences should be utilized to keep the process moving forward, and all efforts should focus on developing student agency. Like Vermont, Henry County also offers a rubric that outlines the stages of implementation for learner profiles. We have adapted this rubric for programs that would like to develop a similar system focused specifically on gifted students and personalized talent development plans (see Figure 4.2).

Colorado also requires what it calls Individual Career and Academic Plans (ICAPs) for all incoming ninth graders. However, Colorado adds an additional layer to this requirement for gifted students. In addition to completing an ICAP, gifted students in K–12 must also complete an Advanced Learning Plan (ALP). Districts may choose to combine the ICAP and the ALP into one document at the high school level to streamline the process. Colorado describes the ALP as "a record of programming options and academic or talent goals that support the student's strength area(s) and affective or behavioral development. Input from parent/guardian, student, teacher/s and gifted education specialist guide the development, implementation, and revisions of the ALP" (Colorado Department of Education, 2020, p.1).

An ALP may look similar to the PLPs described thus far, but it takes a somewhat different stance in stating that one academic goal must be identified each year that is based on the student's area of strength or interest and that one affective goal must also be established each year. Another place in which it differs from the other plans is that it must include evidence of programming options that help build the student's area of strength. Because of this additional element, it requires that school personnel who assist with the development of a combined ICAP/ALP have strong knowledge of various programming options appropriate for gifted students, which at the high school level may include acceleration or concurrent enrollment. Therefore, additional training may be required for the personnel involved in developing a combined ICAP/ALP. A comprehensive worksheet for developing an ALP for gifted students can be found at www.cde.state.co.us/gt/alpworksheet2016. A version we adapted for programs in the beginning stages of this work can be viewed in Figure 4.3.

While it is not typical for states to mandate a differentiated personalized learning plan specifically for gifted students, some gifted programs do currently make use of them. Students at Davidson Academy, a school for highly gifted students, develop PLPs with guidance from staff and families.

	Not Evident	Emerging	Operational	Exemplary
Learner Profile	No evidence exists to indicate that the program is using learner profiles of gifted students in a meaningful way.	The program uses two or more non-integrated platforms for tracking and analyzing gifted students' data. Because information is stored in different files and locations, school personnel, gifted students, and families have difficulty organizing and making sense of it as a coherent whole. Learner profiles, therefore, are infrequently referenced.	Historical, current, and aspirational data for gifted students are considered and work together to comprise a learner profile for each gifted student. The learner profile is housed on a single platform for accessibility and is an integral part of students' decision-making processes and the gifted program.	Learner profiles are based on students' academic and psychosocial strengths, needs, interests, goals, and portfolio. They are used to personalize learning experiences for gifted students. Learner profiles are regularly and easily accessed by students, families, and school personnel, and increase student agency over learning.

Figure 4.2 Assessment Rubric for Gifted Students' Personalized Talent Development Plans

Source: Adapted from Henry County Schools (2018), pp. 9–11

	Not Evident	Emerging	Operational	Exemplary
Goal-Setting	No evidence exists to indicate that the program is fostering gifted students' ability to set and pursue goals in a meaningful way.	Some opportunities exist for gifted students to set their own short- and long-term goals for talent development. These goals may reflect predetermined or superficial outcomes. Goals are infrequently referenced or monitored for progress.	Gifted students have regular opportunities to set their own SMART goals. They also have regular opportunities to demonstrate their ability to meet those goals. Goals are clearly tied to talent development and are regularly reviewed and monitored for progress.	Gifted students as well as their parents/guardians and school personnel collaboratively develop SMART goals that drive decision-making about the students' learning experiences. Goals attend to both the academic and the psychosocial skills required for talent development. Goals are regularly reviewed and monitored for progress, and revised as needed.
Strengths, Interests, and Needs	No evidence exists to indicate that the program is fostering an understanding of gifted	Gifted students are aware of their own strengths, interests, and needs, but are not yet connecting	Gifted students are aware of their own strengths, interests and needs, and use that understanding	Gifted students' strengths, interests, and needs are captured in the learner profile. That information

	students' individual strengths, interests, and needs in a meaningful way.	that knowledge to the further development of their own talent.	to make decisions that positively impact their talent development.	is used collaboratively by the students, their parents/ guardians, and school personnel to make decisions that positively impact students' talent development.
Portfolio	No evidence exists to indicate that the program is using portfolios of student work in a meaningful way.	Portfolio items exist but are not aligned to gifted students' goals or talent development. Portfolios include gifted students' work but not in a way that reflects learning progress over time. Portfolios are not easily accessed by gifted students, their families or their teachers.	Portfolio items are aligned to gifted students' goals and talent development. Portfolio artifacts serve as evidence of gifted students' mastery of skills and content, clearly showing progress and talent development over time. Portfolios are easily accessed by gifted students, their families, and their teachers.	Portfolio items are clearly aligned to gifted students' goals and talent development. Portfolio artifacts serve as a thorough record of gifted students' mastery of both academic and psychosocial skills, clearly showing progress and talent development over time. Digital portfolios are regularly and easily accessed by gifted students, their families, and school personnel.

Figure 4.2 Continued

Core Strategies

	Not Evident	Emerging	Operational	Exemplary
Conferencing	No evidence exists to indicate that the program is using student-led conferencing in a meaningful way.	Student-led conferences happen infrequently. Conferences are heavily scripted and/or require little input from students. They do not differentiate for the needs of gifted students and their personal talent development.	Student-led conferences take place at least two times during the year. Conferences require gifted students to discuss their own progress, needs, and aspirations, and are focused on students demonstrating growth in talent development over time.	Student-led conferences are a regular part of the learning experience. Conferences include multiple members of a gifted student's support team (i.e. parents/guardians, teachers, advisors, mentors, etc.). Gifted students actively drive conversations and decisions about their own learning and growth in talent development over time.
Advisory	No evidence exists to indicate that the program is using advisory in a meaningful way.	The program has implemented an advisory structure for gifted students, but the time is not being maximized to	The program has implemented a system that helps teachers get to know their gifted students well, fosters student agency,	Advisory is an integral part of the program's culture, serving as a learning community, involving

		increase the development of students' academic and psychosocial skills.	builds a sense of community, and helps gifted students improve their academic and psychosocial skills.	all school staff, and connecting every gifted student with a positive adult mentor. Advisory builds a culture of care and self-advocacy, preparing gifted students to effectively continue progressing along the talent development continuum as they move into college and careers.
Agency	No evidence exists that the learner profile is enabling student agency among gifted students.	Gifted students are aware of their learning profile but are not using it to reflect on their own strengths, interests, or needs in ways that benefit their talent development.	Gifted students are leveraging the learner profile to assist them in their talent development.	Gifted students are leveraging the learner profile as a tool that enables them to be the primary decision-makers in their talent development.

Figure 4.2 Continued

Core Strategies

Advanced Learning Plan Worksheet
Student Information

Required:
• Student's name
• Student's ID number
• Date of birth
• Grade level
• School and district
• Identified area(s) of giftedness with dates and methods of identification
   o General/specific intellectual aptitude
   o Academic aptitude: reading, writing, mathematics, science, social studies, and/or world language
   o Talent aptitude: visual arts, performing arts, musical, dance, psychomotor abilities
   o Creative or productive thinking
   o Leadership abilities
• Twice-exceptional designation (IEP or 504) or other educational plans (ELL)
• Date of ALP development

ALP Team Members
Required: • Student • Parent/guardian • Classroom teacher(s) • Gifted education staff or other staff with training in gifted education *Other:* • Additional support staff as appropriate
Parental Engagement and Participation
Required: • Date of parent/guardian notification of ALP development • Evidence of parent engagement and input in ALP development and review of progress

Figure 4.3 Worksheet for Developing an Advanced Learning Plan

Note: ALP, Advanced Learning Plan; ELL, English language learner; IEP, Individualized Education Plan

Source: Adapted from Colorado Department of Education (2020)

Personalized Talent Development Plans

Examples:
- Signature or electronic signature
- Checklist
- Inventory
- Survey
- Questionnaire
- Narrative description

Current Achievement Data

Required:
- Note areas of particular strength or concern, as evidenced in most recent student data

Examples:
- State assessment data
- Nationally-normed testing data (PSAT, SAT, ACT, etc.)
- Classroom data
- Performance data

Current Information About Student's Interests and Activities

Required:
- A list of the student's identified interests as they relate to area(s) of talent development
- A list of participation in classes or activities that develop those interests and talents

Establishment of Annual Goals

Required:
- SMART achievement goal in area(s) of strength and interest
- SMART affective goal in area(s) of strength and interest to address one or more competency: personal, social, communication, leadership, cultural, and college/career planning
- Action steps to be taken during current school year to achieve both goals

Progress Reporting

Required:
- Date(s) and detail(s) of progress reporting, including who is primarily responsible for working with the student to monitor progress towards goals, how often progress reporting will occur, and the method for progress monitoring
- Evidence that indicates how student is progressing towards goals

Figure 4.3 Continued

93

Core Strategies

Examples of Evidence: • Work samples • Achievement data
• Videos or photos of student-created work or performances • Narrative descriptions • Checklists
Final Assessment of Goal Attainment
Required: • Date and details of final assessment of progress towards achievement and affective goals, including who is involved in that final assessment and how that assessment is communicated with parent/guardian • Recommendations for transition to next grade *Examples:* • End--of-year conference • Checkbox for Goal Attained or Goal Not Attained with brief explanation • Narrative description of annual student progress

Figure 4.3 Continued

Secondary students attending ASPIRE Academy for Highly Gifted Students also create them.

ASPIRE Academy is a public school-within-a-school that serves highly gifted students in grades 1–12 at three campuses in Grapevine-Colleyville Independent School District in Texas. Its existence is due, in part, to the district's commitment to personalized learning. Part of the district's personalized learning initiatives include a requirement to develop PLPs for each secondary student in the district. Teachers within ASPIRE Academy adapted the PLP format utilized by their campuses to create documents more appropriate for their student population. While students are primarily responsible for completing these PLPs, they do so with assistance from one of their core ASPIRE teachers, and families are encouraged to discuss them with the students.

At the middle school level, ASPIRE students are asked to create a general profile of themselves based on their strengths, weaknesses, interests, learning preferences, and post-graduation plans. They update their personal profile at least once per year. They then utilize a 1–4 ranking system to evaluate themselves in several core areas related to talent development, including creative thinking, critical thinking, complexity of work, collaborative skills, and social–emotional skills (see Figure 4.4). These specific areas were chosen because they are the same areas that their elementary teachers rate them on in a supplemental, standards-based report card in grades 1–5, so the students are familiar with what they mean in practice. That supplemental report card is discontinued after elementary school for logistical reasons, but the students need to continue to refine these skills as they advance through middle school.

After completing the self-evaluation, middle school students create a specific goal for themselves in two or more areas of their choosing. Along with each goal, the students write an action plan in which they identify the steps they will take to meet that goal. At checkpoints throughout the year, they reevaluate themselves, provide evidence that supports their evaluation (typically in the form of a link to a class assignment or an explanation two or three sentences long), and make adjustments to their goals and plans as needed. These PLPs are digital and housed on a shared platform, so all ASPIRE teachers have access to each one.

At the high school level, the PLP becomes more focused on preparing for college. It is used to track graduation requirements, course selection, and standardized test scores. It also contains links to resources students can use to help them choose a university, a major, and a career, and provides a place for them to document the options they are interested in pursuing further. Students are encouraged to consider their most immediate post-secondary plans around four primary options: highly selective four-year universities, honors colleges housed within four-year universities, liberal arts colleges, and specialized schools, such as military academies, women's colleges, and historically Black colleges and universities. As in middle school, core ASPIRE teachers assist the students as they work on their PLPs, and families are encouraged to help as well.

While ASPIRE Academy has experienced some success with the use of these PLPs, as illustrated by the conversations in this chapter's opening vignettes, implementing them has not been easy. Finding time for students and teachers to discuss them regularly and ensuring that all teachers are comfortable and equipped to have conversations with students about them has been a challenge that the Academy is still working to address. More information about these types of challenges can be found in the discussion of advisory systems in Chapter 8.

Ranking Scale	
4	Demonstrated consistently in all classes
3	Demonstrated consistently in most classes
2	Demonstrated inconsistently or only in a few classes
1	Not demonstrated in classes

Critical Thinking
Asks insightful, authentic questions and seeks answers
Demonstrates evidence of high level reflection
Shows perseverance when challenged
Demonstrates integrity academically and individually

Creative Thinking
Brainstorms fluently and regularly to generate ideas
Thinks flexibly; sees things in new and different ways
Expresses original and unique ideas
Elaborates on ideas to create sophisticated products
Takes risks in own thinking

Complexity of Work
Connects elements of Depth and Complexity to own learning
Works at highest levels of Bloom's Taxonomy regularly and with ease
Views ideas through multiple perspectives

Collaboration
Shows willingness to compromise
Recognizes value in others' opinions in addition to own
Moves group toward completion of tasks and goals
Seeks and accepts opportunities to lead
Contributes ideas for group consideration

Social and Emotional Skills
Demonstrates humility
Uses failure as an opportunity to learn
Shows self-confidence
Demonstrates self-directed learning

Figure 4.4 Skills Self-Assessed and Developed by Middle School Students in ASPIRE Academy's Personalized Learning Plan

Source: Taliaferro et al. (2019)

Shifting the Focus to Personalized Talent Development Plans

While personalized learning plans may vary in purpose and structure, at their core they are all a way to capture and build on each student's individual strengths in a deliberate way. It is our contention that by focusing these plans more intentionally on talent development, educators can help ensure that gifted students are able to actualize the potential represented by whatever qualifications they met to become identified as gifted. The ALPs utilized in Colorado are perhaps the closest that we have seen to something that might be considered a personalized talent development plan, in that they clearly identify the areas of giftedness for each student in the profile section and require that each student have both an academic goal and an affective goal in an area of strength.

A challenge in creating a personalized talent development plan for each student, though, is ensuring that the educators working with them have the requisite knowledge to guide gifted students along varying trajectories in different domains. Some excellent frameworks to assist with that are currently being developed.

Recognizing that the fields of sports and music have long known how to take children displaying exceptional talent in their early years and develop that talent into eminence, researchers in gifted education are now focusing on identifying the specific skills needed to develop eminence in other fields, including academics. Raw talent is certainly a needed ingredient, but by itself, it is not enough. Students must have other skills that propel them to access additional resources and spend the time needed to develop their natural talents into something tangible. To help identify those skills, Olszewski-Kubilius et al. (2019) consulted with 18 international psychologists who study talent development and giftedness, and 13 psychologists who focus on high performance in specific domains (academics, art performance, art production, professions, and sports) to identify the psychosocial skills most important to achieving success in different domains at each stage of the talent development process, from demonstrating ability to achieving eminence. These psychosocial skills are grouped into the following categories, each of which is broken down into further sub-skills: creative risk-taking, social skills, metacognitive self-regulation, motivational self-regulation, emotional self-regulation, cognitive self-regulation, and insider knowledge.

Several psychosocial sub-skills emerged as important across all stages of talent development. Not surprisingly, these skills also correspond to the foci of much of the current social–emotional learning that occurs in schools. These skills include coping with challenges, failure, and anxiety; knowing how to focus one's own attention and concentration; goal-setting; demonstrating self-confidence, commitment, and perseverance; practicing time management and organizational skills; and collaborating well with others.

Because the time spent in K–12 schooling is mostly spent in the first stage of the talent development process, as students ideally move from ability to competence in their area of strength, we suggest that talent development plans include the psychosocial skills most commonly needed by students in that stage, with a focus on those that are needed specifically in academics and mathematics. In addition to the ones identified above, these also include:

- being open to experiences
- eliciting and showing respect
- demonstrating empathy and compassion
- knowing one's own strengths and weaknesses
- being able to capitalize on one's own strengths and compensate for weaknesses
- self-regulating one's arousal and relaxation
- using appropriate learning and practice strategies
- being teachable
- knowing the "game" and how to play it.

In addition to targeting specific psychosocial skills for development, a personalized talent development plan should also target the academic skills that a student needs to strengthen in order to reach the next stage of development in their area of strength and identify opportunities that will help that student develop those skills. Those opportunities may exist within the student's current school system. However, they may also exist outside of it and could include participation in academic competitions, mentorships with local professionals, additional coursework completed in the summer or online, and/or professional publication of the student's

Personalized Talent Development Plans

work. Identifying those opportunities and making sure that the educators involved in co-creating personalized talent plans with students and their families understand them is vital.

As schools and programs work to create templates for these plans, we suggest they begin by answering these questions:

1. What data do we have that indicates what a student's domains of giftedness are?
2. What data do we routinely collect that will indicate whether or not students are advancing in their domains of giftedness?
3. What data do we – or can we – collect to capture students' development in the psychosocial skills required for talent development?
4. What trajectories exist within our school system for students to develop their talents in each of the domains we have identified?
5. What opportunities exist outside of our school system that our students can feasibly access to help them develop their talents in each of the domains we have identified?
6. How can we allocate time and resources (including personnel) to help students create personalized talent development plans and routinely monitor their progress?
7. What training will our staff need to be able to implement personalized talent development plans?
8. How many goals can our students and staff effectively manage?
9. Where will we house our personalized talent development plans so everyone involved can access them?
10. How will we regularly assess our implementation of the personalized talent development plans and make improvements?

Summary

Personalized learning requires that educators know their students well. Individual learner profiles that document students' areas of strength and interest should be easily accessible and updated at least yearly. These learner profiles can be used to create personalized academic and affective goals for gifted students that are documented in a personalized talent development plan. All stakeholders (faculty, administration, student, and parent) should be represented in the creation and implementation of personalized talent development plans. Creating and implementing personalized talent development plans requires staff, student, and family training, as well as regular assessment and adjustments of the process.

References

Bailey, J., Carter, S. C., Schneider, C., & Ark, T. V. (2012). Data backpacks: Portable records & learner profiles. Henry County Schools. https://schoolwires.henry.k12.ga.us/site/handlers/filedownload.ashx?moduleinstanceid=74244&dataid=90012&FileName=DLN-Smart-Series-Databack-Final1.pdf

Bray, B. (2019). *Getting to know you with your learner profile.* Rethinking Learning. https://barbarabray.net/2019/08/16/getting-to-know-you-with-your-learner-profile/

Callahan, C. M. (2018). Considerations for the identification of gifted and talented students. In C. M. Callahan & H. L. Hertberg-Davis (Eds.), *Fundamentals of gifted education: Considering multiple perspectives* (2nd ed.) (pp. 94–102). Routledge.

Colorado Department of Education. (2020). ALP blended with an ICAP. www.cde.state.co.us/postsecondary/crosswalk-icap-alp

Dixson, D. D., Olszewski-Kubilius, P, Subotnik, R. F., & Worrell, F. C. (2020). Developing academic talent as a practicing school psychologist: From potential to expertise. *Psychology in the Schools, 57*(10), 1582–1595. https://doi.org/10.1002/pits.22363

Henry County Schools. (2018). Personalized learning rubric. https://schoolwires.henry.k12.ga.us/cms/lib/GA01000549/Centricity/Domain/7692/PL%20Rubric%20Domains%20and%20Criteria%2010.15.18.pdf

McClaskey, K. (2020). *Empower the learner – building the skills of agency and self-advocacy using the UDL lens.* Make Learning Personal. http://kathleenmcclaskey.com/2020/08/02/part-2-of-3-empower-the-learner/.

Olszewski-Kubilius, P., Subotnik, R. F., Davis, L. C., & Worrell, F. C. (2019). Benchmarking psychosocial skills important for talent development. In

R. F. Subotnik, S. G. Assouline, P. Olszewski Kubilius, H. Stoeger, & A. Ziegler (Eds.), The future of research in talent development: Promising trends, evidence, and implications of innovative scholarship for policy and practice. *New Directions for Child and Adolescent Development*, *168*, 161–176.

Pane, J. F., Steiner, E. D., Baird, M. D., & Hamilton, L. S. (2015). *Continued progress: Promising evidence on personalized learning.* RAND Corporation. www.rand.org/pubs/research_reports/RR1365.html

Pane, J. F., Steiner, E. D., Baird, M. D., Hamilton, L. S., & Pane, J. D. (2017). *Informing progress: Insights on personalized learning implementation and effects.* RAND Corporation. www.rand.org/pubs/research_reports/RR2042.html

RAND Corporation & Bill & Melinda Gates Foundation. (2014). *Early progress: Interim research on personalized learning.* Bill & Melinda Gates Foundation. https://usprogram.gatesfoundation.org/-/media/dataimport/resources/pdf/2016/12/42-early-progress-on-personalized-learning-full-report.pdf

Subotnik, R. F., Stoeger, H., & Olszewski-Kubilius, P. (2017). Talent development research, policy, and practice in Europe and the United States: Outcomes from a summit of international researchers. *Gifted Child Quarterly, 61*(3), 262–269. https://doi.org/10.1177/0016986217701839

Taliaferro, C., Mishoe, G., & Jones-Balsley, K. (November, 2019). Supporting the social-emotional growth of highly gifted middle school students. National Association for Gifted Children Annual Convention, Albuquerque, NM.

US Department of Labor. (2016). Individualized learning plans across the U.S. www.dol.gov/agencies/odep/topics/individualized-learning-plan/map#VT

Vermont Agency of Education. (2019). Personalized learning plans process manual. https://education.vermont.gov/sites/aoe/files/documents/Personalized%20Learning%20Plans%20Manual.pdf

Competency-Based Progressions and Acceleration

In 2003, the University of Iowa hosted a summit on acceleration. With support from the John Templeton Foundation of Pennsylvania, they invited leading scholars and educators from around the country to attend, with the goal of producing a national report on the status of educational acceleration in the United States. The resulting 2-volume report, *A Nation Deceived: How Schools Hold Back America's Brightest Students*, laid bare the various ways in which our school systems regularly ignore research and fail gifted students in classrooms every day. Presenting a viewpoint both grim and alarming, and illustrated vividly with accounts of real students' experiences, this report became perhaps one of the most popularly read pieces on advanced education, capturing the interest of the press, the general public, policy makers, and of course, educators. Defining the issue of the routine stagnation of America's most talented students as one of inherent inequity, the report loudly called for the elimination of all barriers that regularly prevent advanced students from receiving an appropriate education.

As a result, the next decade saw renewed interest in better aligning educational practices with educational research. And the research on acceleration is robust and clear: acceleration is the most effective intervention for academically gifted and motivated students.

In 2015, the group produced a follow-up two-volume report: *A Nation Empowered: Evidence Trumps the Excuses Holding Back America's Brightest Students*. While many encouraging advances were reported, such as the passing of state-level policies that explicitly create pathways for academic acceleration and the expansion of access to advanced coursework through the Advanced Placement (AP) program and partnerships between colleges and high schools, the report also recognized that a great deal of work remains to be done. Misconceptions and biases against acceleration remain entrenched throughout our schools, and far too many educators and policy makers who hold power over the trajectory of students' educational futures remain unfamiliar with the research.

And while policy makers and educators continue to work to catch up to the research, gifted students continue to languish. Yes, many approaches exist for educating gifted students in schools today. However, grade acceleration clearly has yielded the best results. Unfortunately, schools largely continue to rely on student age rather than ability to determine academic placement. Consequently, gifted students regularly attend classes driven by standards that are far too low. Recent research suggests that 20%–49% of English language arts students and 14–37% of math students have already mastered standards one full grade level above their current placement (Peters et al., 2017).

Situated firmly within the context of this renewed discussion about the need for greater access to acceleration, the personalized learning movement began its rise. In its embrace of using actual data to make informed decisions about instruction for individual students, advocates for personalized learning began promoting the same tools that gifted education had long asked schools to offer: the ability to move individual students through their schooling at the pace that is most appropriate for them. Competency-based progression is the method through which that type of personalization can happen.

Personalized Learning and Competency-Based Progressions

Competency-based learning is one of the key features of personalized learning. Also known as mastery-based learning, proficiency-based learning, and performance-based learning (Brodersen et al., 2017), competency-based learning requires students to demonstrate a certain level of mastery of individual concepts or skills before they move on to learn new content. It envisions the classroom as a place where no student will be required to progress to the next unit when they fail a test on concepts that will be built on in the next unit. Implementation requires frequent

Core Strategies

assessments, which may occur at different times for different students according to their personal readiness. In theory, classrooms that embrace competency-based learning practices will structure procedures so that all students are learning at their own pace. This specific type of acceleration is referred to as continuous progress (Assouline et al., 2015; Southern & Jones, 2015), and it inevitably must include advancement to the next grade level of content at non-traditional points within the school year. When a student proves ready to move from second-grade math to third-grade math, the student moves. However, many teachers and schools eschew an all-or-nothing approach to competency-based learning, instead taking some of its principles and modifying them to fit more traditional school structures.

In RAND's study of personalized learning, the majority of teachers in both personalized learning schools and the national sample reported using competency-based practices to either a large or a moderate extent, and it was clear that some degree of competency-based instructional practices were utilized even in schools that had not fully implemented a model of competency-based progressions (Pane et al., 2017; RAND Corporation & Bill & Melinda Gates Foundation, 2014). However, fewer schools were implementing competency-based progressions than other features of personalized learning (Pane et al., 2015).

Teachers in Next Generation Learning Challenges (NGLC) schools did report using these practices more than the national sample of schools; however, their students were less likely to report that these practices were common (Pane et al., 2017), implying that a disconnect existed between the teachers' understanding of these practices and the students' understanding. It is possible that the work that teachers were doing to appropriately level students in their work wasn't visibly seen by the students, so they were, to some extent, unaware of it. However, it is also possible that the teachers believed they were offering flexibility to students but students didn't view it as flexible at all. Lending some credence to the latter interpretation, slightly less than two-thirds of school administrators in RAND's study reported that students could actually advance in their learning based on competency (Pane et al., 2015).

Several constraints emerged as inhibiting the full use of competency-based progressions in schools, including state requirements related to testing, advancement, and how credits are awarded and transferred; grade reporting structures that needed to follow traditional formats for clarity of communication with various stakeholders; the fear of students with poor

Progressions and Acceleration

time management skills falling far behind if they had too much control over the pacing of their own learning; and the utilization of seat time rather than learning to advance students in content (Pane et al., 2015; Pane et al., 2017). One major hindrance was pacing that educators perceived as needing to be aligned with expectations regarding grade-level standardized testing (Pane et al., 2015). Driven by the belief that students' learning needs to conform with traditional grade-level calendars in order to optimally prepare students for end-of-year standardized exams, many teachers paced learning in classrooms so that it was somewhat flexible but controlled. The majority of students reported that they had choices about how they used their time but they had to meet deadlines set by the teacher. Other students reported that they had no control at all over the pacing of their own learning.

One math teacher described the way this looked in her classroom thusly:

> In Algebra, students are broken into basic, proficient, and advanced problems. [The math problems are] not individualized by me, but students can access them and zoom through the easier problems to advanced. Students that have to hone in on the basic can spend more time on that. Students choose what group of questions they want to work on. It's helped some students see where they are at and where they want to go and the advanced kids push the rigor of that.
> (RAND Corporation & Bill & Melinda Gates Foundation, 2014, p. 12)

While this type of practice may be considered a micro version of a competency-based progression insofar as students have some flexibility to progress from basic content to more advanced content within the structure of a lesson or unit, it definitely does not utilize the model to its full effect.

Given the cyclical nature of much learning that happens as students progress from one grade level to the next, this practice also raises important questions about how to determine when "advanced" in one grade level actually translates to "basic" or "proficient" on the same skill in the next grade level. If a student is consistently and successfully completing "advanced" problems in third-grade math, for example, it's logical to infer that the student might be better served by being introduced to fourth-grade math concepts.

105

Core Strategies

If a system utilizes competency-based progressions, it is only reasonable to expect that advanced students will progress to the point that acceleration into another grade level is warranted. However, virtually all of the schools studied by RAND utilized traditional grade levels (Pane et al., 2015), perhaps because they had no other options or were unaware of what other options exist. It's therefore important that schools understand the state and local policies that govern both competency-based progressions and acceleration.

Current State Policies Regarding Competency-Based Progressions

Competency-based progressions have not yet been fully adopted by any state, but many have been experimenting with them as part of personalized learning. A 2017 report describing the landscape of competency-based progressions throughout the United States identifies two ways in which states are engaging with this practice: through pilot programs in competency-based education and through general innovation programs or funds. At the time of the report, 23 states were involved in one or both of these efforts (ExcelinEd & EducationCounsel, 2017). Table 5.1 lists those states and their method of involvement. However, while these efforts have certainly created an environment that allows for greater personalization via competency-based progressions, it does not appear that schools and districts are using them to a significant degree (ExcelinEd & EducationCounsel, 2017). This limited enactment is possibly because school administrators and local education leaders do not yet fully understand how to utilize competency-based progressions most effectively.

One of the early adopters of competency-based progressions and the state that has possibly advanced the furthest in this process is New Hampshire. State regulations require that local school boards ensure that each high school clearly outlines the competencies required for graduation, and all high school "credits shall be based on the demonstration of district and/or graduation competencies not on time spent achieving these competencies" (State of New Hampshire Office of Legislative Services, 2014). Students are, by law, allowed to demonstrate that they have mastered the competencies required for graduation though pre-assessments and through work completed via prior learning activities.

106

Progressions and Acceleration

Table 5.1 States Utilizing Competency-Based Progressions in 2017

Pilot Programs	General Innovation Programs or Funds	Both
Florida	Alabama	Idaho
Illinois	Arkansas	Ohio
Iowa	Colorado	
New Hampshire	Connecticut	
Oregon	Georgia	
Utah	Indiana	
	Kansas	
	Kentucky	
	Massachusetts	
	Minnesota	
	Mississippi	
	Texas	
	Washington	
	West Virginia	
	Wyoming	

Source: Based on ExcelinEd & EducationCounsel (2017)

Colorado is another example of a state that has created a pathway for graduation based on student mastery of competencies. While local school boards are tasked with creating the details for their own schools, state guidelines offer a menu of options that can be utilized in order for students to demonstrate college and career readiness, which is one requirement for graduation (Colorado Department of Education, 2016). These options include obtaining minimum scores on standardized tests, such as AP exams, AccuPlacer tests, the ACT, the SAT, and the Armed Services Vocational Aptitude Battery (ASVAB). In lieu of these test scores, local education agencies may also allow students to demonstrate readiness via standards-based performance assessments or capstone projects. Colorado also allows districts to substitute competency-based progressions for seat time (Colorado Education Initiative, 2015).

Westminster Public Schools is an example of a local school system in Colorado that has embraced these initiatives (Westminster Public Schools, 2020). There, students are assigned to levels rather than to grades for their learning, and these levels are based on the students' mastery of learning. Students are able to advance to a higher level at any time during the year.

It is therefore possible for a student who traditionally would be a fourth-grade student working on fourth-grade reading and fourth-grade math to instead be working simultaneously at level 3 for reading and at level 5 for math.

Maximizing the progress of individual students who are working at different levels does present educators with challenges, and blended learning perhaps shows the most promise as a way in which educators can forge a viable pathway for students to experience continuous progress based on competency-based progressions. Termed a "disruptive innovation" (Horn & Staker, 2014) for the promise it holds to transform education, blended learning seeks to give students more control over the time, place, path, and pace of their learning than they would experience in a traditional school setting. Unlike traditional online courses, however, blended learning intentionally includes components of in-person schooling in order to provide students with instructional support and scaffolding, and to deepen their learning via personal interactions with teachers and other students.

While favorable state policies and local regulations have not yet translated into widespread use of competency-based progressions, they have set the stage for innovative schools to pilot programs that utilize them. Local educators interested in more fully embracing competency-based progressions should consult their state and local policies. It is possible that they will find a mechanism already exists for allowing their broader use.

Closely related to policies on competency-based progressions are policies related to acceleration.

Current State Policies Regarding Acceleration

Understanding that for gifted students, competency-based progressions must give way to acceleration, it's also important for educators to have an understanding of their own states' policies regarding acceleration. According to the latest *State of the States* report on policies governing gifted education by the National Association for Gifted Children (NAGC), ten states have policies that explicitly allow for acceleration, and 16 states allow local education agencies (LEAs) to determine acceleration policies (Rinn et al., 2020). Those states are listed in Table 5.2. Two states – Idaho

Progressions and Acceleration

Table 5.2 State Policies for Acceleration

State Policy Allows for Acceleration	State Policy Allows LEAs to Determine Acceleration Policies	State Policy Does Not Address Acceleration
Alabama	Alaska	Connecticut
Florida	Arizona	Delaware
Idaho*	Arkansas	District of Columbia
Illinois	California	Hawaii
Kentucky	Colorado	Iowa
Minnesota	Georgia	Kansas
Missouri	Indiana	Michigan
New Mexico	Louisiana	Mississippi
North Carolina	Maine	Montana
Ohio	Maryland	Nebraska
Texas	Massachusetts*	New Hampshire
	Nevada	New York
	New Jersey	North Dakota
	Oklahoma	Oregon
	Pennsylvania	Rhode Island
	Washington	South Carolina
	West Virginia	South Dakota
		Tennessee
		Utah
		Vermont
		Virginia
		Wisconsin
		Wyoming

Note: LEA, local education agency * This state did not respond to surveys for the most recent *State of the States* report. However, information from 2014–2015 (Belin-Blank, 2020) indicates that Idaho allows for acceleration. ** This state did not respond to surveys for the most recent *State of the States* report. However, information from 2014–2015 (Belin-Blank, 2020) indicates that Massachusetts allows LEAs to determine acceleration policies
Source: Based on Belin-Blank (2020) and Rin, Mun, & Hodges (2020)

and Massachusetts – did not respond to surveys for this most recent report. However, information from 2014–2015 (Belin-Blank, 2020) indicates that Idaho allows for acceleration and Massachusetts allows LEAs to make those determinations, so we have included them in Table 5.2 in those categories. While the remaining states do not have policies that explicitly allow for acceleration at either the state or local level, they also do not have policies that prohibit it (Belin-Blank, 2020). It is therefore likely that local administrators who want to create stronger pathways for acceleration for the students they serve can find a means to do so.

However, the difficulties encountered when first trying to forge an unfamiliar pathway for a student should not be minimized. School bureaucracies can be slow, unwieldy, and unwelcoming to suggestions for change, particularly when the proposed changes may only benefit a small number of students within the system. Compounding these difficulties is the general lack of familiarity that most educational administrators and counselors have with the wealth of research that exists on acceleration. Unfortunately, most colleges of education do not routinely teach undergraduate or graduate students about pedagogy appropriate for gifted learners as part of the curriculum for all preservice teachers. Instead, separate classes or programs of study are offered specifically for educators interested in gifted education, which are not accessed by the majority of students seeking to work in education.

To illustrate the depth of this problem, 18 states currently have no requirement that teachers of gifted students be trained in gifted education (Rinn et al., 2020). In addition, only four states – Arizona, Iowa, South Carolina, and Texas – require professional learning in gifted education for administrators and counselors (Rinn et al., 2020). This system understandably results in entire school systems having a very small percentage of professionals within them who are well versed in policies and practices related to gifted education.

The acknowledgement of these difficulties is certainly not meant to discourage professionals (or, for that matter, families) from advocating within the system for more appropriate policies and opportunities for gifted students when those do not exist. Rather, it is meant to temper expectations as that advocacy work is being done. Once a new path is forged and a new policy is written, the benefit to future students will be immense. While that path is being created, however, students whose needs are not being met still exist, and during that time, it is helpful to consider other options that may be accessed more immediately. Fortunately, when it comes to acceleration, many such options exist.

Types of Acceleration

A Nation Empowered identifies 20 different types of acceleration that currently exist for students (Assouline et al., 2015; Southern & Jones, 2015). The one that this chapter has focused on the most thus far has been continuous progress, yet it is also one that is currently not widely used to its full potential. Therefore, it may be necessary for educators and families to consider other forms of acceleration that reap similar benefits for gifted students. These acceleration methods can be grouped into two broad categories: acceleration by whole grade levels and acceleration by content. These methods are listed in Table 5.3. Of the 20 types of acceleration identified, we are going to focus on the ones that most directly relate to formal schooling, where educators and administrators can have the most impact. Those that involve acceleration by whole grade levels include early admission to kindergarten, early admission to first grade, grade-skipping, early graduation from high school, and early college entrance. Methods that allow for acceleration by content include combined classes, credit by

Table 5.3 Types of Acceleration

By Whole Grade Level	By Content Area
accelerated/honors high school or residential high school on a college campus	acceleration in college
	Advanced Placement (AP) courses
	combined classes
early admission to first grade	concurrent/dual enrollment
early admission to kindergarten	continuous progress
early entrance into middle school, high school, or college	credit by examination
	curriculum compacting
early graduation from high school or college	distance-learning courses
	extracurricular programs
grade-skipping	International Baccalaureate (IB) courses
	mentoring/tutoring
	self-paced instruction
	subject-matter acceleration
	telescoping curriculum

Source: Based on Southern & Jones (2015).

exam, curriculum compacting, telescoping, AP courses, and International Baccalaureate (IB) courses.

Advancing Students Whole Grade Levels

Three of the acceleration options that exist within traditional K–12 schools involve advancing students by an entire grade level or more: early admission to kindergarten, early admission to first grade, and grade-skipping. All of these options are best implemented at the beginning of a new school year to make the transition as smooth as possible for the student. Early admissions to kindergarten and to first grade allow for students – especially those who may be entering school with strong reading and math skills already in place – to begin their education at the grade level that most closely aligns with their existing academic skills and knowledge rather than based simply on their age. Stories abound of gifted students entering school already knowing how to read or count, and then spending a full year simply reviewing information that they already know, with no way to move forward in their learning.

The psychological and academic impacts of this type of situation can be quite detrimental, as students' earliest and most formative experiences with school may involve boredom, disengagement, and/or the feeling that school is supposed to be easy. If the boredom and disengagement continue, students may respond by behaving in inappropriate ways that get them in trouble, beginning a cycle of negative school experiences that may be hard to break.

However, it's not just students who behave inappropriately who may be harmed. Students whose behavior conforms to desired expectations and who outwardly appear to be handling the situation well may also suffer in the long term. Some of them may continue to advance through their schooling for years, remaining consistently ahead of their peers and finding "new" lessons in class familiar and easy. It may not be until these students enter advanced high school classes that they encounter truly unfamiliar or challenging content for the first time in school, and at that point, psychologically, they may not know how to respond to that challenge. Since school has always been easy for them, some of these students internalize their first encounter with difficult work as their own failing,

Progressions and Acceleration

believing that they are somehow no longer gifted or not very smart because they do not already know all of the right answers or are not able to quickly figure them out. The very core of their self-concepts may be questioned and irrevocably damaged as they decide the most appropriate course of action is just to give up when academic material feels hard. Schools that allow for early entrance to kindergarten or first grade play a significant role in preventing these types of long-term problems by placing students in their earliest classes based on their readiness for the work rather than solely based on their birth date.

Yet even when students are appropriately placed in kindergarten and first grade, sometimes they still reach a point in their education when teachers and/or family members recognize that not enough new learning is occurring. In this case, grade-skipping may be the best option. In localities that have procedures in place for this need, students are often required to take a series of tests to demonstrate that they have already acquired the knowledge and skills that are taught at the grade level that they are seeking to skip. In some cases, radical acceleration may occur, with students skipping two or more entire years of their K–12 schooling.

A common barrier encountered when students seek to skip one or more grades is the erroneous assumption on the part of well-meaning administrators and counselors that skipping entire grade levels will result in negative social and psychological impacts. It is difficult for many people to envision a scenario, for example, in which a nine-year-old student may enter high school and not be psychologically damaged by the lack of a same-age peer group and, by extension, friends of any kind. An abundance of research proves, however, that this concern is not valid. Gifted students typically thrive by being among their intellectual peers, regardless of age. Affording them the opportunity to spend their days with others who can converse with them about topics of mutual interest is a benefit that can actually enhance their social skills, and it is one that can't be replicated by attending classes with same-age peers.

For secondary students, early graduation from high school is another acceleration option that in many ways is similar to whole grade-skipping. High school graduation is typically dependent on the number of credits earned rather than the number of years spent in high school, and most high schools offer yearly schedules that contain plenty of room for students to take elective courses and participate in activities that are not graduation requirements. This means gifted students may find that their educational interests will be better served by completing their graduation requirements in less than four years and starting their college classes earlier than others.

While state and local graduation requirements do vary, the only discipline that typically requires four full years of study is English. In cases where four full years of science or social studies are required, students can often take multiple courses within those disciplines concurrently. For example, a student might take Biology, Chemistry, World History, and United States History all in the same year. Because of this option, it is possible for students to have all but one of their required courses completed before they begin their senior year of high school. While it may take some work to determine how to get credit for the fourth required English class within the local system, students may be able to take a summer course or online class in order to earn that credit. If the high school that the student attends does not offer those options, the student may be able to take the course through an accredited online school or a local community college. Some schools may also allow the students to earn the credit by taking an exam to demonstrate mastery of the material.

In addition to the benefits that accelerating by a grade level or more can provide for students academically, socially, and emotionally, acceleration can also result in economic benefits. Research shows that students who accelerate a full grade level have higher incomes than otherwise similar adults who did not accelerate in school (McClarty, 2015; Warne & Lieu, 2017). While this income difference is more pronounced for males than for females, adults who accelerated a full grade level in school earn, on average, 4.66% more than similar same-age peers who did not accelerate in school (Warne, 2017). Not only does this difference in income exist in initial salaries, but yearly increases in salaries are also greater for the students who accelerated, as is job satisfaction, job prestige, and work productivity (McClarty, 2015).

Despite all of the advantages that accelerating a full grade level or more provides, acceleration remains underutilized as an option for gifted students. Families and educators who are considering full grade acceleration but are not certain if it is an appropriate option for a child have a tool to guide them. The Iowa Acceleration Scale (IAS) was developed by the Belin-Blank Center (Assouline et al., 2009) to assist families, students, and educators in determining whether or not acceleration will be in the best interest of a child. Now in its third edition, the IAS-3 lays out the procedures to follow and data to consult when making a determination.

Acceleration to College

It is impossible to have a discussion about gifted students who need some form of whole grade acceleration without acknowledging that at some point, whole grade acceleration leads to the need for early access to college courses. In this section, we would like to discuss two distinct types of accelerated experiences that can benefit gifted students: early college entrance, which may occur via a specific program or may be accessed by students individually, and Early College High Schools. Other options for accessing college classes on a more limited basis will be described in the next section.

Early college entrance may occur for some students via preexisting programs designed specifically for this purpose. Many of these are supported at least in part through state funding, and admission is generally competitive. While characteristics of these programs vary, most of them allow students to complete their final years of high school concurrently with university-level courses, and they typically fall into two categories: autonomous programs and programs that are located on universities. Autonomous programs have their own campus, facilities and staff who are content experts. Examples of autonomous programs include Indiana Academy for Science, Mathematics, and Humanities; Louisiana School for Math, Science, and the Arts; North Carolina School of Science and Math; and South Carolina Governor's Schools. In contrast, at university-based programs, students in the program are housed together at a university and take classes taught by university faculty, oftentimes alongside other college students. They also have a group of dedicated staff members overseeing their experience. Since early college students are minors, they may have more restrictions than typical college students have, such as nightly curfews and more professional oversight of their behavior and work. Examples of university-based programs include Gatton Academy in Kentucky and Texas Academy of Mathematics and Science.

Unlike early college students who begin their college careers through a specialized program, some early college entrance students simply begin

Core Strategies

college on their own at an earlier age than is typical. Their experience is identical to the experience of other college students; the only difference is their age. This early entrance may occur as a result of grade-skipping, homeschooling, early graduation from high school, the earning of a general equivalency diploma (GED) rather than a high school diploma, or a number of other unique situations.

A subset of early college students is those who are radically accelerated, meaning that they are entering college two or more years earlier than the typical student. Radically accelerated college students are often the ones who make headlines, and public interest in them may be high, partially because these students seem to be anomalies and partially because people are curious about how minors – especially those 16 or younger – navigate college campuses where so many young adults are experiencing freedoms that these minors don't necessarily have. In graduate programs, students aged 22–60 may attend the same classes without anyone finding it odd, but the particular implications of minors mixing with undergraduate students can create a lot of worry and concern. Sometimes, that concern, while well-meaning, can actually hurt students.

One adult, reflecting on the experience of enduring such well-meaning comments from others as an early college student, described it as follows:

> I definitely remember having that feeling as a kid, being like, 'Everybody is so concerned about my well-being, is something wrong and I just don't know?' And looking back on it now, no it was just me doing my thing. But the assumption that you just doing your thing is something that cannot possibly exist in the world is really harmful.
>
> (Jett & Rinn, 2019, p. 317)

As this student points out, much of that concern seems to be unwarranted, and as with other forms of acceleration, research indicates that students who enter college even radically early tend to do very well. These students, on average, are academically motivated, socially well rounded, successful in college, and thankful for the opportunities afforded to them to start college early (Jett & Rinn, 2019).

In contrast to early college entrance, early college high schools typically enroll students for all four years of high school, at the end of which students emerge with both a high school diploma and an associate's degree. During their four years of study, students take a mixture of high school and college courses, with the college classes often substituting for typical high school course requirements. Originally founded in the early 2000s through an initiative funded in part by the Bill & Melinda Gates Foundation, over 200 of these programs now exist, the oldest example of which is Bard High School Early Colleges.

Acceleration continues to be a viable option for gifted students even after they begin college. Honors colleges and honors programs at various universities provide pathways for undergraduate students to access more advanced content, with specialized courses often replacing core requirements within the university's curricula. College credits earned while in high school, as well as scores on university placement exams also allow newly full-time college students to skip basic courses and enter advanced classes their first year. Options also readily exist for students to double major – or even triple major, in some cases – in the same amount of time in which a typical student completes one major course of study. In addition to accelerating through multiple majors, additional pathways exist for undergraduate students to earn more than one degree simultaneously and for them to combine their undergraduate studies with graduate studies in accelerated, compacted programs.

Acceleration within K–12 Schools: Advancing Students by Content Area

Because asynchronous development can be a characteristic of gifted students, it is not appropriate for all gifted students to advance full grade levels. Some gifted students may have highly advanced math and science skills but be on grade level for humanities, or vice versa. In these cases, methods of acceleration that allow for content-specific advancement may be needed. Different methods of content-specific acceleration can currently be found within K–12 schools: combined classes, curriculum compacting, telescoping, AP courses, and IB courses.

Some schools are able to achieve content-specific acceleration through combined classes, another form of acceleration in which students of multiple ages are served in the same classroom. Montessori schools are one example of this method. In a Montessori primary classroom, students aged

Core Strategies

3–6 are grouped together, and they typically stay with the same teacher for three years. Because the teacher is trained to provide instruction in what would traditionally be three different grade levels of work, and materials for all of those different levels are available within the classroom, it's easy for students to access advanced content when they are ready. And because the entire school is structured in this manner, when a student masters all of the work that a teacher has available in one core subject, the teacher might send the student to another, higher-level classroom to receive new lessons in that subject area from a different teacher. In this scenario, a six-year-old primary student with advanced math skills remains with their primary teacher for all but a portion of the day; during a designated time each day, that student joins a junior level classroom, which serves students who would traditionally be in grades 1–3, for math instruction.

Another form of subject-specific acceleration is curriculum compacting. This method requires that students be given pre-assessments at the beginning of new units so that they do not have to complete lessons that focus on material they have already mastered. Instead, they use the extra time to work on more advanced material. Baltimore schools utilize this method to serve gifted students in general education classrooms, with each student using their extra time in the school day to complete an individualized, problem-based project that connects to their areas of strength. While curriculum compacting allows students to work at an advanced level, it typically does not result in advanced grade placement.

Unlike standard curriculum compacting, telescoping is an acceleration method that does result in advanced grade placement. A student who telescopes in math may, for example, take math classes that are designed to teach more than one year of math standards in a year. Given the amount of review that typically occurs in math classes each year, a telescoping option is a good one for gifted students who want to move at a faster pace. In Grapevine-Colleyville Independent School District in Texas, for example, students may take a telescoping exam at the end of a school year and, if they score well enough, skip the next grade level of math entirely. In addition, specific accelerated math courses are offered in sixth and seventh grade. Students in these classes are taught all of the sixth-, seventh-, and eighth-grade math standards in those two years, and they take the state's required standardized test for eighth-grade math at the end of seventh grade. This specific pathway allows students to then take Algebra I in eighth grade. Another telescoping option exists that combines Algebra II

118

Progressions and Acceleration

and Pre-Calculus into one year of formal study, thus preparing students to enroll in AP Calculus AB a year earlier than the typical pathway.

The last few acceleration methods we are going to discuss are particular to secondary students. The first is credit by exam. In instances where a gifted student already knows the content of a required course and wants to be excused from taking it – typically so that more advanced content can be accessed prior to graduation – a student may be allowed to take an exam demonstrating mastery in order to earn the credit. These exams may be offered and administered directly through the local school system. However, in some cases, a student may be able to take a College Board College-Level Examination Program® (CLEP) test on their own and have their score considered by the local school for granting of credit. If a local school does not have a specific policy in place for students to earn credit by exam, we recommend that interested educators or families check with their state policies to see if a provision exists that allows for this option to occur. It is possible that the local school has simply never been asked to provide a pathway that the state allows them to offer.

Once students enroll in high school, they may choose to enroll in a number of different courses designed to teach college-level content to high school students. Two specific programs provide structures and curricula for these courses: Advanced Placement (AP) and International Baccalaureate (IB). By far the most prolific and popular of the two are classes offered through the College Board's AP program.

Recent decades have seen tremendous growth in the number of schools offering AP courses on their campuses. While the College Board controls the content that is taught in each of these classes and offers training to all teachers, local schools hire their own teachers for AP classes and can tailor the pacing and assignments in each course to meet the needs of the students taking it. In addition to having a trained high school teacher providing support for high school students, the content may be taught over a longer period of time than it would be in college. For example, the content of an AP Calculus AB class may be taught over the course of a full year at a high school, whereas at a university, the course's content would be covered in one semester. At the end of each AP course, students have the option of taking an AP exam, which is written and graded by the College Board. The exams are usually a combination of multiple choice and short answers or short essays. Students who score well on an AP exam may be granted college credit for the courses when they enroll in college.

119

Core Strategies

Universities' policies for awarding credit based on AP exams differ, but these policies can usually be found with a quick search on the university's admissions website.

It is important to note that while AP curriculum is accelerated, it does not always meet standards set for gifted education. Some courses are so prescribed in their curriculum that they do not leave room for students to explore deeply the academic content in specific areas of high interest to them. For example, a student in AP World History might be highly intrigued by the work of Enlightenment thinkers, but the pacing of the course may only allow for two class periods to read and discuss their work before moving on to nationalism and revolutions.

In addition, AP classes are primarily designed to be the equivalent of introductory college courses. Gifted students who are able to do so are increasingly taking AP courses as early as their freshman year of high school, and we find it a bit disingenuous to suggest that the best educational pathway for gifted students is to spend four years taking introductory college courses, especially since we would never suggest that college students do the same.

With a similar purpose and structure as the AP program, the IB program also offers students college-level courses starting in high school. IB courses focus more heavily on research and writing than AP courses do, and they delve more deeply into disciplinary content. An IB course on the History of the Americas, for example, may spend several weeks analyzing the Cold War and its impact on Central America. Therefore, IB may be more appropriate for gifted students who typically crave depth in their studies and who will benefit from an earlier focus on the types of learning experiences that are typical in highly selective universities and in graduate programs.

In addition to taking end-of-course exams created by IB, students in all IB courses are required to complete and submit work (such as original research projects, 7–15-page research essays, and artistic creations) that they spend months developing. Students seeking to earn an IB Diploma must receive a minimum score on all of their individual assignments and achieve a certain number of points cumulatively for their work. Because of the expense and work associated with the program, however, it is less common for students to have access to IB classes.

Another way that high schools are currently offering college-level courses to high school students is through partnerships with local colleges. Two ways that these partnerships exist are through dual credit courses and concurrent enrollment. While these terms are sometimes used interchangeably, we are defining them here as separate and distinct.

Dual credit courses are typically offered on high school campuses and are attended only by high school students. As the term "dual" implies, these courses count for two types of credit: high school and college. Depending on the arrangement that the college and high school have, the courses may be taught by high school teachers or by college faculty, but the content of the courses is controlled by the college. Unlike AP and IB courses, dual credit courses do not have organizations with an international presence creating course standards or ensuring that they are upheld. Therefore, the quality and content of these classes may vary considerably from one school to the next. Additionally, the number of different courses high schools offer for dual credit may be much smaller than the number of courses offered for AP or IB credit.

What draws many students to dual credit courses is the guarantee of college credit at a significantly reduced price. A student only has to pass the class to earn that credit; there is no external mechanism through which the student has to demonstrate their learning. It is therefore important that students who want that credit to apply to another university from which they hope to earn a degree understand that college's transfer credit policies. While it is usually simple to find the page on a university website that indicates its policies for granting credit for AP and IB scores, policies for transfer credits may be more difficult to locate and are sometimes subject to approval from specific academic department chairs.

In contrast to dual credit, concurrent enrollment means that a student is fully enrolled in both a college and a high school at the same time. Students with concurrent enrollment typically take their college courses on a college campus with college students. They may not receive any high school credit at all for these college courses, or they may have to individually negotiate that credit with their local school. However, they do receive college credit and often a more authentic college experience. The variety of different courses a student may take via concurrent enrollment can be significantly larger than what is offered through dual credit.

One of our own children began taking classes at a local university via concurrent enrollment while still in high school, and it was undoubtedly a positive experience. An initial foreign language placement exam given by the university awarded her 16 credit hours of Spanish prior to her registering for classes, and additional credits were awarded based on her AP exam scores. At age 17, she

Core Strategies

was a high school senior taking senior-level college Spanish courses, college Calculus 2, and advanced college English courses.

Students who opt to take classes through concurrent enrollment do so for a number of reasons: to get ahead on their education, to better prepare for university (especially if their goal is to obtain a degree from a more selective university), because they love to learn, because they seek challenge, for self-fulfillment, for socialization, and to demonstrate their initiative (Dare et al., 2017). These are characteristics that all educators should actively seek to encourage in students.

Summary

Competency-based progressions personalize learning for students by allowing them to advance through academic material according to their own needs. For gifted students, these progressions can naturally lead to acceleration, which is the most broadly supported educational intervention for gifted students but remains underutilized. The positive cognitive, social, and psychological outcomes of acceleration are well-established by decades of research and warrant its broader use. Twenty different forms of acceleration have been identified by experts in gifted education that educators and families can draw on. While many systemic barriers currently exist which inhibit the broad use of acceleration, a personalized learning framework can provide the structure to expand its use within schools.

References

Assouline, S. G., Coangelo, N., Lupkowski-Shoplik, A., Lipscomb, J., & Forstadt, L. (2009). Iowa Acceleration Scale (3rd ed). Belin-Blank Center.

Assouline, S. G., Colangelo, N. & VanTassel-Baska, J. (2015). *A nation empowered: Evidence trumps the excuses holding back America's brightest students* (Vol. 1). Belin-Blank Center.

Belin-Blank Center. (2020). *State acceleration policy*. Acceleration Institute, Belin-Blank Center.

Brodersen, R. M., Yonaski, D., Mason, K., Apthorp, H., & Piscatelli, J. (2017). *Overview of selected state policies and supports related to K-12 competency-based education.* US Department of Education, Institute of Education Sciences, National Center for Education Evaluation and Regional Assistance, Regional Educational Laboratory Central. https://ies.ed.gov/ncee/edlabs/projects/project.asp?projectID=1458

Colorado Department of Education. (2016). *Graduation guidelines engagement toolkit.* www.cde.state.co.us/postsecondary/graduationguidelinesengagementtoolkit

Colorado Education Initiative. (2015). Igniting the unique potential of Colorado's students: Designing learning environments for the future of learning. www.coloradoedinitiative.org/wp-content/uploads/2019/02/NGL-TOOLKIT_SinglePage.pdf

Dare, A., Dare, L., & Nowicki, E. (2017). Concurrent enrollment: Comparing how educators and students categorize students' motivations. *Social Psychology of Education, 20,* 195–213. https://doi.org/10.1007/s11218-016-9364-8

ExcelinEd & EducationCounsel. (2017). *Policy, pilots, and the path to competency-based education: A national landscape. A survey of current state law and policy on competency-based education in K-12 systems.* Foundation for Excellence in Education and EducationCounsel. https://excelined.org/wp-content/uploads/2017/05/CBE.NationalLandscape.Final_.pdf

Horn, M. B. & Staker, H. (2014). *Blended: Using disruptive innovation to improve schools.* Jossey-Bass.

Jett, N. & Rinn, A. N. (2019). Radically early college entrants on radically early college entrance: A heuristic inquiry. *Journal for the Education of the Gifted, 42*(2), 303–335. https://doi.org/10.1177/0162353219874430

McClarty, K. L. (2015). Early to rise: The effects of acceleration on occupational prestige, earnings and satisfaction. In S. G. Assouline, N. Colangelo, J. VanTassel-Baska, & A. Lupkowski-Shoplik (Eds.), *A nation empowered: Evidence trumps the excuses holding back America's brightest students* (Vol. 2) (pp. 171–180). Belin-Blank Center.

Pane, J. F., Steiner, E. D., Baird, M. D., & Hamilton, L. S. (2015). *Continued progress: Promising evidence on personalized learning.* RAND Corporation. www.rand.org/pubs/research_reports/RR1365.html

Core Strategies

Pane, J. F., Steiner, E. D., Baird, M. D., Hamilton, L. S., & Pane, J. D. (2017). *Informing progress: Insights on personalized learning implementation and effects*. RAND Corporation. www.rand.org/pubs/research_reports/RR2042.html

Peters, S. J., Rambo-Hernandez, K., Makel, M. C., Matthews, M. S., & Plucker, J. A. (2017). Should millions of students take a gap year? Large numbers of students start the school year above grade level. *Gifted Child Quarterly, 61*(3), 229–238. http://doi.org/10.1177/0016986217701834

RAND Corporation & Bill & Melinda Gates Foundation. (2014). *Early progress: Interim research on personalized learning.* Bill & Melinda Gates Foundation https://usprogram.gatesfoundation.org/-/media/dataimport/resources/pdf/2016/12/42-early-progress-on-personalized-learning-full-report.pdf

Rin, A. N., Mun, R. U., & Hodges, J. (2020). *2018–2019 State of the States in Gifted Education.* National Association for Gifted Children, Council of State Directors of Programs for the Gifted. www.nagc.org/2018-2019-state-states-gifted-education

Southern, T. & Jones, E. D. (2015). Types of acceleration: Dimensions and issues. In S. G. Assouline, N. Colangelo, J. VanTassel-Baska, & A. Lupkowski-Shoplik (Eds.), *A nation empowered: Evidence trumps the excuses holding back America's brightest students* (Vol. 2) (pp. 9–18). Belin-Blank Center.

State of New Hampshire Office of Legislative Services. (2014). Chapter ed 300 administration of minimum standards in public schools; Ed 306.27 high school curriculum, credits, graduation requirements, and cocurricular program. www.gencourt.state.nh.us/rules/state_agencies/ed.html

Warne, R. T. (2017). Possible economic benefits of full-grade acceleration. *Journal of School Psychology, 65,* 54–68. https://doi.org/10.1016/j.jsp.2017.07.001

Warne, R. T., & Liu, J. K. (2017). Income differences among grade skippers and non-grade skippers across genders in the Terman sample, 1936–1976. *Learning and Instruction, 47,* 1–12. http://dx.doi.org/10.1016/j.learninstruc.2016.10.004

Westminster Public Schools. (2020). *About our* competency-based system. www.westminsterpublicschools.org/Page/9094

Inquiry Models of Learning

Personalized learning is a distinct pedagogy that differs from differentiation and individualization. At the heart of personalized learning is a serious commitment to authentic, student-centered learning. In personalized learning, students are afforded more autonomy than in typical differentiation or individualization approaches. With this autonomy, students make some of the decisions about their learning pathways; in fact, students tend to have more voice and choice in personalized learning than other pedagogical models (Song et al., 2012). Voice and choice are somewhat developmental; students in older grade levels may have more substantive voice and choice than primary students. However, the developmental nature of voice and choice assumes students have had opportunities to mature by practicing self-direction and making learning decisions.

As students become active agents in the learning design process, they will have input with their teachers on what is included in the learning cycle. At more mature levels, learners may have full control over aspects of the learning cycle. This shared responsibility for planning learning is a paradigm change for many educational settings. When students are co-designers, or co-creators of learning content, the concept of curriculum becomes more fluid and responsive. Specifically, the curriculum becomes more authentic, more engaging, and more personal for students. Inquiry models of learning are essential features of co-created learning spaces serving the educational goals of deep learning, increased student self-direction, and personalized pathways of engagement.

DOI: 10.4324/9781003237136-8

Core Strategies

 # Inquiry Learning Pedagogy

Inquiry learning began in earnest in the mid-20th century, though its educational roots run much deeper in Progressive education and philosophy. A key feature of inquiry learning is moving students from passive recipients to active investigators. Educational tasks are designed to arouse students' curiosity so that they actively pursue answers to their own questions and in the process master critical content knowledge. Broadly speaking, inquiry learning is active investigation in response to a task, a problem, or a need. Students engaged in inquiry learning are expected to actively generate questions, seek answers through their own research, and communicate coherently what they found in response to those questions and sub-questions. Inquiry learning often involves problem definition, problem-solving, creative thinking, and design. Four general principles of inquiry learning are presented in Table 6.1.

Pappas (2014) described four general forms that inquiry learning might take. These forms represent a range from narrowly focused to open-ended inquiry. The forms may be applied to several inquiry-based teaching models, and the conceptual goal of the four forms is to help teachers understand a range of ways to develop inquiry learning in their curriculum. The four forms are:

Table 6.1 Principles of Inquiry Learning

Principle 1	Inquiry learning is student-centered. The student drives the process as teachers provide support and resources.
Principle 2	Inquiry learning requires information gathering, information processing, and conceptual understanding.
Principle 3	Inquiry learning expects teachers to facilitate the process of inquiry learning. Teachers are constantly gathering data about students' skills, work habits, and collaboration efforts.
Principle 4	Inquiry learning involves evaluation techniques that measure students' process skills, as well as content acquisition and conceptual understanding.

Note: These four principles describe the student-centered process of active learning during inquiry-based learning. Inquiry learning requires students to generate questions, seek information in response to those questions, and synthesize that information into coherent solutions, explanations, or designs (Bell et al., 2010; Pappas, 2014)

- *Confirmatory Inquiry*

  Students are given a driving question and a method of responding to the question for a result that is already known. Through inquiry they gather information to confirm the results. The focus of confirmatory inquiry is developing investigation skills.

- *Structured Inquiry*

  Students are given a driving question and a method of responding to the question. Through inquiry they develop a solution or explanation that is supported by evidence gathered during the inquiry process. The focus of structured inquiry is investigation and data synthesis.

- *Guided Inquiry*

  Students are given only a driving question. They then design a method of investigation and determine if that method is sufficient to respond to the question. The focus of guided inquiry is generating a method, investigation skills, and data synthesis.

- *Open Inquiry*

  Students are confronted with a scenario. They form their own questions, design a method of investigation, and determine if that method is sufficient to respond to their questions. The focus of open inquiry is asking questions or defining problems, generating a method, investigation skills, and data synthesis.

The four forms of inquiry put forward by Pappas (2014) demonstrate how teachers can utilize inquiry learning from simple, structured designs to complex, open-ended designs. These forms also highlight the essential features of inquiry learning: (a) asking questions, (b) developing a method of investigation, (c) gathering data, (d) analyzing data or synthesizing information, and (e) communicating results.

Inquiry Models in Personalized Learning and Gifted Education

The gifted education programming standards of the National Association for Gifted Children (NAGC) recommend using inquiry models of learning (NAGC, 2019), and inquiry models have similarly

Core Strategies

been advocated as an implementation vehicle for personalized learning (Lee, 2014). We will demonstrate how the following inquiry models can support personalized learning and achievement outcomes in gifted education: (a) problem-based learning, (b) project-based learning, (c) independent or team-based research, (d) design-based learning, and (e) creative problem-solving.

Problem-Based Learning

Problem-based learning (PrBL) originated in medical education in the 1980s (Barrows & Tamblyn, 1980). This teaching model was designed to address the complexity of knowledge transfer, critical thinking, and decision-making. In the 1980s, PrBL was an innovative pedagogy in the inquiry learning tradition, and while it seems less innovative today, it remains popular in professional education (Savery, 2006). Multiple studies and meta-analyses were conducted in the 1990s and early 2000s that provided evidence that medical students taught in PrBL environments performed as well as medical students in traditional learning environments on typical measures of medical competencies (see Albanese & Mitchell, 1993; Denton et al., 2000; Vernon & Blake, 1993).

By 2021, PrBL had permeated all levels of education, including elementary and secondary education. PrBL has been lauded for its potential high levels of student engagement, inquiry, problem-solving, and domain-specific complex thinking and application. Research on the effectiveness of PrBL indicates that students in PrBL conditions perform at least as well as students in non-PrBL conditions on standardized tests of achievement (De Witte & Rogge, 2016). However, the primary benefits of PrBL may go beyond standardized tests of achievement (Gallagher & Gallagher, 2013). Students engaged in PrBL improve in creative thinking, critical thinking, and problem-solving (Albanese & Mitchell, 1993; Bell, 2010; Gallagher et al., 1992). PrBL learning designs have even impacted students' career awareness and motivation in science, technology, engineering, and mathematics (STEM) (LaForce et al., 2017).

Gallagher (2015) and Tan (2009) explained how the use of ill-structured problems requires students to pose questions, define problems, and personally investigate those questions and problems.

128

Inquiry Models of Learning

There are some variations in how PrBL is implemented, but some common features of PrBL learning design include the steps listed below. Typically, students:

- examine and define a problem within an ill-structured scenario
- explore what they currently know about the topic and issues
- determine what they need to know to design a solution
- search and find the information needed to develop a solution
- identify and evaluate possible ways to solve the problem
- clearly explain and defend a solution
- present their solution to an audience.

What is needed to make PrBL a legitimate practice of personalized learning? Most inquiry models, including PrBL, could be implemented without rising to the level of personalized learning. Similarly, inquiry models are used with students at all levels, including gifted and talented students. These models are flexible and can be implemented in a way that supports personalized learning for gifted and talented students. The following guidelines should be considered when applying PrBL at the intersection of personalized learning, and gifted and talented education:

1. The problem space is a knowledge and skill match to the student's high ability. The problem space is ill-defined, conceptually complex, requiring critical thinking, creative thinking, and analytical thinking.

2. The problem space is ill-defined but addresses two additional criteria: (a) it is domain-based, meaning that it reflects the learning standards of the subject domain; and (b) it is open-ended enough to allow the student to define and investigate a narrowed problem that matches the student's interest.

3. Most implementations of PrBL include students working together as a team. Yet, sometimes the need to accommodate a team contradicts the principles of personalized learning. There are a few ways to adjust for this. First, a team of students could work in the same problem space, but each student individually defines

129

and addresses a problem that is personalized. Second, the team could work on a group-defined problem, but each student individually approaches the problem from a personalized lens. This personalization could reflect the student's career interests or particular talent strengths. Third, it is possible to have students work on a PrBL individually. In that case, the process is quite similar to an independent study that originates in an ill-defined problem space and the steps in the PrBL process are followed.

The role of the teacher in PrBL involves preparation and real-time support as needed. Teachers are scenario creators. They design the problem, including structures and constraints that will impact the work of the students. In personalized learning, the design of the PrBL should also consider students' profiles, interests, and strengths (see Table 6.2).

Project-Based Learning

Project-based learning (PBL) is student-centered inquiry associated with Constructivist learning principles and 21st-century learning design. Three fundamental PBL principles of teaching and learning include: (1) learning is context specific, (2) students are actively involved in the learning process, and (3) students achieve group and personal goals through social interactions and the sharing of knowledge and understandings (Kokotsaki et al., 2016). Students often work in teams to engage authentic questions or real-world challenges (Blumenfeld et al., 2000).

Learning designs in PBL develop students' capacity for creative thinking, critical thinking, and problem-solving. Students engaged in sustained PBL tend to display greater work-readiness, as well as problem finding and focused inquiry skills (Jollands et al., 2012). Additionally, students who learn in PBL environments improve skills in divergent thinking, planning, and knowledge transfer (Saunders-Stewart et al., 2012). PBL can be a highly engaging way for students to learn complex content through application-oriented projects.

There are numerous models of PBL used in learning designs across all disciplines and grade levels. Some models are more personalized than others. The intersection of PBL and personalized learning blends essential elements of both approaches. We recommend emphasizing the following characteristics of PBL that honor personalized learning principles.

Inquiry Models of Learning

Table 6.2 Teacher Role Using the Problem-Based Learning Inquiry Model

Learning Outcomes	• Articulate learning outcomes for the problem-based learning. • Specify what students will know and be able to do as a result of the problem-based learning. • When developmentally appropriate, students assume a role in defining the learning outcomes.
Ill-Structured Problem Space	• Create the ill-structured problem space that will drive the inquiry. • The problem should resemble a real-world situation or something students may encounter in their future work or lives. • The problem should be closely related to standards in the discipline(s).
Audience	• Determine the real-world audience for whom the students are designing a solution. Students may assist in determining the audience. • Develop an entry event – a document, video, or presentation that exposes the students to both the problem and the audience.
Ground Rules and Group Processes	• Develop relevant ground rules for the project (timelines, expectations for assessment, details of the final product/ presentation). • Clarify expectations for group work, as well as independent work.
Secure Relevant Resources	• Much of the determining of resources ought to be left to the students. • Identify resources that will be made available for individuals or teams.
Personalized Scaffolding	• Personalized scaffolding should match the student's learning progressions and zone of proximal development. • Anticipate and prepare any tools that the teacher will use to facilitate learning.
Assessment	• Establish how the students will be assessed. • Consider ways that students can be individually assessed, as well as how the group/team will be assessed. • Assess conceptual knowledge, domains skills, as well as creativity, problem-solving, and analytical thinking.

Source: Adapted from Kettler et al. (2018)

Core Strategies

Essential Questions

Almost every model of PBL begins with an essential question. The essential question should be rooted in the content of the curriculum, while also intersecting real-world application and student interests. The essential question drives the inquiry process. It should be open-ended with multiple possible answers. Examples of essential questions include:

(a) In stories, what makes a hero a hero?
(b) In what ways is geometry applied to sports?
(c) How would you design a new playground using only sustainable materials?
(d) How can a community improve resident engagement in local government?
(e) How can you use science to inspire people to make healthier eating decisions?

To make the essential question more personalized, involve students in the development of the question by using question stems. Widely used question stems include:

(a) How can ___ improve ___?
(b) How would you design a new ___?
(c) How might we use ___ to change ___?
(d) What impact did ___ have on ___?
(e) What is the relationship between ___ and ___?

Students are more engaged in the PBL when they play a part in developing the essential question.

Sustained Inquiry

Inquiry is systematic investigation in response to a question, problem, issue, topic, or idea. Inquiry involves exploration, asking more questions, making discoveries, and/or seeking new or better understanding. In personalized PBL, students engage in inquiry so that they may respond to the essential question. The amount of time spent in the inquiry phase can vary from a couple of days to several weeks. Typically, the amount of inquiry time

132

Inquiry Models of Learning

increases as students age and develop, and build capacity for sustained attention. Similarly, the level of independence in inquiry increases as students develop. Students learn to systematically collect data in the inquiry process. Sometimes the data are secondary, such as information published digitally or in print. Other times the data are primary, meaning the student gathers and synthesizes through the use of interviews, surveys, archival content analyses, etc. As students develop and mature, they should learn increasingly sophisticated and domain-specific forms of inquiry and data analyses.

Authenticity

Authentic learning requires students to explore, study, and discuss meaningful concepts through real-world problems and projects that are relevant and interesting to the learners. Personalized learning in PBL inherently values the authentic nature of the essential question and the outcome of the inquiry. Authentic learning tasks expect students to experience learning and apply information in real-world contexts on topics that are applicable beyond school. Designing PBL to be personalized and authentic requires deep understanding of how the content and skills of the curriculum apply in real-world contexts. Authentic PBL may involve career education and exploration so that students experience what it is like to think, answer questions, innovate, or problem solve as a political scientist, historian, mathematician, artist, or engineer.

Student Voice and Choice

The term "voice and choice" means giving students agency, allowing them to take ownership or make decisions in the learning process. Voice and choice have been widely associated with personalized learning and are used somewhat in PBL design and implementation. In the PBL process, students may have voice and choice in the essential questions they pursue, the types of data they collect in the inquiry process, or the final product that will be developed to culminate the learning process. Voice and choice tend to raise student engagement and support the development of self-directed learning skills. The more experience students have participating in the learning design, the more they will improve their skills as independent learners. Voice and choice may include both procedural aspects of the PBL,

Core Strategies

as well as content-focused choices. For instance, a student with a strong interest in health sciences may engage in social studies PBL and emphasize aspects of public health, while a student with an interest in engineering may approach the same PBL and emphasize aspects of public infrastructure.

Multi-Phase Final Product

All PBL culminates in a final product. In some cases, the final product is publicly presented to an audience, but in other cases it may be presented with little fanfare in the classroom. Personalized PBL work should allow students to have input on the final product, including participating in the development of the rubric or quality indicators for the product or performance. The term "multi-phase product" is often used to show that the product is more of a process that emphasizes some or all of the following components: proposal, first draft, revised draft, and final product. The PBL product should involve self-assessment components. Peer review with constructive feedback is also beneficial. The decision to make the final product multi-phased makes it more authentic; rarely do real world products culminate in a single draft product or performance. Authentic work is almost always a draft–feedback–revise process.

Independent or Team-Based Research

Gifted programming standards (NAGC, 2019) and common models of gifted education recommend opportunities for students to engage in independent research, and independent research may be the most personalized of all the inquiry models. Long-standing protocols for independent research in gifted education have included the Purdue three-stage model (Feldhusen & Kolloff, 1986), the autonomous learner model (Betts, 1985), and the independent study model (Johnsen & Goree, 2015). Each of these inquiry models can vary from less to more structured in their support systems. These approaches to independent research share the goal of engaging students in systematic study of a topic/question employing authentic methods of research and production.

To emphasize the principles of personalized learning, independent or team-based research ought to prioritize students' interest-driven research. Interest-driven research accomplishes academic goals of planning, inquiry, data analysis, and concept formation. Additionally, interest-driven research can help students form or strengthen emerging identities, career interests, and self-regulation. When independent research is implemented within a content-specific course (mathematics, science, language arts, social studies), the research should merge content-specific content with student interests. Independent research may also be implemented through a domain-general inquiry space such as pull-out programs or specialized independent research courses.

A great example of blending personalized learning and independent research was developed by Fischer (2016) working with high school students in Montana. This approach to independent research maximizes personal interest and is best implemented in domain-neutral environments (e.g. specialized independent research courses). Fischer's model for personalized independent research (Fischer, 2016) emphasizes four essential features, which are listed below.

Blank Slate of Opportunity

Allow the students to begin with a blank slate that becomes personal and interest-driven. This can be facilitated by having students complete interest inventories, career profile surveys, or other tools designed to clarify interests worth pursuing. The blank slate opportunity becomes a space where students are free to explore their identity, what they care most about, or what they want to become. As they imagine their future, they color the blank slate with personalized learning opportunities. The role of the teacher is to facilitate the students' self-reflection and exploration.

Student Freedom to Choose

Students choose their topics based on their interests. As they select topical areas, they engage in clarifying and narrowing their potential study. Again, the teacher serves as a resource to facilitate this narrowing process to help the students land at a viable research space. In some cases, students may choose to study in one area over and over, constantly focusing on one or two areas. Other times, students will move from topic to topic as they explore multiple areas of interest in search of the one that captivates them most. The point of emphasis is the freedom to choose – to make it personal.

Core Strategies

Flexibly Structured Support from the Teacher

The role of the teacher is to offer support and stand back. Students' independence and self-direction are developed through opportunities to practice, improve, and develop over time. Teachers actively support the students through probing questions, suggestions, formative feedback, and guidance. As students mature in their independence, the role of the teacher evolves with them. The teacher may think of themselves as a mirror to help students see themselves more clearly and pursue studies that support identity development and self-direction.

Time, Space, and Resources

When independent research is systematically implemented, students develop the capacity for more extended studies as they move upward in grade levels. High school programs may offer year-long independent study courses with the option to continue the study for a second year or even a third year. Students who win prestigious scientific research contests have often been engaged in their study for two, or even three years. Independent workspaces with technology resources are also necessary to support quality personalized research endeavors. Additionally, high school personalized research programs often have policies and procedures to support students working with mentors outside of school.

Programs Supporting Personalized Research

Genius hour (McNair, 2017; Smith, 2017) and maker spaces (Cooper, 2013; Krueger, 2021) are potential personalized research models when they afford personalized approaches to work. Genius hour is inherently personalized, allowing students an opportunity to pursue their unique curiosities. Similarly, maker spaces encourage students to explore and create physical products related to independent research. Both of these relatively new programs can be incorporated into personalized learning as long as they support systematic inquiry in students' areas of interest.

The College Board's Advanced Placement (AP) Capstone program and AP Seminar and AP Research courses offer advanced high school students a structured and validated opportunity for personalized independent research. The courses are intended as a two-year sequence

Inquiry Models of Learning

in the final two years of high school, though some advanced students may take the courses earlier than that. Students research a topic of personal interest, synthesize information, and apply authentic research methodologies. Students make presentations and produce an extended essay that presents the results of their research. Gifted education programs with a personalized learning approach may want to sequence additional research courses that precede the AP Seminar and AP Research courses so that independent research on topics of personal interest span more than just two years of high school.

While most personalized learning implies working independently, students may work in research teams of other high ability students with similar interests. Emphasis on personalized learning should not contradict the typical authentic structures of work, and most authentic research is conducted through research teams. Research teams should connect with personal interests to the extent possible, but students have important opportunities to learn collaborative research and productivity skills as they work with others.

Design-Based Learning

Design-based learning is a specialized form of project-based learning that has most commonly been applied in STEM education (Barron et al., 1998; Fortus et al., 2005; Silk et al., 2009). The hallmark feature of design-based learning is the creation of a product prototype in response to a challenge or problem. The development of the prototype is followed by phases of testing and evaluation, which lead to improvements and redesigns reflective of authentic engineering and design work.

Design-based learning is a specialized STEM inquiry model that applies a cyclical problem-solving process. This inquiry process was derived from engineering fields and innovative thinking models. Multiple descriptions of the steps in the cyclical model exist, but a few elements are consistent across the variations: (a) generation of ideas, (b) developing a prototype, and (c) evaluating and improving the prototype. An example of the cyclical process is presented in Figure 6.1. The design process is iterative, and students repeat the steps multiple times as needed to complete the project. One of the learning premises of STEM design work is learning from failed attempts. In the design model, students are expected

137

Core Strategies

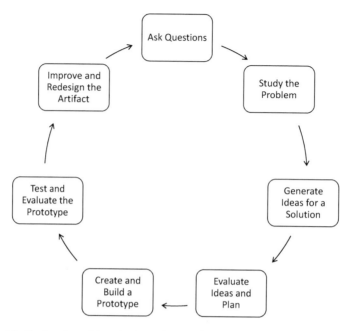

Figure 6.1 Design-Based Inquiry Learning Cycle
Note: Design-based learning is a seven-phase specialized approach to project-based learning in which students respond to design-based challenges or problems that result in the development of a physical product that solves the problem or satisfies the design need (Kettler et al., 2018). (Used with permission)

to develop prototypes that fail to meet initial expectations but continue to improve after feedback.

Design-based learning within personalized learning may be most appropriate for students with specific interests in STEM areas or design arts (e.g. visual arts, fashion, architecture). The seven phases are briefly described below.

- ***Phase 1: Ask Questions***

    Students encounter a design problem space that is either teacher-initiated or student-initiated. They proceed by asking clarifying questions to focus their plan and intended outcome. Questions may include: (a) What are the goals of the project?; (b) Who is the audience?; (c) What am I going to design?; (d) What are the constraints in which I must work?; and (e) What are critical aspects of the design?

Inquiry Models of Learning

- ***Phase 2: Study the Problem***

  Students engage in inquiry to gain a deeper understanding of the problem/challenge. Inquiry may involve gathering data from digital resources, interviews with experts, or experiments in which they simulate attempts to solve the problem. The main purpose of this phase is to achieve deep understanding of the problem and its constraints.

- ***Phase 3: Generate Ideas for a Solution***

  Students apply divergent thinking techniques to generate possible solutions. They may use techniques such as brainstorming, SCAMPER (substitute, combine, adapt, modify, put to another use, eliminate, reverse), or lateral thinking when seeking many possible solutions. The main idea here is to imagine a product that can elegantly meet the requirements of the solution.

- ***Phase 4: Evaluate Ideas and Plan***

  Students use analytical tools (e.g. T-charts, strengths–weaknesses comparisons, feasibility estimates) to analyze the possible ideas for a solution. The main idea of this phase is to use an analytical process to identify the best possible idea and make a plan for developing the artifact/solution.

- ***Phase 5: Create and Build a Prototype***

  Students create drawings or blueprints for their design. Using those plans, they build early iterations of the solution. Students need to document the design process in a way that could be replicated or modified as needed. The main idea of this phase is to develop the product while understanding that it will require revision after testing and evaluation.

- ***Phase 6: Test and Evaluate the Prototype***

  Students develop a way to test their product to verify how effectively it solves the problem. The main idea of this phase is to use data to determine if or how the prototype could be refined or redesigned.

- ***Phase 7: Improve and Redesign the Product***

  Students learn from the evaluations in the previous phase and design improvements to the product. These two final phases can be repeated as many times as necessary.

139

Core Strategies

The design-based inquiry model can be personalized according to students' topics of interest when applied in domain-neutral learning environments (e.g. pull-out programs, specialized independent research courses). The model may also be used in STEM-based gifted education programs that emphasize authentic learning and career exploration. Additionally, schools that offer design-based arts courses as part of their gifted education services (e.g. combining gifted education with career and technology education) could use design-based personalized learning to engage students in authentic and meaningful learning in those courses.

Creative Problem-Solving

Creative problem-solving (CPS) is an inquiry model that emphasizes creative thinking and problem-solving. During CPS students apply both divergent and convergent thinking skills to identify/clarify problems and develop viable solutions (Treffinger & Isaksen, 2005; Treffinger et al., 2006). CPS has been recommended and applied to gifted education (Treffinger, 2004), and it is a viable inquiry model to apply within a personalized learning approach to gifted education. Like the previous models described, the personalized learning emphasis is seen in the following two ways: (1) students apply CPS to problems of their own personal interest, and (2) students take an active role in planning the inquiry process, with voice and choice in the final product and evaluation criteria of that final product.

Mumford et al. (2018) describe an eight-step process to characterize how people solve problems that require creative or non-heuristic thinking (see Figure 6.2). The eight steps in the CPS process are dynamic in that students move through the steps but at any time may circle back to repeat or redo one of the steps. The CPS model is an accurate reflection of how experts in business, industry, and professional services typically solve complex problems. When students routinely use this process to apply knowledge and skills in school, they are prepared to transfer those skills and use the model in authentic settings as well.

Students begin the CPS process by clearly defining the problem (step 1) in a way that narrowly describes the challenge with clearly defined variables and relevant constraints. After the problem is clearly defined, students actively engage in inquiry – information gathering for the purpose of understanding the problem from multiple points of view,

140

Inquiry Models of Learning

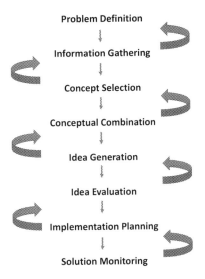

Figure 6.2 Creative Problem-Solving Inquiry Model
Note: The creative problem-solving process (adapted from Mumford et al., 2018) involves eight phases through which individuals move both forward and backward as needed to move from initial definitions of the problem to the implementation and monitoring of the solution

as well as how others may have attempted to solve this exact problem or a similar problem (step 2). Concept selection (step 3) involves identifying conceptual frameworks that contribute to the understanding of the problem. For example, if a student were trying to solve the problem of increasing vaccination uptake, one possible concept may be personality traits – are some personality profiles more likely to avoid vaccinations? Conceptual combination (step 4) is considered a complex, creative thinking task. Students consider all the possible concepts generated in step 3 and look for ways to combine them to form a new conceptual framework at the intersection of two or more concepts. Perhaps another concept related to vaccination uptake is scientific misunderstanding. The student may combine personality traits with scientific misunderstanding to better understand personal barriers to vaccinations. The next two steps are the beginning of solution-seeking. Students generate ideas (step 5) for solutions based on those conceptual understandings, and then they develop systematic ways to evaluate those ideas (step 6). They may evaluate them for feasibility, effectiveness, costs, and resource availability; the point is systematic evaluation of the possibilities rather than hasty selection of a solution. The final two steps involve implementing the solution (step 7) through a well-defined plan that is detailed to the degree possible. The last step is solution monitoring (step 8) where students have a plan for how to monitor and evaluate whether the plan is successful at solving the problem defined in step 1.

CPS is a high-demand skill in most workplaces; thus, it is well worth implementing at all levels of learning even if it is not personalized. Combining this inquiry model with personalized learning involves students identifying problems that they personally care to solve. Students should also be involved in planning their inquiry methods and the evaluation process for their work. CPS can be used to study domain-specific content through personalized connections, but CPS can also be used as a tool for addressing personal problem spaces, such as career planning, how to afford college, finding ideal summer internships, or post-secondary transitions.

Summary

Inquiry models of learning are recommended for gifted education because the models engage high ability students in self-directed learning, information processing, creative thinking, and problem-solving. These models can be used effectively at impersonal levels, but more importantly they are also a great fit within a personalized learning framework in gifted education. Personalized learning is implemented in big decisions, such as using personalized learning plans, data-driven learning progressions, and adaptive technologies to support customized pathways. This chapter has revealed the other side of implementing personalized learning in the micro-moments of the teaching and learning cycle. Student inquiry is driven by student interests. Students exercise voice and choice in decisions regarding learning outcomes and assessment protocols. Inquiry-based learning provides a viable pedagogical space for the merging of student-centered learning and personalization without any sacrifice in rigor or engagement. Additionally, as students internalize the steps of these models, they are building skills for future learning and complex work in environments that require problem-solving, creativity, design, and independent achievement of results.

References

Albanese, M. A., & Mitchell, S. (1993). Problem-based learning: A review of the literature on its outcomes and implementation issues. *Academic Medicine, 68* (1), 52–81.

Barron, B. J. S., Schwartz, D. L., Vye, N. J., Moore, A., Petrosino, A., Zech, L., & Bransford, J. D. (1998). Doing with understanding: Lessons from research on problem- and project-based learning. *Journal of the Learning Sciences, 7*(3–4), 271–311. https://doi.org/10.1080/10508406.1998.9672056

Barrows, H. S., & Tamblyn, R. M. (1980). *Problem-based learning: An approach to medical education.* Springer.

Bell, S. (2010). Project-based learning for the 21st century: Skills for the future. *The Clearing House: A Journal of Educational Strategies, Issues, and Ideas, 83*(2), 39–43. https://doi.org/10.1080/00098650903505415

Bell, T., Urhahne, D., Schanze, S., & Ploetzner, R. (2010). Collaborative inquiry learning: models, tools, and challenges. *International Journal of Science Education, 32*(3), 349–377. https://doi.org/10.1080/09500690802582241

Betts, G. T. (1985). *The Autonomous Learner model for the gifted and talented.* Autonomous Learning Publications and Specialists.

Blumenfeld, P., Fishman, B. J., Krajcik, J., Marx, R. W., & Soloway, E. (2000). Creating usable innovations in systemic reform: Scaling up technology-embedded project-based science in urban schools. *Educational Psychologist, 35*(3), 149–164.

Cooper, J. (2013, September). *Designing a school makerspace: An approach to defining and designing the right space for your school.* Edutopia. www.edutopia.org/blog/designing-a-school-makerspace-jennifer-cooper

De Witte, K., & Rogge, N. (2016). Problem-based learning in secondary education: Evaluation by an experiment. *Education Economics, 24*(1), 58–82.

Denton, B. G., Adams, C. C., Blatt, P. J., & Lorish, C. D. (2000). Does the introduction of problem-based learning change graduate performance outcomes in a professional curriculum? *Journal on Excellence in College Teaching, 11*(2–3), 147–162.

Feldhusen, J. F., & Kolloff, M. B. (1986). The Purdue three-stage model. In J. S. Renzulli (Ed.), *Systems and models for developing programs for the gifted and talented* (pp. 126–152). Creative Learning Press.

Fischer, T. (2016). Independent research, creative productivity, and personalization of learning: A student-centered pedagogy of gifted education. In T. Kettler (Ed.), *Modern curriculum for gifted and advanced academic students* (pp. 171–187). Prufrock Press.

Fortus, D., Krajcik, J. S., Dershimer, R. C., Marx, R. W., & Mamlok-Naaman, R. (2005). Design-based science and real-world problem-solving. *International Journal of Science Education, 27*(7), 855–879. https://doi.org/10.1080/09500690500038165

Gallagher, S. A. (2015). The role of problem-based learning in developing creative expertise. *Asia Pacific Education Review, 16*, 225–235. https://doi.org/10.1007/s12564-015-9367-8

Gallagher, S. A., & Gallagher, J. J. (2013). Using problem-based learning to explore unseen academic potential. *Interdisciplinary Journal of Problem-Based Learning, 7*(1), 111–131. https://doi.org/10.7771/1541-5015.1322

Gallagher, S. A., Stepien, W. J., & Rosenthal, H. (1992). The effects of problem-based learning on problem solving. *Gifted Child Quarterly, 36*(4), 195–201.

Johnsen, S. K., & Goree, K. K. (2015). Teaching gifted students through independent study. In F. A. Karnes & S. M. Bean (Eds.), *Method and materials for teaching the gifted* (4th ed.) (pp. 445–478). Prufrock Press.

Jollands, M., Jolly, L., & Molyneaux, T. (2012). Project-based learning as a contributing factor to graduates' work readiness. *European Journal of Engineering Education, 37*(2), 143–154.

Kettler, T., Lamb, K. N., & Mullet, D. R. (2018). *Developing creativity in the classroom: Learning and innovation for 21st-century schools.* Prufrock Press.

Kokotsaki, D., Menzies, V., & Wiggins, A. (2016). Project-based learning: A review of the literature. *Improving Schools, 19*(3), 267–277.

Krueger, N. (2021, April). Create a school makerspace in 3 simple steps. International Society for Technology in Education. www.iste.org/explore/ArticleDetail?articleid=103

LaForce, M., Nobel, E., & Blackwell, C. (2017). Problem-based learning (PBL) and student interest in STEM careers: The roles of motivation and ability beliefs. *Education Sciences, 7*(4) 92–114. https://doi.org/10.3390/educsci7040092

Lee, D. (2014). How to personalize learning in K-12 schools: Five essential design features. *Educational Technology, 54*(3), 12–17.

McNair, A. (2017). *Genius hour: Passion projects that ignite innovation and student inquiry.* Prufrock Press.

Mumford, M. D., Martin, R., Elliott, S., & McIntosh, T. (2018). Creative thinking in the real world: Processing in context. In R. J. Sternberg & J. C. Kaufman (Eds.), *The nature of human creativity* (pp. 147–165). Cambridge University Press.

NAGC. (2019). Pre-K to grade 12 gifted programming standards. The National Association for Gifted Children. www.nagc.org/resources-publications/resources/national-standards-gifted-and-talented-education/pre-k-grade-12

Pappas, C. (2014, June 18). *Instructional design models and theories: Inquiry-based learning model.* eLearning Industry. https://elearningindustry.com/inquiry-based-learning-model

Saunders-Stewart, K. S., Gyles, P. D. T., & Shore, B. M. (2012). Student outcomes in inquiry instruction: A literature-derived inventory. *Journal of Advanced Academics, 23*(1), 5–31.

Savery, J. R. (2006). Overview of problem-based learning: Definitions and distinctions. *The Interdisciplinary* Journal of Problem-Based Learning, 1(1), 9–20. https://doi.org/10.7771/1541-5015.1002

Silk, E. M., Schunn, C. D., & Cary, M. S. (2009). The impact of an engineering design curriculum on science reasoning in an urban setting. *Journal of Science Education and Technology, 18*, 209–223. https://doi.org/10.1007/s10956-009-9144-8

Smith, M. (2017, September). *Genius hour in elementary school.* Edutopia. www.edutopia.org/article/genius-hour-elementary-school

Song, Y., Wong, L.-H., & Looi, C.-K. (2012). Fostering personalized learning in science inquiry supported by mobile technologies. *Educational Technology Research and Development, 60*(4), 679–701.

Tan, O. S. (2009). *Problem-based learning and creativity.* Cengage Learning Asia.

Core Strategies

Treffinger, D. J. (2004). Introduction to creativity and giftedness: Three decades of inquiry and development. In D. J. Treffinger (Ed.), *Creativity and giftedness* (pp. xxiii–xxx). Corwin Press.

Treffinger, D. J., & Isaksen, S. G. (2005). Creative problem solving: The history, development, and implications for gifted education and talent development. *Gifted Child Quarterly, 49*(4), 342–353.

Treffinger, D. J., Isaksen, S. G., & Stead-Dorval, K. B. (2006). *Creative problem solving: An introduction.* Prufrock Press.

Vernon, D. T. A., & Blake, R. L. (1993). Does problem-based learning work? A meta-analysis of evaluation research. *Academic Medicine, 68*(7), 550–563.

Criterion-Referenced Assessment of Student Progress

Personalized learning is a 21st-century education innovation made viable by disruptive technology and brought into being as part of the subsequent widespread social acceptance of personalization in general. For instance, most people receive daily personalized advertisements, news feeds, and commercial recommendations based on individual data. This personalized world is so ubiquitous, it may be difficult to conceive of one-size-fits-all anything. Yet, one-size-fits-all education remains the prevalent model of teaching and learning today. Advocacy for personalized learning predates the technology that tends to drive it at this time. For instance, more than half a century ago, Keller (1968) suggested the following guidelines for personalized approaches to learning: (1) make time flexible so that students progress at their own pace; (2) allow students to move on as soon as they master a topic/skill/concept – no more waiting; (3) utilize self-directed models that allow students to access content so that the teacher is not the primary deliverer of information; and (4) assess students often, and use the assessment data to make immediate decisions about what comes next.

Making time flexible may be the most disruptive idea in modern education. Traditionally, schools are structured with schedules, grading periods, and bells telling everyone when to move to the next stop. Most school systems record and structure student progress via a strictly time-based system. For example, Algebra is a 36-week course. After 36 weeks, students move on to Geometry or repeat Algebra for 36 more weeks. Time is constant but student mastery varies. Surely some students can master Algebra in less than 36 weeks. Just as surely, some students might need 45 weeks. Time-based education had been criticized well before the

DOI: 10.4324/9781003237136-9

modern personalized learning models appeared. For instance, Carroll (1963) gathered extensive data to show that when all students spend the same amount of time in a course of study, the result is a high correlation between achievement and ability. High ability leads to high achievement and low ability to low achievement quite consistently. Bloom (1968) argued that time-based schooling was designed to fail those with lower ability.

Many would argue today that time-based schooling tends to fail students at both ends of the ability distribution, including gifted students. By the 1980s, Bloom (1984) found that when time was allotted flexibly, schools could improve the achievement and overall attitudes toward learning of all students. Bloom's approach was termed "mastery learning." While mastery learning is supported with research and common sense, it most often proves too disruptive to school systems dedicated to the efficiency of time-based education.

One of the personalized learning schools we visited as research for this book intentionally made time flexible and achievement constant. Students worked on a course until it was mastered. In some cases, that was as quick as 12 weeks or in others, as long as 42 weeks. For students in that school, time flexibility reflected their domain strengths and interests. Some students at the school mastered mathematics and science courses in 20–25 weeks but spent the full 36 weeks to master social studies and language arts courses. Time flexibility proved a great match for high ability students with particular strengths in either science, technology, engineering, and mathematics (STEM) or humanities. The critical feature for the time-flexibility principle in this school was moving students on to the next topic/course as soon as they mastered the content. Peine and Coleman (2010) studied the experiences of gifted students in school, and described sitting and waiting as a universal experience for most gifted students in a typical school structure. Personalized learning with time flexibility has the potential to eliminate the learning inefficiencies of waiting, just as Keller suggested more than 50 years ago.

Applying flexible time principles in personalized learning requires procedural prioritizations that harken back to Keller's fourth guideline mentioned above – assess students often and use the data to make decisions about what comes next (Keller, 1968). Gifted students generally master new content faster than average students. That's why they almost universally describe school as periods of waiting – waiting for the teacher, waiting for the other students. However, in spite of its clear benefits, personalized learning is underutilized for gifted students because it requires assessment that produces rich data combined with flexible structures to facilitate differentiated learning for gifted students.

Assessing versus Grading

Our discussion of assessment must begin with an important clarification. Assessing students on their work is not the same thing as assigning them a grade. Assessment at its core is meant to provide students with feedback about how they are progressing with their learning. It is meant to be constructive and to help guide students toward their next steps: Is there a particular skill or concept that needs more work? Is the student ready to move on to new material? While grades certainly can offer this type of feedback to students, they don't always. These and other weaknesses in traditional grading systems are why standards-based grading has been embraced by many schools and teachers, and why it has an important role in personalized learning systems.

Traditional grading systems that assign students numbers or letters for their work and then average all of scores together to obtain a report card grade can be quite problematic. One source of such problems is that teachers do not always agree about how assignments should be scored. To illustrate this problem, we would like to describe a system that does a particularly good job of training teachers to score student work consistently and offer it as a contrast to what typically occurs in schools.

When the College Board prepares to score essays that students write as part of their Advanced Placement (AP) exams each year, they begin by bringing all of the graders together and discussing the scoring guidelines. The graders all read several essays together and come to agreement on how different types of responses will be scored. This calibration is a vital part of ensuring that students' scores are consistent, regardless of who actually grades them. During the subsequent grading, a lead grader spot-checks the work of the other graders, and, whenever needed, the grading pauses so that group or individual recalibration can occur. The process is designed to ensure the integrity of the scores, which may be used by colleges to award course credit. However, individual schools rarely have time to devote to teachers engaging in this type of calibration or to ensuring that grades are consistently assigned across all sections of a given course. Because of this

Core Strategies

lack of calibration, an essay that might be scored as an A by one teacher could feasibly be scored as a B by the teacher in the next classroom, even when they are using the same rubrics and grading scales.

Another factor that contributes to the problems of traditional grading systems is the practice of averaging grades for a report card. When a student or a parent sees that a student earned an A or a 95 in science, what useful information is conveyed? The only thing we know is that the student did about 95% of whatever the teacher wanted the student to do cumulatively throughout the grading period. The grade itself does not convey information about the student's specific strengths or areas in need of improvement.

Compounding both of these problems are additional concerns about grade inflation, which results in students receiving grades that do not correspond with the student's actual level of mastery of the content or skills taught. It is certainly not uncommon for students to receive grades based on work completion or participation rather than on mastery of skills or content. In addition, some teachers regularly curve grades or add bonus points to them through a variety of methods, so that when the student and family sees the final grade, it is much higher than the grade that the student actually earned. We've seen numerous situations in which a student actually fails a test but receives an A or B due to the addition of bonus points of some kind. We've also seen instances of students consistently failing tests but ending up with an A or B for the class on their report card.

While grading is certainly an activity with which schools and teachers continue to wrestle, we want to make it clear that this chapter is not about grading. It is about assessment. It is about providing students and their families with the feedback that they need to understand where students are in their learning and what they need to do in order to continue to grow their knowledge and their academic skills.

Principles of Assessment for Gifted Students

To be effective, assessment must be clearly aligned with standards and instruction. Furthermore, instruction for gifted students must be differentiated from the core curriculum. While a certain murkiness regarding the role of gifted education curricula has most likely always existed, it has become especially exacerbated in recent years as standards-based education has moved to the forefront of many local departments of curriculum and

150

instruction. Kaplan (2020) describes four different approaches that local programs often take:

1. *Complete the regular curriculum first and "reward" gifted students who finish it quickly with more complex work.* This approach is frequently taken, but the cost is that it relegates the deeper, more meaningful work that gifted students need to something that is "extra" rather than something that is necessary.

2. *Instruct students with a differentiated curriculum from the beginning.* People opposed to this approach often cite a concern that gifted students will miss some of the basic or foundational concepts of learning.

3. *Present both the regular curriculum and the gifted curriculum in parallel with one another.* This approach allows elements of each curriculum to reinforce elements of the other.

4. *Integrate the gifted curriculum with the regular curriculum, so that both are intentionally interwoven.* Teachers utilizing this approach become curriculum developers themselves as they determine where, when, and how the integration occurs.

While no single approach is going to satisfy all stakeholders, the key to implementation lies in ensuring that the goals of both the core and the differentiated curricula are clearly identified and met, and that assessment aligns with the instructional approach taken.

Whichever approach is utilized, assessments must include standards from both the differentiated curriculum and the core curriculum. While details of the core curriculum are typically determined by the state and local schools, in most cases any or all of the following three different options exist for identifying the differentiated standards:

1. Draw from above-grade level standards in the subject.

2. Include state-required standards for gifted education where those exist.

3. Ensure that elements from the programming standards of the National Association for Gifted Children (NAGC) are included and met.

Even when acceleration is the primary mode of differentiation, it is vital that standards for gifted education still be incorporated into the curriculum and assessed. While allowing students access to above-grade level courses is an excellent way of meeting their needs, even above-level standards may fail to capture the depth of knowledge and skills that gifted students need. In our own experiences, we have worked with gifted middle school and high school students intellectually capable of performing some work at the introductory level of graduate courses. One of us even taught a seventh-grade student who earned a near perfect verbal score on the SAT. As an eighth-grade student, she audited an undergraduate literature course at a four-year university in the fall, and based on her work in that class, the university allowed her to audit a graduate literature course in the spring. Many similar students exist in our schools. In these circumstances, the standards in traditional secondary courses are simply not complex enough to meet the students' full academic needs.

Unfortunately, it is not uncommon, especially in schools with a strong focus on preparation for standardized state tests, that standards from the differentiated curriculum are not meaningfully assessed because they are not part of what will be tested at the end of the year in state assessments. The amount of resistance and fear related to assessing students on standards that are not tested by the state simply cannot be understated, and this resistance wreaks havoc on gifted programs and students. When gifted standards are not adequately assessed, students and their families are deprived of valuable feedback about how the students can improve in their development of advanced skills and concepts. Students may also begin to internalize the unspoken message that the advanced part of their curriculum is not of real value. However, society at large also suffers from the lack of talent development that is a certain result of this neglect.

In both the core and the differentiated curriculum, standard principles of good assessment must be followed. Reutzel and Cooter (2019, pp. 406–408) succinctly identified five principles of assessment for reading teachers that can also serve as good practices for teachers of gifted students in all subject areas. Their principles are stated as follows:

1. choose the right assessment tool for your purpose
2. measure the right things
3. leverage assessment as a means for continuous improvement

4. do not supplant instruction with assessment
5. use valid and reliable instruments.

Types of Assessments

Two types of assessments are commonly utilized in gifted education: norm-based assessments and criterion-based assessments. Norm-based assessments give us valuable information about how students perform in relationship to others, with results often reported in scaled scores, stanines, and percentiles. CogAT, NNAT, PSAT, SAT, and ACT are all examples of norm-based assessments through which we learn how students rank against their peers on tasks that are typically required for advanced academic success. In contrast to norm-based assessments, criterion-based assessments tell us how students perform in relationship to expectations set by academic standards. It is through criterion-based assessments that we obtain detailed information about whether or not students have acquired the skills and knowledge that have been taught to them. These types of assessments, therefore, are crucial to help teachers decide appropriate pacing of instruction for individual students, how quickly and how far to accelerate students in their content learning, and to what extent students are able to perform at advanced levels in the content.

Among criterion-based assessments typically used in schools, two additional categories emerge: formative assessments and summative assessments. Formative assessments should be low-stakes and frequent, as they provide information during the learning process as to how well the students are understanding the content or mastering the skills. Formative assessments are often compared to the practices that athletes must attend in order to prepare for a game. They are tasks or activities that students complete in order to help them achieve mastery of knowledge or skills. The results of these assessments should be utilized by teachers to determine the next steps for instruction. Typical formative assessments may include solving math practice problems, analyzing the data from a science lab, participating in a class discussion about a reading assignment, completing an exit ticket that demonstrates an understanding of that day's lesson, or taking a short quiz. In contrast, a summative assessment is more high-stakes, as it is meant to be a culminating activity through which a student

Core Strategies

demonstrates mastery of material learned throughout a unit of study. It is the equivalent of the athlete's big game. Tests, essays, creative writing, projects, and presentations are all common types of summative assessments.

It is worth noting that some assessments that are particularly meaningful and useful to gifted students straddle middle ground between the formative and the summative. This is because some types of assessment are designed not only for students to demonstrate their deep knowledge and advanced skills, but also to provide additional learning experiences in and of themselves. Performance-based assessments and project-based assessments, when constructed well, fall into this category.

Also referred to as authentic assessments, these activities require students to actually use the knowledge and skills that they have learned in the same way that professionals in the field do, and as they do so, they continually become better at it. This type of assessment may involve students strengthening their research and writing skills as they work to produce a paper that is submitted for publication. It may involve students in a science class designing and conducting an original experiment and presenting the results of that experiment at a symposium. It could also require students studying civics or economics to propose a solution to a problem that their community is experiencing and to engage in a public debate about their proposal. What all of these activities importantly share is that they provide students an opportunity to demonstrate the depth to which they understand the subject matter, as well as the advanced skills that they have developed to work within that subject matter. As students complete their final product, they continue to stretch themselves, identify new obstacles, and experiment with ways to overcome those obstacles, thereby extending their own learning and development throughout the entire process. These types of activities are often scored using rubrics which capture both the essential knowledge and skills of the core curriculum, and the advanced knowledge and skills that gifted students are given the opportunity to showcase. Examples of how those rubrics might be structured will be given later in this chapter.

The Role of Pre-Tests

One type of criterion-based formative assessment that we strongly encourage gifted programs to utilize is the pre-test. When constructed well,

Criterion-Referenced Assessment

pre-tests serve as powerful diagnostic tools that educators can use to plan the pacing and compacting of their curriculum, and to thereby reduce or even eliminate time that gifted students spend waiting in class to learn something new. By assessing students on the knowledge and skills that will be introduced in a new unit prior to any instruction taking place, teachers gain valuable knowledge about how to best personalize instruction for each student. Whereas some students may need a great deal of instruction on new material, others may need none at all, and those students should be allowed to move on to material that is truly new to them.

However, we do recommend that the items on the assessment be constructed as open-response rather than multiple choice, true/false, matching, or any other type of question in which students simply have to select from among a set of pre-constructed responses. While it is certainly easier and quicker to assess answers that are based on pre-constructed responses, these types of assessments also increase the likelihood that students will guess correctly. Moreover, since many gifted students were initially identified to receive services based at least in part on scores they earned on standardized aptitude and achievement tests, we know that many of them have strong test-taking skills.

The following example, which is a composite based on experiences from our own work, provides a good illustration of this potential pitfall. At School X, a group of eighth-grade gifted students were enrolled in a high school Pre-AP Chemistry course. At the end of Pre-AP Chemistry, all of the students were required to take a state exam associated with the course. The teacher, who was well trained in gifted pedagogy, began each unit with a short pre-assessment that contained multiple choice questions about each standard that would be covered in the new unit. She then used the results of the pre-assessments to compact the curriculum. This compacting moved the students along at a faster pace than the traditional Pre-AP Chemistry students taking the course and created more time for the eighth-grade students to delve into advanced concepts and ideas, and to extend their learning. Some of that advanced learning drew directly from the AP Chemistry curriculum.

While, in theory, there should not have been a problem with this design, in practice, several of the students experienced significant struggles. In discussing their difficulties, students articulated quite clearly that they often knew which answer choice was correct on the pre-assessments based solely on their knowledge of how multiple-choice questions work. They

155

would oftentimes select the right answer without having a clear idea of why it was the right answer. Since the teacher thought they understood those concepts much better than they actually did, each time she moved on to more advanced topics that were based on those concepts, the students experienced a great deal of anxiety. That anxiety manifested as blame on the teacher for "not teaching" them things that they clearly needed to know.

To compensate for what they perceived to be their teacher's shortcomings, the students would then spend a great deal of time at home researching concepts online and trying to fill in their own learning gaps. When the teacher realized that the pre-assessments were creating a false positive about the students' level of understanding, the situation was easily remedied.

The teacher began opening each unit with a discussion of the Pre-AP Chemistry standards that would be covered, letting the students talk through what they already knew and what was completely unfamiliar. As part of this discussion, she allowed the students to suggest how much time they might need to spend on each standard and the order in which they wanted to address each standard. Also included in that initial discussion were elements of the AP Chemistry curriculum that might serve as extensions when time allowed. The explicitness of this procedure ensured that the students knew the distinction between what they would be required to know for the state test that was required for Pre-AP Chemistry, what was an extension of that information, and what they would learn in more depth during a future AP course. It was a good solution for all involved. However, a great deal of stress and anxiety had been caused for both the students and the teacher as they sought to determine the source of the problem and how to fix it.

Using Assessment Results for Acceleration

In the scenario described above, an experienced teacher effectively utilized pre-tests in each unit in order to compact a Pre-AP curriculum and accelerate her gifted students into AP standards. An issue that often arises when criterion-referenced assessments are utilized within a model of acceleration – whether that acceleration involves a unit of study within a course or a course in its entirety – is how much mastery a student should be able to demonstrate before moving on to new content.

In traditional school settings, students are typically expected to demonstrate mastery of 60% or 70% of the content in order to receive a passing grade for the class and move on. In instances where state tests are required at the end of the year, the level of mastery required for a passing score may be even lower. For example, in Texas, students receive a designation of "did not meet," "approaches," "meets," or "masters" to indicate their level of academic attainment on each standardized state exam. A student whose score is "approaches" is typically considered to have passed the content and be ready for the next level of instruction in that subject. In 2019, students who took the seventh-grade mathematics exam only had to answer 16 of the 40 questions correctly (40%) in order to receive a score of "approaches" and thus to pass the test by state standards (Texas Education Agency, 2020). However, Texas students in grades 6–12 who wish to accelerate in a content area in which they have not received formal instruction by utilizing a credit by exam option must score at least 80% on the exam in order to receive credit (Texas Administrative Code, 2018). In situations in which students are allowed to accelerate through units or standards but not entire courses, the determination about how much mastery a student is required to demonstrate (and how) is oftentimes left solely to the discretion of the individual teacher or the teacher's department.

Several concerns arise as we consider how much mastery should be required to be demonstrated before acceleration occurs. Of course, nobody wants to place students in a learning environment in which the standards being taught are so far above a student's instructional level that the student gives up or fails. However, we also have concerns about setting a standard of mastery so high that we reinforce the inappropriate and unattainable idea that gifted students should be perfect at everything they do. It seems particularly harmful and cruel to tell students that they can only access new learning or new content when they demonstrate mastery of 90% or more of the standards, as sometimes occurs when teachers utilize pre-tests for instructional decisions. In our current educational environments in which grades and self-worth have become conflated for so many students, and in which anxiety related to perfectionism can result in a myriad of forms of self-harm, we want to make sure students know that sometimes, 60% or 70% is good enough. We are reminded here of the medical school adage "Ds get MDs." Sometimes it really is appropriate to allow a student with a smaller degree of mastery to go ahead and move on to the more complex

Core Strategies

work that the student is more interested in completing. In the course of doing that more complex work, many gifted students will even correct their own deficiencies as they encounter an authentic need to do so.

Another concern we have regarding the inconsistencies that exist regarding how much mastery is "enough" for a student to achieve before moving on to new content is intimately tied to equity. At a time in which more educators are actively seeking to remove barriers to learning and to ensure that all students have equitable educational experiences, holding students who want to advance to more complex work to a different set of requirements than students who choose to remain on a traditional track seems particularly unjust.

Assessment Tools for Depth and Complexity

As previously described, it is important that all gifted students be assessed not only on the core curriculum and standards that every student in their school is taught, but also on the differentiated curriculum that their program provides to serve the specific, personalized needs of its gifted students. One way in which the gifted curriculum can be differentiated from the standard curriculum is through the addition of depth and complexity (Kaplan et al., 1994; Kaplan, 2008).

Working with a Javits grant in 1994, the California Department of Education and California Association for the Gifted developed a framework that outlines specific ways in which depth and complexity can be operationalized as tools for differentiation in all subjects. Depth can be added as students move beyond grade-level standards and work with patterns, trends, rules, details, big ideas, unanswered questions, ethics, and the language of the discipline. Complexity is increased as students consider connections across disciplines, multiple perspectives, and changes over time. Additional content imperatives ground the depth and complexity elements into advanced content; these imperatives encourage students to consider the origin and contribution of a piece of content, and any parallels, paradoxes, and/or convergence it may have with other pieces of content. Twenty-five years after this original work was published, the icons developed to help students visualize these processes have become ubiquitous in professional development sessions and in gifted classrooms. They can also be utilized as a framework for criterion-based assessments.

158

As teachers utilize the depth and complexity icons in the daily work that gifted students complete in various subjects, assessments should be created to determine whether or not students are working with content in deeper, more complex ways. Frames in various formats have been a fairly common way of structuring work with the icons, and a variety of these frames can be found with a quick internet search. In addition to facilitating group and individual work, depth and complexity frames can also serve as fairly quick and easy assessment tools that allow teachers valuable insight into a student's thought processes and knowledge about a topic.

Depending on the topic, the frame may address a single content standard in depth, or it may address multiple standards, with each assessed by a different part of the frame. The frames can be produced in a variety of mediums, and students can even quickly draw their own. We have seen them produced by hand on paper, created with word processing programs, drawn on small individual whiteboards that allow students to erase and rewrite their work, designed on a presentation slide that students can edit, and outlined on electronic whiteboards that allow students to add their comments via electronic sticky notes. The format and look of frames are far less important than the content that the students produce when utilizing them. An example from social studies, modified for students to utilize as a word processing document, is provided in Table 7.1.

Additional templates can be utilized that require students to combine the icons in some sort of logical progression that emphasizes the connections among them. One example is a template (Rodriguez, 2020) that helps students cite and analyze textual evidence in order to make inferences and determine themes, a skill that appears as an anchor standard in Common Core State Standards for English Language Arts (ELA) (CCSS.ELA-LITERACY.CCRA.R.1, ELA-LITERACY.CCRA.R.2) (Common Core State Standards Initiative, 2020). With this template, students begin by identifying several quotes from the text that seem to express important ideas. These quotes become the foundational details of the text that the students then use for further analysis. For each quote, students generate one word that encapsulates the topic of the quote; this word should be drawn from the language of the discipline, representing a concept or idea that professionals within the discipline seek to understand. The students then combine those words to create one sentence, a big idea that expresses a personal interpretation of the connections among those concepts and

Core Strategies

Table 7.1 Modified Depth and Complexity Frame

Topic: The Mission System

	Why did Spain create the mission system in North America?
	What was daily life like in the mission system?
	Contrast the Spaniards' views of the missions with the Native Americans' views of the missions.
	Was it ethical for the Spaniards to create the mission system? Why or why not?
	Were the missions ultimately successful? Why or why not?

is supported by the text. Figure 7.1 provides a template for this activity. Figure 7.2 provides an example from ELA that is based on a reading of Kurt Vonnegut's *Harrison Bergeron*.

Elements of the depth and complexity framework can also be intentionally tied to creative thinking skills. For example, students might analyze the multiple perspectives that various stakeholders hold surrounding an issue that is of current importance in the field. As part of that analysis, students can identify who the stakeholders are, what other stakeholders want, what obstacles other stakeholders might present, and how those obstacles might be overcome. A stakeholder chart, such as

Criterion-Referenced Assessment

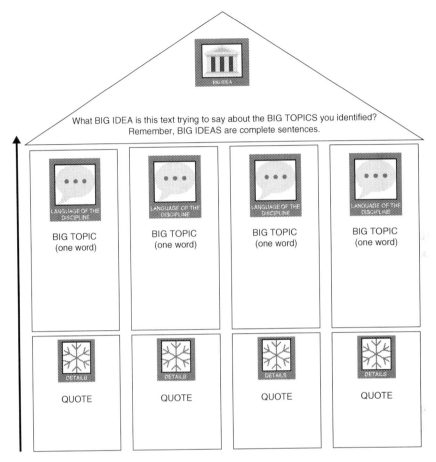

Figure 7.1 Template for English Language Arts Depth and Complexity Text Analysis

Source: Adapted from Rodriguez (2020)

the one in Table 7.2, can be used as an assessment tool through which students document their analysis and demonstrate their understanding of the multiple perspectives surrounding an issue. As a further step, a teacher might turn this into a performance assessment by having students adopt the roles of different stakeholders and participate in a simulated stakeholder meeting.

We have seen such simulations run quite effectively in gifted science and social studies classrooms, particularly when they capture the connections between the two disciplines. Such activities might focus on

Core Strategies

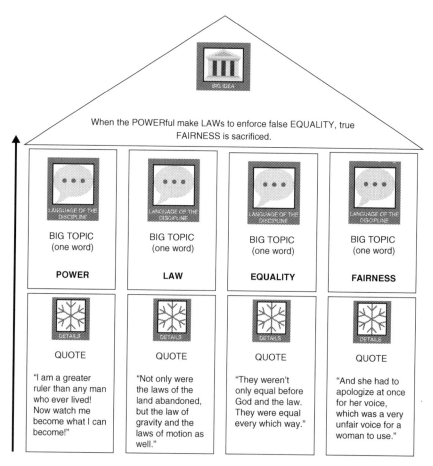

Figure 7.2 English Language Arts Depth and Complexity Text Analysis: *Harrison Bergeron*

Source: Template adapted from Rodriguez (2020); quotations from Vonnegut (1961)

a specific community's disaster relief efforts prior to, during, and after a natural disaster; on issues pertaining to property rights and standards of living when businesses with large footprints (such as hog farms, gas and oil drilling companies, airports, and hot sauce factories) interfere with nearby residents' perceived quality of life; or on topics that pit economic interests against conservation efforts. As an illustrative example, we will describe one stakeholder activity that we helped design for a science class that was taught to gifted high school students.

Criterion-Referenced Assessment

Table 7.2 Stakeholder Meeting Chart

Personal Stakeholder Group			Personal Position on Issue
Other Stakeholder Group(s)	*This Group's Position on Issue*	*Obstacle Presented by This Group's Position*	*Strategy to Address That Obstacle*

One of the course's instructors had recently completed a summer field internship in the Galápagos islands and centered the stakeholder activity around that experience, using her professional expertise to frame a simulation based on existing stakeholder conflicts. The central question explored in the activity was how much (if any) of the Galápagos islands should be protected and how. The students were tasked with resolving the following questions during the stakeholder meeting:

- How much of the Galápagos islands should be designated as a marine protected area?
- How much of the area can be fished?

Core Strategies

- Will there be any restrictions or protections on fishing?
- Will there be any restrictions or protections on tourism?
- How will those restrictions and protections be enforced?

After researching and discussing the political, social, cultural, and economic elements at work in the Galápagos islands, students were assigned to one of the following stakeholder groups:

- longline fishermen from the mainland, who depend on longline fishing to support their families and to feed their communities, but who aren't allowed to move to the Galápagos islands because they were not born there
- sport fishermen, who are native to the Galápagos islands and earn their livelihoods through tourism and who compete with the longline fishermen for catches
- Galápagos National Park workers, who are charged with enforcing regulations but have limited funding and manpower
- scientists, who want to preserve the marine life and are concerned about damage to the ecosystem
- politicians, who need to pass policies that benefit as many constituents as possible in order to remain in office and/or retain allies
- tourism groups, who bring economic benefits to the area and who need to ensure that the ecosystem remains healthy enough to sustain their businesses.

Working in small groups with members of their assigned stakeholder groups, students completed additional research, decided what they would advocate for during the meeting, and attempted to make back channel deals with other groups prior to the formal meeting's commencement. When the meeting began, the teacher served as moderator. Each group began by giving a short speech to advocate for their position and then answered questions asked by the other groups. When all groups finished their presentations, a period of open discussion/debate ensued. The teacher then called for a formal vote on each question.

After the simulation concluded, the class had a whole-group debrief in which they discussed both the policies that they had passed and the

Criterion-Referenced Assessment

processes by which those policies had been developed. It is not uncommon during these debriefs for students to realize that they passed some policies that conflict with one another and/or that some of their policies may result in unintended negative consequences. The first time that students engage in this type of activity, they may feel somewhat disillusioned that it was so difficult to get policies passed with so many different stakeholders' interests at play. Ethical questions often arise naturally as part of the process, and students may, for the first time in their lives, experience vicariously but strongly the conflict that comes with knowing that there is not a single solution that solves everyone's problems and that most policies cause harm in some way. Though these feelings may challenge students' sense of themselves and their world, when handled reflectively, deep learning occurs that ultimately makes this experience a positive one.

Another assessment tool that can help structure students' considerations of the long-term consequences of human actions is a table that encourages them to think through both the intended and unintended consequences of their actions in a stakeholder experience (see Table 7.3). This activity focuses students on looking at changes over time while still engaging their

Table 7.3 Intended and Unintended Consequences

Policy or Action	
Consequence #1	*Consequence #2*
Intended Consequence / *Unintended Consequence*	*Intended Consequence* / *Unintended Consequence*

Core Strategies

creative thought processes. After a stakeholder meeting, students can take one policy that has been passed and brainstorm the possible consequences of that policy. Rather than stopping there, though, they can then take those initial consequences and identify both the intended and unintended consequences that may result. This activity strengthens the students' creative and critical thinking skills.

Rubrics for Summative Assessments

In evaluating gifted students' summative work within the differentiated curriculum in a way that is meaningful and that continues to orient the students toward further growth, teachers should construct rubrics that capture a wide range of proficiency levels. Rather than labeling each performance level with a standard numerical or letter scale or with quality indicators such as "needs improvement," "average," or "excellent," each level instead might be labeled as "novice," "apprentice," "practitioner," or "expert." The description of what constitutes expert performance on the rubric should clearly indicate how professionals in the field use that skill or work with that information. For example, an essay rubric might include a row that assesses the writer's thesis statement in this way:

- novice: the thesis statement is unclear
- apprentice: the thesis statement accurately identifies the topic of the essay
- practitioner: the thesis statement explains what the central argument of the essay is
- expert: the thesis statement sets up a complex argument and takes a clear position on that argument.

The benefit to choosing specific standards and assessing them on this type of scale is that students know that working authentically as professionals in the field do is the ultimate goal – not a letter grade or a numerical grade or a descriptive word (such as "excellent") that contains unavoidable elements of subjectivity. It also clearly explains the traits that define each of those levels and thus gives students a clear idea of what they need to do to continue to personally develop along the talent continuum.

166

Since developing advanced and sophisticated professional products is a gifted standard identified by the NAGC, we also recommend that programs create specific rubrics that identify what those types of products should include at different grade levels. The Texas Education Agency, working with experts in gifted education, created and piloted the Texas Performance Standards Project across 67 school districts from 2000–2006 in order to do just that. Lauded by Sally Reis as "an assessment system that adequately measures the highest levels of achievement of gifted and talented students" (Texas Education Agency, 2007), the performance tasks and their associated rubrics can be publicly accessed via the Texas Performance Standards Project website. Educators can search for performance tasks by grade level and subject. Developed for different grade bands (K–2, 3–5, 6–8, and 9–12), the rubrics are designed to help teachers evaluate students on specific elements of their research plan, as well as on their final product and their communication skills. For example, the rubric for grades 6–8 evaluates students on the elements listed in Table 7.4 (Texas Education Agency, 2011). Each rubric contains grade-level appropriate expectations for gifted students and descriptors of what each element looks like at the novice, apprentice, practitioner, and expert level. Complete rubrics for each grade band can be found at www. texaspsp.org.

Table 7.4 Elements Assessed in Middle School Texas Performance Standards Project

Developing and Implementing a Research Plan: Research Process	Development of Questions
	Research Methodology
	Sources of Information
	Collection of Data
	Analysis and Interpretation of Data
	Multiple Perspectives
Presentation of Learning: Product and Communication	Organization
	Depth of Understanding
	Impact
	Delivery
	Vocabulary of Disciplinarian

Source: Adapted from Texas Education Agency (2011)

Core Strategies

 Summary

Personalized learning for gifted students should embrace time-flexible learning, frequent assessments that provide rich data, and continuous progress through an aligned curriculum. Assessments should provide students with specific feedback about their level of mastery of specific skills and content knowledge, and should intentionally help students move along a talent development trajectory, from novice to apprentice, to practitioner, to expert. To this end, gifted students should be assessed on skills and content required in both the standard curriculum and the gifted curriculum. The NAGC programming standards, as well as state standards for gifted education, where those exist, can provide a starting point for developing assessments aligned with gifted curriculum.

References

Bloom, B. S. (1968). Learning for mastery. *Instruction and Curriculum*, *1*(2), 1–10.

Bloom, B. S. (1984). The 2-sigma problem: The search for methods of group instruction as effective as one-to-one tutoring. *Educational Researcher*, *13*(6), 4–16.

Carroll, J. B. (1963). A model of school learning. *Teachers College Record*, *64*(8), 723–733.

Common Core State Standards Initiative. (2020). *English language arts standards >> anchor standards >> college and career readiness anchor standards for reading*. www.corestandards.org/ELA-Literacy/CCRA/R/

Kaplan, S. (2008). Layering differentiated curricula for the gifted and talented. In F. A. Karnes & S. M. Bean (Eds.), *Methods and materials for teaching the gifted* (3rd ed.) (pp. 107–135). Prufrock Press.

Kaplan, S. (2020). The curriculum dilemma. *Gifted Child Today*, *43*(3), 199–201. https://doi.org/10.1177/1076217520916212

Kaplan, S., Cassity, M., Fontaine, R., Hunt, H., Tempes, F., Brandes, B., Abbott, B., & Barkett, C. (1994). *Differentiating the core curriculum and instruction to provide advanced learning opportunities*. California Department of Education, California Association for the Gifted.

Keller, F. S. (1968). Good-bye, teacher... *Journal of Applied Behavior Analysis, 1*(1), 79–89. https://doi.org/10.1901/jaba.1968.1-79

Peine, M. E., & Coleman, L. J. (2010). The phenomenon of waiting in class. *Journal for the Education of the Gifted, 34*(2), 220–244.

Reutzel, D. R., & Cooter, R. B. (2019). *Teaching children to read: The teacher makes the difference* (8th ed.). Pearson.

Rodriguez, C. (2020, December 2). *Teaching to the top: An advanced depth and complexity boot camp* [Conference session]. Texas Association for the Gifted & Talented, giftED20, online, Austin, TX.

Texas Administrative Code. (2018). *Chapter 74: Curriculum requirements. Subchapter C: Other provisions. Paragraph 24: Credit by examination.* https://tea.texas.gov/sites/default/files/ch074c.pdf

Texas Education Agency. (2007). *The Texas Education Agency's Texas Performance Standards Project: Summary of success.* www.texaspsp. org/assets/uploads/docs/TPSPmagazine_web.pdf

Texas Education Agency. (2011). *Middle school TPSP assessment rubric overview.* www.texaspsp.org/assets/uploads/docs/Middle_School_Rubric.pdf

Texas Education Agency. (2020). *State of Texas assessments of academic readiness. Raw score conversion table, grade 7 mathematics.* https://tea.texas.gov/sites/default/files/2019_STAAR_Spring_7M_RS-SS_tagged.pdf

Vonnegut, K. (1961). Harrison Bergeron. The Magazine of Fantasy and Science Fiction, 21(4), 5–10.

Multi-Year Mentoring for Talent Development

The role of mentors in furthering individuals' education and knowledge has been well-established for centuries. A trusted advisor, often a family member or friend who takes responsibility for overseeing the development and well-being of someone younger or less experienced, can often be the source of advice and wisdom that helps a young person achieve their goals and find success. Effective mentors are plentiful in popular culture, with many people wondering how their own lives might be different if they had had a Yoda, a Dumbledore, or a Mr. Miyagi guiding them along the way.

The word "mentor" derives from the character Mentor in Homer's *The Odyssey* (Homer, 2018, originally published 1614). A friend of Odysseus, Mentor is entrusted to care for Odysseus' son, Telemachus, while Odysseus is fighting the Trojan War. Due to a variety of misfortunes, Odysseus spends 20 long years away from home, during which time his whereabouts become unknown and his son grows to adulthood. During Odysseus' prolonged absence, his wife is beset by suitors hoping to take his throne and his kingdom along with his wife's hand in marriage. In the opening books of *The Odyssey*, Athena, the Goddess of Wisdom, assumes first the form of Mentes, whose name is etymologically tied to "mentor," and then the form of Mentor in order to give Telemachus sage advice and assistance, instilling in him the mental courage and the direction he needs to protect his father's kingdom from the many men attempting to overtake it. Athena appears again in Mentor's form at the end of the epic, after Odysseus finally arrives home, encouraging Odysseus as he and Telemachus engage in their final battle to restore his rightful position as king. Athena's assistance as

Mentor enables peace to be restored to the kingdom and the epic's hero to retain his throne. The message is clear that oftentimes help and wisdom are needed for even the best to achieve success.

For centuries, mentors have served as natural teachers and advisors to people for whom they cared. Outside of the realm of immediate family and friends, mentors have also long served as experts who provided content knowledge and oversaw skill development in young adults – sometimes apprentices – learning new trades and professions. Historically, these types of mentorships were often substitutes for formal education. Today, they are widely viewed as supplements to formal education, as modern mentors often come in the form of both academic advisors and professionals overseeing a young adult's internship or research project within a particular field of study.

The majority of elementary and secondary schools today employ well-trained counselors whose responsibilities include guiding their students successfully through their schooling. However, gifted students, whose cognitive skills, intellectual curiosity, and need for meaningful intellectual stimulation lie outside of the group norm present in their own schools, often find themselves in need of more specialized assistance. In elementary and secondary schools, gifted students need school-based advisors who are highly trained in advanced and gifted education, and who will remain with the student for multiple years, analyzing their work and interests, helping them understand their own strengths and needs, and co-creating educational plans with them and their families. As these gifted students outgrow their own school systems' resources, their advisors should know how to connect them with outside mentors and opportunities to help them to continue to grow in their areas of talent and interest.

Defining Mentorship

Most understanding of mentors and mentorship is based on informal knowledge and narrative understandings of mentors. However, mentorship is studied as an empirical social science construct as well. Research work on the mentorship process has been largely conducted in studies of career development and managerial studies, and some educational research has focused on mentorship as well. A well regarded, social science definition of mentoring comes from Bozeman and Feeney (2007):

Mentoring: a process for the informal transmission of knowledge, social capital, and psychological support perceived by the recipient as relevant to work, career, or professional development; mentoring entails informal communication, usually face-to-face and during a sustained period of time, between a person who is perceived to have greater relevant knowledge, wisdom, or experience (the mentor) and a person who is perceived to have less (the protégé).

(Bozeman & Feeney, 2007, p. 731)

Mentoring in most settings is one-to-one, but group mentoring is viable and effective as well (Huizing, 2012). Group mentoring may be beneficial in educational environments, and some research has found group mentoring effective with gifted students (Stoeger, 2017). In group mentoring, one or more mentees interact with and form relationships with one or more mentors. There are five typologies of group mentoring that can be used in the process of talent development with high ability, gifted students (see Table 8.1). Mentorship in all of these typologies has typically occurred in face-to-face interactions, but digital/online mentoring is increasingly being used as the technologies needed for this type of mentoring are becoming more commonplace (Packard, 2003). A blend of digital and in-person mentoring is also recommended, and a blend of digital and in-person is an effective way to use the many-to-one mentorship typology.

Supplemental programs beyond the classroom are effective for increased personalization of learning and talent development in a particular domain (Olszewski-Kubilius et al., 2020), and mentorship opportunities are included in the list of recommended supplemental programs. Mentorships with gifted students have been effective for career development in science, technology, engineering, and mathematics (STEM) (Stoeger et al., 2013) among gifted students, including those categories of student typically underrepresented in STEM fields (Stoeger et al., 2017). In fact, mentorship has been considered by some to be the gold standard of pedagogy and learning (Eby et al., 2008; Stoeger et al., 2013; Underhill, 2006). Multi-year mentorship is one of the most powerful educational interventions for personalizing learning and developing exceptional talent over time. Figure 8.1 presents the intended outcomes of multi-year mentoring as a component of personalized gifted and talented education. Mentorship programs are most effective with (a) thoughtful matches of mentors/mentees, (b) clarity of the purpose of the mentorship, and (c) consistent and frequent interaction.

Multi-Year Mentoring

Table 8.1 Mentorship Typology

Type of Mentorship	Description
One-on-One	• one mentor works with one mentee • hierarchical relationship where the purpose of the influence is from mentor to mentee • example: student with STEM talent is actively mentored by a biomedical engineer working at a local pharmaceutical firm
One-to-Many	• one mentor works with multiple mentees • hierarchical relationship where the purpose of the influence is from the mentor to all of the mentees • example: a lawyer in the community meets regularly to mentor a group of students interested in future careers in the legal profession
Many-to-One	• constellation of mentors working with one mentee • hierarchical relationship where the purpose of the influence is from the mentors to the mentee • each mentor typically has a specific expertise that is different from the other mentors • example: student with exceptional math talent is mentored by three mentors working in different math-intensive industries: one in the financial industry, one in computer science, and one in academia
Many-to-Many	• multiple mentors work with multiple mentees • hierarchical relationship where the purpose of the influence is from the mentors to all of the mentees • mentors are clearly defined with distinct roles differentiating them from the mentees • example: three graduate students in a writing MFA program mentor a group of 20 students in the creative writing club at a high school
Peer Mentoring	• non-hierarchical group of peers mentoring each other • roles of mentor and mentee may shift as the peer groups influence each other • example: a group of gifted high school students interested in engineering meet weekly to mentor each other in career exploration and preparing for college

Note: MFA, Master of Fine Arts; STEM, science, technology, engineering, and mathematics

Core Strategies

Figure 8.1 Seven Facets of Mentoring for Talent Development
Note: Mentoring supports talent development in seven areas where mentorship is effectively implemented with appropriate mentors over sufficient time. When implemented in a personalized learning framework, multi-year mentoring can significantly impact student achievement, motivation, and focus.

Models of Mentorship for High Ability Students

Mentoring in Higher Education

Perhaps one of the most effective examples of modern mentoring within advanced academic settings currently occurs on university campuses. When undergraduate students enroll in universities, they are immediately assigned to an advisor whose job is to help the students successfully navigate the university system and achieve their academic goals. A good advisor reviews each student's test scores, course grades, and career goals, and helps each student develop and follow a four-year plan for graduation. Advisors will also connect their students with additional university resources, such as tutoring, counseling, and career services, as needed.

Additional services offered by universities that students can access, often on the advice of an advisor who sees a need for them, become part of the valuable mentoring system that benefits students. Tutoring centers and writing centers help strengthen targeted academic skills. Counseling services frequently include sessions to help students strengthen their executive functioning through direct instruction and assistance with time management skills and organization. Career service offices administer tests that help match students' interests, academic strengths, and personality types to potential careers that could be a good fit for them. In addition, they assist students with resume writing, help them strengthen their interview skills, and connect them with internships that will help them gain professional experience while still in college.

Depending on the university model, college students may have more than one advisor guiding them, with each advisor specializing in a different aspect of the student's education. For example, a student in an honors college may have an honors advisor who focuses the student on specialized honors courses and symposiums that substitute for the university's regular core requirements. That same student may also have an advisor from the college of their chosen major, who ensures that the student is taking an appropriate sequence of courses within the major, and connects the student to relevant professional organizations, internships and research opportunities.

In addition to these formal mentors, it is not uncommon for university students to connect informally with at least one professor who also provides guidance and support to the student throughout their tenure at the university. This is particularly the case for those attending liberal arts colleges, private universities, and honors colleges, where the undergraduate experience is more likely to be a primary focus for professors. A science professor may become a research mentor, inviting an interested student to participate in their current research project and to attend a professional conference to help present the results. A humanities professor may encourage an especially talented student to submit a piece of writing for professional publication or to present it at a professional symposium. These professors may also steer their students towards specific graduate programs or job opportunities that will help them continue to thrive in their fields post-graduation.

175

Core Strategies

Some universities actively facilitate the process of creating these informal mentorships between faculty and undergraduate students through their use of residential colleges, which are essentially dorms that are structured similarly to the Houses described in the *Harry Potter* books. Residential colleges may have university faculty living in the dorms with students as well as faculty members who keep evening office hours in the dorms' common areas and who regularly dine with students. This type of system creates additional opportunities for students to interact with experts, and to receive not only professional advice about how to advance in specific fields, but also personal advice about how to navigate higher education, professional fields, and life in general in ways that are personally beneficial. For students who may not have personal connections to people in the fields they hope to enter, and for those who may be the first in their families to attend college, these relationships can certainly have life-altering impacts.

While the university experience – and the depth of mentoring that often accompanies it – typically is reserved for students who have graduated high school, some early college experiences do exist for advanced secondary students. While these are explored in more detail in the chapter on acceleration, it is worth noting here that, like the typical university model, these programs also include mentoring components. For example, the Texas Academy of Mathematics and Science (TAMS), a program that allows students to complete their last two years of high school while enrolled as full-time residential students at the University of North Texas, provides students with academic advising, college advising for their years beyond the two in which they are TAMS students, and career counseling. In addition to the types of services offered by many university advisors and described above, advisors at TAMS also collect peer references and parent assessments to help them guide students along their educational pathways ((University of North Texas, 2020).

Mentoring in Non-School-Based Gifted Programs

Within the field of gifted K–12 education specifically, the need for specialized mentors has been widely acknowledged for decades. To date, much of this mentorship has existed outside of traditional K–12 schools. One prominent example of this is seen in the work of Julian Stanley, a

176

Multi-Year Mentoring

cognitive science researcher at Johns Hopkins University, who, in 1968, was introduced to a 12-year-old who was so advanced in his regular math classes that his parents enrolled him in a coding class at the university. When the student outperformed many of his classmates in the coding class, his instructor introduced him to Stanley. Stanley performed a series of cognitive tests on the student and, after determining that no other options were available for meeting the student's academic needs within his existing school system, successfully advocated for his admission to the university at age 13. (In fact, one often finds in the trajectory of many students who enter college at a very young age a significant influence played by a mentor – in this case, someone with the authority and knowledge to have traditional rules waived or amended in order to meet the needs of the exceptional student.) As a direct result of this relationship, Stanley began the Study for Mathematically Precocious Youth in 1971 and founded the Center for Talented Youth (CTY) in 1979. Duke University followed suit with its own Talent Identification Program (TIP) in 1981, and throughout the 1980s and 1990s numerous other talent search programs were developed by universities across the United States.

As part of their programming, talent search programs typically provide gifted students with more opportunities to learn advanced content from actual content experts than most secondary schools logistically can. Secondary students who qualify for these programs can spend several weeks during the summer intensively studying one course in a field of interest, taught by an instructor who has completed graduate work in that field. Courses are taught on university campuses, where students also have access to specialized facilities and equipment that most secondary schools cannot afford. For example, a student with an interest in marine science who enrolls in a three-week summer course through CTY can board a sailing vessel and complete field work related to the watershed and marine life in the Chesapeake Bay or travel the East Coast from Baltimore to Rhode Island to study whales and estuary systems. Within the talent development program models, instructors become short-term academic mentors, not only teaching students about the content of the course, but also setting aside time in class for students to learn about college programs and career pathways within that particular field should they choose to pursue it further.

In collaboration with some of these talent search programs, a number of notable groups also work to provide resources to selected gifted students as part of their goal of helping advanced students develop to their potential.

Core Strategies

Mentoring is included as a resource by some of the most prestigious programs.

The Young Scholars Program of the Jack Kent Cooke Foundation offers both financial assistance and mentoring to high performing seventh-grade students with financial need. Students who are selected for the program work with an advisor for five years, with the student and family communicating with the advisor at least once every four to six weeks. The advisor helps each student develop an individualized learning plan and provides each student with assistance choosing (and potentially applying to) a high school, developing a four-year high school plan that includes both academics and extracurriculars, selecting summer programs to attend, and applying to colleges. In a similar manner, their College Scholarship Program offers personal advising and financial assistance to seniors in high school throughout their college experience. In the past 20 years, the Jack Kent Cooke Foundation has supported approximately 2,800 students with advising and provided over $222 million in scholarships (Jack Kent Cooke Foundation, 2020).

In a similar vein, Davidson Young Scholars for the Highly Gifted offers support to profoundly gifted students between the ages of 5 and 18. In addition to selecting from a number of different educational opportunities offered through the program, students who are selected may elect to work with a Family Consultant. The Family Consultant can assist with planning related to academics, talent development, college, and the student's social and emotional needs. Additionally, the Family Consultant can help students navigate their current school and will speak directly with teachers, counselors, and administrators at the school (Davidson Institute, 2020).

Lastly, the Special Populations Network of the National Association for Gifted Children and the Gifted Racial Accountability and Commitment to Equity Special Interest Group sponsor the Dr. Martin D. Jenkins Scholar Award each year. This award was created to assist highly gifted, high-achieving Black students in grades 6–12. Students who receive this award have the option of participating in an ambassador program, peer mentoring opportunities, and an alumni network. Through these programs, students may be mentored by former award recipients in activities such as the college application process and various opportunities available in their local communities.

Thus far, the models discussed all exist outside of the traditional school setting that the majority of students – even gifted ones – encounter as

178

part of their K–12 schooling. Indeed, not many models currently exist for providing these levels of support for students within traditional schools. However, some structures do exist within looping models, advisory models, and school-facilitated internships that can be built on by schools seeking to strengthen the level of support provided to gifted learners.

Looping

The type of mentoring that we propose will work best for gifted students requires that the mentor work with the student over multiple years. This timeframe will allow the mentor to get to know the student on a deeper level and to track the student's growth and interests over a longer period of time. In traditional K–12 school settings, the only people who typically work with students over several years, however, are counselors and administrators. Unfortunately, the size of their typical load of students, as well as their additional job responsibilities do not generally allow for the time needed to get to know each student well. Rather, their time is generally devoted to a myriad of administrative duties – such as scheduling, testing, and large-scale student group activities – that are essential to the smooth running of the school but leave little time for personally learning about each student. Time that is spent getting to know students and families well focuses heavily on at-risk students.

The school personnel who do see all students daily and have the best opportunity, therefore, to get to know them well are their teachers. However, at the secondary level, teachers typically see so many students each day that it is also difficult for them to develop a deep understanding of each one during the course of one school year. One method that some schools use to help students and teachers develop the deeper type of relationship that is often fostered on university campuses and that helps make for more meaningful guidance and advising is "looping," a term used to describe the situation when teachers and students stay together for more than one year. Looping is typically accomplished by cohorting a group of students and teachers together and having them advance from one grade level to the next together. However, some of the same effects of looping can also be achieved through multi-age classrooms, in which students remain with the same teacher for several years, with each new year seeing some students leave and some new students enter.

179

In the early history of American schools, keeping teachers and students together for multiple years was fairly common practice as a matter of necessity. As communities and thus school sizes grew, having students and teachers remain together for more than a year became less common. Today, looping can be found sporadically throughout American schools, especially elementary schools and smaller secondary schools in which teachers may need to teach multiple grade levels for logistical reasons.

Looping provides many benefits, including creating a stronger sense of community among teachers, students, and families, and greater academic performance, which is more easily accomplished when teachers know their students well (The Northeast and Islands Regional Educational Laboratory at Brown University, 1997). When Indian Hills Middle School in Shawnee Mission, Kansas, intentionally implemented looping to help its students, it realized many of these benefits (McCown & Sherman, 2002). Since teachers already knew the students after their first year together, learning progressed much more rapidly at the start of school for the groups that looped. Teachers were also able to customize learning for the students from the first day of school. Discipline referrals were less frequent within the looped groups, and parent support was stronger, probably because expectations and relationships had already been firmly established. The primary disadvantage noted at the school was that the looping students were so far ahead in the curriculum that members of the non-looping group felt like they were receiving a lesser quality education.

While looping is not the norm in most schools in the United States, two school systems do exist that intentionally utilize it for full effect: Waldorf and Montessori.

First established in Germany in 1919, Waldorf schools are based on experiential education, with the arts fully integrated into a classical academic experience. As part of their program's design, Waldorf teachers stay with the same students for 5–8 years, which allows them to better assess and address each student's development and needs. Waldorf schools expanded to North America in 1925, and 1,214 schools currently operate worldwide, with over 150 schools in the United States (Association of Waldorf Schools of North America, 2020). Its practice of looping became a staple of German elementary education, as students throughout the country remain with the same teacher from grades 1–4 for the same effects.

With more than 20,000 schools around the world and over 5,000 in the United States, Montessori schools are more readily accessible to Americans than Waldorf schools (National Center for Montessori in the Public Sector, 2020). Montessori schools group students together into multi-age classrooms, ideally with the same teacher for a period of at least three years, in order to help teachers build deeper knowledge of their students' interests and needs. Primary classes include preschool and kindergarten students aged 3–6 years. Elementary students are grouped together into ages 6–9, 9–12, or sometimes 6–12. Secondary students are typically grouped into ages 12–15 and 15–18. In addition to having the benefit of a teacher who knows each student well, in these mixed age classrooms, older students themselves become peer mentors for the younger students in the room.

Advisory Models

While traditional school systems are not typically set up to support looping, they have attempted to gain some of the same benefits through advisory models, which are intended to group a small number of students with one advisor who will similarly get to know each student well. Advisory models came about as educators realized that large, comprehensive secondary schools were failing to meet many students' needs.

In analyzing the development of America's high schools, Ted Sizer (1999), a prominent, lifelong advocate for smaller, more personalized school systems, acknowledges that they were designed to increase students' options, and those seemingly limitless options remain the appeal of them to many families. However, much of what we perceive as an option in these schools isn't truly an option at all. Most high school students remain restricted to courses offered at their current grade level, which are largely taught with curricula designed to meet the needs of an average learner of a specific age. In addition, students commonly have difficulty being scheduled into courses they want to take. The large class loads that are maintained at these schools also naturally inhibit teachers from knowing their students well. To illustrate this point, Sizer (1999) runs us through the following scenario: if the average teacher sets aside ten minutes per week to review one student's work and to meet individually with that student, the teacher could work with six students in the course of one hour. A teacher with 120 students would need 20 hours per week to touch base with all of those students. Teachers simply do not have that amount of time. In making his argument for smaller schools, he reminds us that "personalization requires knowing each young person well. If we can achieve that goal, then flexible options among programs make sense. However, options offered without knowing the students well are not authentic options at all" (Sizer, 1999, p. 8).

In order to truly be effective, Sizer (1999) maintains that secondary teachers need to be assigned to a smaller number of students, and part of their regular schedule should include time for them to talk to each one. A necessary corollary to this is that teachers also need to be given the authority to act on behalf of their students' needs. Referring students to school administrators or counselors in order to get permission for a change in a student's educational plan means that the person who is making the decision about the student is actually the person who knows the student least. Additionally, Sizer (1999) advocates for traditional grade levels to be replaced by progress based on student performance and for all students to have a documented individualized education program. While it may seem to people who have never experienced such a system that these goals are lofty and even unrealistic, we do have examples of schools achieving success with them through the implementation of advisory programs.

Advisory programs have been utilized, especially in private schools and in middle schools, for decades. For example, Carleton Washburne Middle School in Winnetka, Illinois, has run an advisory program since the 1920s (Benson & Poliner, 2013). The popularity of advisory programs grew considerably during the mid-1980s as part of the middle school reform movement, when educators began to realize more widely that adolescents in the middle grades have unique social and emotional needs, and benefit from a closer relationship with adults; advisories built into middle school programs may also be called homerooms, mentoring periods, or teacher-based guidance times (McClure et al., 2010). Today, the Association for Middle Level Education explicitly mentions advisory in their standards for preparing teacher candidates to teach in the middle grades: "[middle level teacher candidates should] demonstrate their ability to participate successfully in effective middle level school organizational practices such as interdisciplinary team organization and advisory programs" (Association for Middle Level Education, 2020, p. 1). Furthermore, a great deal of literature exists to guide schools in their use and development.

Advisories typically assign a small group of students to one teacher. Group sizes of 20 or less may be the most effective, and ideally, the same advisor will work with the same students for multiple years, thereby looping with their advisees (Benson & Poliner, 2013). Time is then structured into the school day for the advisor to meet regularly with their advisees. Depending on the school, advisory periods may occur daily, similarly to a regular class but sometimes shorter in duration, or they may occur periodically, with the school running a different schedule on advisory days. For example, one private school administrator who advises all middle school heads to create a strong advisory program and to require each teacher to serve as an advisor, structures his school's advisory time to occur every Wednesday after lunch; advisors who want more time can envelop the lunch period into their advisory time (Newlin, 2009). While effective advisories are definitely not one-size-fits-all programs, they do tend to share some common goals and structures.

Advisories can be used for a variety of purposes. Some affective purposes may include helping students learn to deal with their emotions, manage stress, build self-esteem, and develop positive relationships. Community-building and self-understanding are frequently part of the programs. While these softer skills are sometimes dismissed by critics as beyond the scope of what should occur during the school day, these skills do impact students' academic success. Academically, advisories can be used to help students develop study skills and strategies that are targeted to specific courses and assignments where they may be struggling, to help students develop and analyze portfolios of their work, and to conduct regular one-on-one conferences about the student's academic progress, growth, and needs. They can also be used for post-secondary planning, as advisors help students learn more about careers that may be well-suited to their personal strengths and the academic pathways required for those careers.

Several characteristics of highly effective advisories and advisors were identified in a research study encompassing the advisory programs of three diverse middle schools (Shulkind & Foote, 2009). These characteristics are echoed in much of the literature about advisories. The researchers found that effective advisors demonstrated care for their advisees; closely supervised their advisees' academic progress by checking progress reports, talking with advisees' teachers, and conferencing with the advisees; and adopted a role of problem-solver and advice-giver. The advisory groups

Core Strategies

included activities that intentionally built community by fostering positive relationships among one another and intentionally guiding students to develop their communication skills and conflict resolution strategies. They promoted open communication through circle times and team-building games. The students in the advisory functioned as a community of learners, forming study groups and helping one another with their work. These advisories dedicated at least one day per week to work time. Finally, everyone in the group believed that strong advisories lead to stronger academic performance.

Advisory structures should not be just for middle school students, though. The positive impact that can be seen from them has also been successfully utilized in some high schools. In fact, the Bill & Melinda Gates Foundation and the Carnegie Foundation invested hundreds of millions of dollars to reduce the size of high schools in large urban districts in order to promote greater personalization and a stronger connection between students and teachers. A three-year study of students' perceptions of personalization and advisory, and their relationship to academic progress in 14 schools in California provided quantitative evidence that positive social and emotional relations between and among students and teachers were correlated with higher weighted GPAs and standardized test scores (McClure et al., 2010). Paradoxically, while students who reported high levels of personalization within their schools clearly were students who had higher GPAs and test scores, the inverse relationship was true for advisory systems; students who reported the highest satisfaction with their advisory systems tended to be among the lowest academic performers.

And herein lies a potential problem with advisories. To be effective, they must be tailored to the specific students within them. A one-size-fits-all program does not exist. Teachers must be adept at understanding what their students need and make adjustments accordingly, and students who are high performers will certainly have different needs than those who are struggling. The researchers of the high school study (McClure et al., 2010) speculate that struggling students in the schools they studied were the ones who needed the advisory systems the most, which is why they reported satisfaction with them. While higher performing students clearly appreciated and benefited from having positive relationships with teachers, they did not necessarily like the formal, class-like structure of their own advisories, and their personal needs were not being met by them. This

184

research supports our argument that gifted students need specialized advisors who understand their needs and know how to respond to them. Schools that do implement advisories will also benefit from understanding a few of the potential pitfalls of implementation.

Schools utilizing an advisory model must understand that advisories are not academic classes. To differentiate advisory from other school structures, it's important to use the words "advisor" and "advisory;" this language explicitly helps teachers and students make that shift from teaching and regular classroom experiences to the advisory experience (Benson & Poliner, 2013). However, advisories are not just free time. They should have clear goals that tie to the school's mission and the students' needs. They should also be low pressure, supportive environments that focus on activities and discussions that build students' skills and increase their connections to the school environment. Soliciting feedback from students and staff, and regularly making adjustments are vital. It's also important to recognize that some teachers are uncomfortable working with students in ways that do not explicitly focus on their academic content. Teachers who serve as advisors should be skilled at ascertaining their specific students' needs, and creating activities and relationships that meet those specific needs. Teachers who are not well-equipped for this work need to be provided with the resources and training to help them become effective advisors. Placing ill-equipped teachers in a room with students and simply telling them to "teach an advisory section" or to follow scripted lessons created by other teachers for other students is a recipe for disaster. Additionally, turning an advisory period into a response to intervention (RtI) time or mandatory study hall will never meet the goals of an advisory system.

At a high school where one of us worked for many years, students were asked at the beginning of each school year to select an advisor from among their high school teachers. They thus had the option of choosing someone whose own personality and work style was a good match for their own. At regular periods throughout the year, the school schedule was modified to allow for whole group advisory meetings and activities, and each of these meetings looked different depending on the advisor and the group. Sometimes they involved grade checks and organization tips; sometimes they included students discussing their highs and lows of school and offering one another support and advice; sometimes they focused on SAT prep or college planning.

Core Strategies

A few common activities provided cohesion within the system, bonded the students within advisory groups, and at times provided for some friendly competition among advisory groups. For example, each Halloween, a room-decorating contest was held in which advisory groups vied to outdo one another as they decorated their advisor's classroom or a common space. Each group also planned and sponsored a booth at an evening Halloween Carnival held for elementary students. At semester exam time, whole groups met to review what was required in each of their classes and to formulate study plans.

Additional small group meetings and one-on-one meetings were held between advisors and advisees before and after school, during lunches, and during advisors' conference periods, with students being excused from classes as needed for those meetings to occur. Advisors were expected to be knowledgeable about their advisees' grades and test scores, to help advisees develop plans of action if their performance fell, to communicate with parents, and to assist advisees with selecting classes each school year and worthwhile activities during the summer. A monthly faculty meeting helped to facilitate communication among teachers about the students. As students entered their junior and senior years, advisors helped with college planning, applications, essays, resumes, interviews, scholarships, and financial aid applications. While students had the option of changing advisors each year, most remained with the same advisor, which allowed advisors to help their advisees develop post-secondary plans that best fit each one's academic strengths, academic needs, and family finances. It is our contention that this type of mentoring should be available for every gifted student in secondary schools to help ensure their growth and success.

Outside Mentors

Regardless of how much mentoring gifted students receive in their elementary and secondary school settings, a time is likely to come when school-based advisors no longer have all of the information that students need to continue to grow and develop in an area of interest. Specialized and technical knowledge about fields outside of education is best known and delivered by people who participate full-time in those fields. No matter how knowledgeable and well-trained educators are, there are simply some questions gifted students will need answered as they consider future careers and areas of study that will fall outside of educators' areas of expertise. Therefore, connecting gifted students with outside mentors is also an important role of the school-based advisor whenever students' learning and skills outpace the resources available within the school system. Outside mentors can help precocious students continue to learn when they have exhausted their own school system's resources, and they can help underachieving and disadvantaged gifted students engage with topics that hold more interest and relevance to them than what is offered in their standard school-based curriculum. Several existing models and programs provide insights and lessons into ways in which these connections might be incorporated into schools.

In the Enrichment Triad Model that comprises part of the Schoolwide Enrichment Model (Renzulli & Reis, 1994), Type III enrichment opportunities allow students to investigate topics of deep interest to them, problem-solving an issue of importance and creating authentic products for real audiences. Students engaging in Type III enrichment often need the assistance of professional mentors. In a recent case study of ten ninth-grade gifted students enrolled in a Type III Enrichment course, mentors who were knowledgeable in the specific topics of study clearly contributed to the students' academic performance (Brigandi et al., 2018). Furthermore, those mentors whom students perceived as offering positive guidance, commitment to the project, and a personal connection, helped create the broader environment that led to students' achievement and success. Schools can intentionally build into their existing curriculum opportunities for Type III Enrichment that require students to consult with mentors, either as parts of existing courses or as entire courses on their own. When utilized as a part of an existing course, these may be units of study that require students to synthesize and apply skills learned as part of the course's content in a meaningful way and may be conceptualized as passion projects or independent study units. As full courses, they may be independent study electives, offered either within a specific discipline (such as "Science Topics and Research") or more broadly in a class that focuses on the overarching skills needed to conduct authentic research in multiple disciplines, such as Advanced Placement (AP) Seminar, AP Research, and Independent Study and Mentorship. These types of experiences are also prominent components of many STEM academies.

Founded in 1980 as the nation's first residential STEM school, the North Carolina School of Science and Mathematics (NCSSM) is a public residential high school currently serving over 650 juniors and seniors who demonstrate interest and talent in STEM fields (NCSSM, 2020). Located within the Research Triangle in Durham, the school's students have local access to professionals in a variety of fields. Duke University, University of North Carolina at Chapel Hill (UNC Chapel Hill), and North Carolina State University are all nearby, as are a number of STEM-based corporations. Since 2012, an average of 58% of NCSSM students have participated in research, and a stated goal of the school is for students to participate in real-world experiences that allow them to apply their learning to real problems (Shoemaker et al., 2016).

While students have multiple pathways to help them accomplish this goal, the largest is the school's Mentorship Program, which students apply for separately and, if accepted, participate in for two years. Students in the program take required courses that assist them in framing and implementing their research, and students are responsible for reaching out to area professionals and finding a mentor to work with them. They are released from school for two afternoons per week for 21 weeks in order to work on their projects and meet with their mentors. NCSSM instructors regularly monitor the students' progress. In addition to the depth of academic learning that occurs through this program, the experience also fosters students' curiosity, resourcefulness, ownership of their work, professional communication, collaboration skills, and awareness of the world (Shoemaker et al., 2016). Today, 17 state residential math and science schools like NCSMM exist (Jones, 2011), with many of them offering similar experiences.

Similar to NCSMM but housed on a college campus, TAMS was the nation's first early college entrance academy, in which high school juniors and seniors complete their last two years of high school in a residential college setting. TAMS students working either on their own or through the TAMS Research Organization begin working with professional mentors as early as their first semester in the program (Jones, 2011). During their second semester, students may begin applying for one of approximately 65 TAMS Summer Research Scholarships, which provide stipends for summer travel and living expenses to conduct research under the guidance of a mentor at a university, health science center, or NASA. Students completing research may also participate in a colloquium, publish their work in a journal, and/or create a research poster for public display. Some research projects are submitted for awards in national competitions, such as the Intel Science

Talent Search and the Siemens Westinghouse Competition in Math, Science, & Technology.

Another early college institution, The Gatton Academy serves gifted and talented STEM students in their final two years of high school at Western Kentucky University. Gatton offers two formal programs to help mentor students as they make decisions about their eventual careers. Panoply of Possibilities, also known as POP!, connects students to professionals in different fields to learn about their work and their own career paths. The Gatton Sponsored Internship Program (GSIP) invites organizations and businesses throughout Kentucky to sponsor an intern from Gatton for eight weeks during the summer. The intern must be involved in work on a specific project at the organization and must have an assigned mentor–supervisor to support them on the job and to provide a final evaluation of their work (Western Kentucky University, 2020).

Recommendations for Using Mentorships in Personalized Gifted Education

Multi-year mentorships are a hallmark of a personalized learning program for gifted students. For schools wishing to implement an effective mentorship program, we offer the following recommendations:

- Clearly identify the goals and expected outcomes of the mentorship program. Figure 8.1 provides guidance on the areas that might be of particular focus.
- Identify who within your school will serve as multi-year mentors for your students and how students will be assigned to them.
- Dedicate a specific time for in-school mentors to regularly meet with their students. This time may be a regular part of each school day, or it may be incorporated as part of a special schedule that the school runs periodically.
- Ensure that all in-school mentors are trained in gifted education and that they receive additional specialized training from your school regarding the goals, structure, and expected outcomes of the new mentorship program. Equip them with the tools and knowledge they will need to work with the students successfully.

Core Strategies

- Determine how professional mentors outside of school will be utilized. Ideally, one or two people on campus will help coordinate these efforts by maintaining lists of professionals in the community who have volunteered to work with students and by developing standards and expectations about what contact between professionals and students might look like.

- Maintain a list of outside opportunities for students and share it with in-school mentors so that they can reference it as they work with their students.

- During the first months and years of the program, regularly solicit feedback from mentors and students, and make adjustments accordingly.

Summary

Gifted programs exist within K–12 schools because gifted students have talents and needs that are not well served within the traditional school structure. While much attention has been paid to developing these programs so that gifted students can have access to learning activities and materials that will provide more appropriate academic challenges, far less attention has been given to the guidance that gifted students and their families need over time as they progress through these programs. Gifted students need advisors who are trained in advanced and gifted education to work with them for multiple years, to help them develop both the academic and affective skills needed to achieve success in advanced courses, to assist them in selecting appropriately challenging courses and experiences both inside and outside of their secondary school settings, and to guide them in their post-secondary planning. In schools where hiring specialized counselors to do this work is not feasible, teachers trained to serve as advisors to gifted students and a modified school structure that allows time for advisory meetings to occur can serve this purpose.

References

Association for Middle Level Education. (2020). 2012 approved standards: Middle level teacher preparation standards with rubrics and supporting explanations. www.amle.org/AboutAMLE/Professional Preparation/AMLEStandards/tabid/263/Default.aspx

Association of Waldorf Schools of North America. (2020). *Waldorf education*. www.waldorfeducation.org/waldorf-education

Benson, J., & Poliner, R. E. (2013). Designing advisories for resilience. *Educational Leadership, 71*(1), 50–55.

Bozeman, B., & Feeney, M. K. (2007). Toward a useful theory of mentoring: A conceptual analysis and critique. *Administration & Society, 39*(6), 719–739. https://doi.org/10.1177%2F0095399707304119

Brigandi, C. B., Weiner, J. M., Siegle, D., Gubbins, E. J., & Little, C. A. (2018). Environmental perceptions of gifted secondary school students engaged in an evidence-based enrichment practice. *Gifted Child Quarterly, 62*(3), 289–305. https://doi.org/10.1177/0016986218758441

Davidson Institute. (2020). *Young Scholars – program benefits – consulting services.* www.davidsongifted.org/gifted-programs/young-scholars/program-benefits

Eby, L. T., Allen, T. D., Evans, S. C., Ng, T., & DuBois, D. L. (2008). Does mentoring matter? A multidisciplinary meta-analysis comparing mentored and non-mentored individuals. *Journal of Vocational Behavior, 72*(2), 254–267. https://doi.org/10.1016/j.jvb.2007.04.005

Homer. (2018). The Odyssey. (E. Wilson, Trans.). Norton. (Original work published 1614)

Huizing, R. L. (2012). Mentoring together: A literature review of group mentoring. *Mentoring & Tutoring: Partnership in Learning, 20*(1), 27–55. https://doi.org/10.1080/13611267.2012.645599

Jack Kent Cooke Foundation. (2020). *Our scholarships.* www.jkcf.org/

Jones, B. M. (2011). The Texas Academy of Mathematics and Science: A 20-year perspective. *Journal for the Education of the Gifted, 34*(3), 513–543.

McClure, L., Yonezawa, S., & Jones, M. (2010). Can school structures improve teacher-student relationships? The relationship between advisory programs, personalization and students' academic achievement. *Education Policy Analysis Archives, 18*(17). https://doi.org/10.14507/epaa.v18n17.2010

McCown, C., & Sherman, S. (2002). Looping for better performance in the middle grades. *Middle School Journal, 33*(4), 17–21. https://doi.org/10.1080/00940771.2002.11494679

National Center for Montessori Education in the Public Sector. (2020). *Montessori helps children reach their full potential in schools all around the world.* www.public-montessori.org/montessori/

NCSSM. (2020). North Carolina School of Science and Mathematics. www.ncssm.edu

Newlin, J. (2009). Keys to success for the middle school head. *Independent School, 68*(4), 113–117.

Northeast and Islands Regional Educational Laboratory at Brown University. (1997). *Looping: Supporting student learning through long-term relationships.* Brown University. www.brown.edu/academics/education-alliance/sites/brown.edu.academics.education-alliance/files/publications/looping.pdf

Olszewski-Kubilius, P., Subotnik, R. F., & Worrell, F. C. (2020). Programming for talent development beyond the classroom. In J. H. Robins, J. L. Jolly, F. A. Karnes, & S. M. Bean (Eds.), *Methods and materials for teaching the gifted* (5th ed.) (pp. 439–456). Prufrock Press.

Packard, B. W. (2003). Web-based mentoring: Challenging traditional models to increase women's access. *Mentoring & Tutoring, 11*(1), 53–65. https://doi.org/10.1080/1361126032000054808

Renzulli, J. S., & Reis, S. M. (1994). Research related to the Schoolwide Enrichment Triad Model. *Gifted Child Quarterly, 38*(1), 7–20. https://doi.org/10.1177%2F001698629403800102

Shoemaker, S. E., Thomas, C., Roberts, T. & Boltz, R. (2016). Building a mentorship-based research program focused on individual interests, curiosity, and professional skills at the North Carolina School of Science and Mathematics. *Gifted Child Today, 39*(4), 191–204. https://doi.org/10.1177/1076217516661591

Shulkind, S. B., & Foote, J. (2009). Creating a culture of connectedness through middle school advisory programs. Middle School Journal, 41(1), 20–27. https://doi.org/10.1080/00940771.2009.11461700

Sizer, T. R. (1999). No two are quite alike. *Educational Leadership, 57*(1), 6–11.

Stoeger, H., Duan, X., Schirner, S., Greindl, T., & Ziegler, A. (2013). The effectiveness of a one-year mentoring program for girls in STEM. *Computers & Education, 69,* 408–418. https://doi.org/10.1016/j.compedu.2013.07.032

Stoeger, H., Hopp, M., & Ziegler, A. (2017). Online mentoring as an extracurricular measure to encourage talented girls in STEM (Science, Technology, Engineering, and Mathematics): An empirical study of one-on-one versus group mentoring. *Gifted Child Quarterly, 61*(3), 239–249. https://doi.org/10.1177/0016986217702215

Underhill, C. M. (2006). The effectiveness of mentoring programs in corporate settings: A meta-analytical review of the literature. *Journal of Vocational Behavior, 68*(2), 292–307. https://doi.org/10.1016/j.jvb.2005.05.003

University of North Texas. (2020). *Texas Academy of Mathematics and Science.* https://tams.unt.edu/

Western Kentucky University. (2020). *The Gatton Academy.* www.wku.edu/academy/

PART

III

Applying Personalized Learning in Gifted Education

Personalized Learning Examples in Gifted Education

Throughout this book we have described elements of personalized learning that can help gifted education programs and gifted students thrive. Those elements have centered around five main features: personalized learning plans, competency-based learning, inquiry-based learning, criterion-referenced assessments, and multi-year mentoring. In this chapter, we will describe how those elements are being implemented in a few elementary and secondary programs that are each structured differently.

Baltimore City Public Schools

District Information

Baltimore City Public Schools serve approximately 79,000 students. In terms of race and ethnicity, 77% of the students in the district are African American, 14% are Hispanic/Latinx, 8% are White, and 1% are Asian. Slightly more than 50% of the students come from low-income families, and the graduation rate is approximately 70% (Baltimore City Public Schools, 2021). The district has a growing population of English language learners and a large number of Title I and charter schools.

Over the past several decades, City Schools have experienced a number of economic, social, and political difficulties. New leadership and structural changes that began in 2007 focused on reconnecting families and community members with their schools, and by 2010 had brought about some significant improvements (Mapp & Noonan, 2015; Tavernise,

Application

2010). Nine years ago, though, the Gifted Education Office was eliminated completely. It was brought back two years later in response to state legislation requiring identification of and services for gifted students. Gifted elementary students currently are clustered together in heterogeneous classrooms, with the expectation that teachers will differentiate for their learning needs.

Individualized Learning Plans

Individualized learning plans (ILPs) that are connected to problem-based learning are utilized in order to ensure that gifted students are receiving appropriate learning experiences (Lymer & Jutras, 2020). Criterion-referenced pre-assessments provide the mechanism for compacting learning within each class so that gifted students have time to work on the goals in their ILPs.

Like the personalized learning plans (PLPs) described earlier in this book, City School's ILPs contain information about the specific strengths and interests of each student and include data from academic assessments and affective surveys. Utilizing this information, stakeholders (typically consisting of the student, teacher(s), parent(s), and an administrator) establish 1–4 goals for each student to achieve for the school year. The goals must involve the completion of an independent problem-based project that requires divergent thinking. This project also must be tied to the student's strengths, so that it provides an intentional, personalized pathway through which each student can grow in an existing area of talent and interest. If a weakness exists that needs to be addressed, then one of the goals might be tied to strengthening that area of weakness in a way that leverages one of the student's strengths and/or interests.

Students in grades K–2 typically work in small groups on these projects so that the work is more developmentally appropriate for them. Older elementary students may work on their projects individually. Classroom teachers monitor and assist students on meeting their goals throughout the year. Because teachers pre-test students on knowledge and skills prior to starting each new unit of study, they are able to compact student learning and thus free up time in class for gifted students to work on these projects and goals.

While City Schools do not place these ILPs within a formal, institutionalized framework of personalized learning, they do capture several essential elements of personalized learning. Furthermore, they offer an effective example of a low-cost method of infusing personalized learning into existing gifted programs, regardless of how those programs are structured. Not only do the ILPs serve many of the same functions as a PLP, but they also utilize problem-based learning and ensure that gifted students have the time and the opportunity to further grow their talents in an area of interest. While City Schools began these ILPs as a pilot project at ten schools, the success they have experienced with them has led to their expansion to all of their campuses.

ASPIRE Academy

Grapevine-Colleyville ISD and Personalized Learning

Located in the Dallas–Fort Worth metroplex area, Grapevine-Colleyville Independent School District (GCISD) is a suburban district serving approximately 14,000 students. In terms of race and ethnicity, 53% of the district's students are White, 25% are Hispanic/Latinx, 10% are Asian, 6% are African American, and 6% are two or more races. A high percentage of these students – approximately 21% – have been identified as gifted and are served through a variety of tiered services. Economically, the district is comprised of families coming from both high levels of wealth and high poverty, with 22% of its students designated as economically disadvantaged and 24% of the students designated as at-risk. The district, however, has a 97% graduation rate, and based on a record of student success and strong initiatives to continually improve, GCISD has been designated as a District of Innovation by the Texas Education Agency. This designation increases its ability to exercise more local control over its schools. Working with hundreds of stakeholders throughout the community, in recent years, the district implemented two long-range strategic plans for its continued development: LEAD 2021 (GCISD, 2017a) and its successor LEAD 2.0 (GCISD, 2017b).

The district's strategic plans have been ambitious and intimately tied to principles of personalized learning. In 2010, LEAD 2021 laid foundational goals for the upcoming decade. Included among a set of 11 goals and

Application

strategies were the creation of PLPs for each student, transforming classroom instruction from a teacher platform to a learner platform, and fully integrating technology into instruction.

As the district worked to achieve its goals, several notable outcomes occurred. The entire district became 1:1 for technology. PLPs were formalized to help guide students toward college and career readiness. Standards-based report cards were introduced in elementary schools, and teachers and administrators were trained in learner platforms and encouraged to collect student voice to inform instructional decision-making. In addition, several personalized programs were created within the district. These programs included a science, technology, engineering, and mathematics (STEM) academy, a dual language program, an arts-integrated elementary campus, an online school, an early college high school, and ASPIRE Academy for highly gifted students.

ASPIRE Academy

In 2013, ASPIRE Academy was founded to meet the unique needs of students who score at the 99th percentile on nationally normed aptitude and achievement tests. Structured as a school-within-a-school, ASPIRE currently serves over 450 students on three different campuses: Glenhope Elementary (grades 1–5), Cross Timbers Middle School (grades 6–8), and Grapevine High School (grades 9–12). Students in ASPIRE attend specialized core academic courses with other ASPIRE students, and they take electives, such as music and art, with the general student population.

While each ASPIRE classroom has its own character and rhythm to it, defined by the unique personalities of the teachers and students who inhabit it, some elements are common to all. Students are engaged and interested in their work, and they are willing to share it with visitors, whom they expect to take it as seriously as they do.

Humanities

Reading workshops and writing workshops are integral components of the language arts curriculum at all grade levels. Both are well-suited for personalized learning for gifted students, as they capture two important

Personalized Learning Examples

elements of personalized learning and gifted education: they provide a great deal of choice that students can use to tailor their work to their own needs and interests, and they create environments in which students work as professionals in the field do. Passion projects are woven into the curriculum in grade-appropriate ways so students regularly have dedicated time to research, create, and present about topics of personal interest. These projects provide a foundation for students' participation in Advanced Placement (AP) Capstone in high school. Opportunities for professional publication also abound. High school students present their work at a locally-hosted symposium, and several students have been published in *The New York Times* and through the Scholastic Art and Writing program.

Student choice and voice are hallmarks of ASPIRE humanities classes. The Socratic method and the Harkness method are frequently utilized to facilitate student discussion. While state standards provide the foundation for the work that the students complete, they are considered the floor from which students learn rather than the ceiling that could otherwise stop their further advancement. Student interest guides the development of many of the activities. Standards are elevated with additional depth and complexity to meet the students' advanced cognitive needs.

Math

Student voice and choice are also at the forefront of math. Mini lessons in math can cover a lot of content, but they are typically short, and depth and complexity are intentionally layered into the lessons. Class discussions are rich, as teachers focus on developing students' conceptual understanding of mathematics in addition to their procedural knowledge. At the conclusion of lessons, students may be presented with three different options for their individual practice, depending on whether their current level of knowledge about a topic mirrors that of a novice, a practitioner, or an expert.

In recognition of the myriad of benefits of acceleration, the district's math department offers all students the opportunity to telescope in math, and more than half of the ASPIRE students enroll in a math class that is at least one grade level higher than their actual grade level. Approximately 10% of them qualify to take math classes two grade levels or higher than their actual grade. The district is able to serve these students via a "floating" math teacher who works on different campuses and a busing system that transports groups of students between campuses throughout the day.

ASPIRE students who are not formally telescoped in math still receive accelerated math instruction once they enter middle school. ASPIRE's sixth and seventh grade accelerated math classes combine all of the state's standards for sixth, seventh, and eighth grade math into two years of instruction, thus ensuring that all students are prepared to take Algebra I by eighth grade. Once students complete Algebra I and Geometry, they may then test into another accelerated course that covers the state standards for both Algebra II and Pre-Calculus in one year.

Science

Similar to math, science also provides formal pathways for acceleration. Beginning in sixth grade, all ASPIRE students take a two-year program of accelerated science classes that compact four years of science standards into two years. At the end of their seventh-grade year, the students take the state test for eighth grade science and qualify for a high school credit for Integrated Physics and Chemistry. In eighth grade, they take high school Biology I. A pathway also exists for students to test out of middle school science partially or completely via credit by exam and thus begin Biology I as sixth- or seventh-grade students. These students then travel to the high school to continue their science courses in subsequent years.

Some ASPIRE students take their first AP science course in ninth grade, and almost all take at least one AP science class in tenth grade. In addition to offering several different options for AP science classes, the district also offers post-AP science classes that allow students who have successfully completed AP work to independently conduct research and/or learn about topics in specific science fields at a deeper level. Some ASPIRE students will earn seven or eight high school science credits by the time they graduate.

One of the notable elements of the ASPIRE science program is its use of argument driven inquiry (ADI), beginning in elementary school and continuing through high school. ADI is a research-based instructional approach that supports the teaching of both science and language arts standards. It requires students to work as professional scientists do, designing their own experiments and engaging in a peer review process to present and publish their findings.

Throughout the process of completing an ADI assignment, students not only improve their science knowledge and skills but also their written and oral communication skills. The ADI cycle (ADI, 2010) can be applied to any unit of learning and is comprised of the following eight steps:

1. Identify the task and guiding question.
2. Design a method and collect data.
3. Develop an argument, which includes a claim, evidence that supports the claim, and a justification.
4. Share the argument with others and provide critiques of each other's work. Use the feedback to make revisions.
5. Share in a reflective discussion what they learned about both the content and the process of their investigation.
6. Write a formal investigative report.
7. Engage in a double-blind group peer review.
8. Revise and submit the report.

Both the ADI process itself and the number of science courses and pathways available for students create opportunities for strong personalization within ASPIRE's science program.

Social–Emotional Supports

Another mechanism that helps create strong personalization is the social–emotional support provided for students in ASPIRE. In fact, two of the goals of LEAD 2.0 directly address this work:

- Goal 2: "design learning environments that support social and emotional well-being"
- Goal 3: "create a culture that fosters learning environments that reflect student voice and promote student engagement." (GCISD, 2017c)

Some commonalities exist regarding the ways in which these supports are actualized across ASPIRE classrooms. First and foremost, these supports

Application

come from teachers knowing their students well and taking a genuine interest in their students' lives and development. Additionally, all of the campuses offer structural supports that facilitate the creation of positive teacher–student relationships. Several of these were described in Chapter 8, and we will offer some specific examples of how ASPIRE teachers utilize them now.

One structure that ASPIRE teachers commonly use is the "circle-up." Based on a restorative practices framework that maintains that positive relationships are central to student success in school (Texas Education Agency, 2020; Thorsborne & Blood, 2013), circle-ups serve two primary purposes: (1) building a trusting, supportive community within the classroom, and (2) helping students problem-solve any issues that could be negatively impacting their ability to be successful in school. These circle-ups essentially function as a type of advisory; advisory models are described in Chapter 8.

Another important structure campuses provide is a scheduled time for teachers to offer explicit instruction and guidance in the development of the psychosocial skills that are necessary for academic success. In elementary school and middle school, this guidance may focus on self-regulation, as students learn to appropriately handle frustrations that they experience, often as a result of their asynchronous development. Sometimes their frustration is because they clearly see that something is "right" when others do not, and they have not yet developed the ability to artfully persuade others to see their viewpoints or to keep differences of opinion in their proper perspective. Sometimes, this frustration is a result of their bodies not being able to keep up with their brains; they cannot type or write quickly enough to capture their thoughts on paper without slowing down their thinking process, or they cannot draw a picture that realistically captures the image that is in their heads. Other times, their life experiences simply are not yet sufficient to help them contextualize current or historical events, or a particularly vivid passage from a book. Whatever the cause may be, the teachers help students practice self-regulation techniques by teaching them to recognize when they start to feel overly frustrated, and they give them strategies to use that will prevent a potentially negative feeling from escalating into a larger problem. As students transition into middle school, time management, organization, collaboration skills, and study skills all become areas in which students receive support.

204

In high school, the focus hones in more specifically on time management, course selection, and college preparation and guidance. High school students' PLPs tie specifically to their college goals, and time is regularly scheduled for teachers and district personnel to conference individually with students about different elements of their PLPs. In addition, various facets of the college application process are woven into the regular curriculum, and after-school workshops are held for students to guide and assist them in their college selection process.

Given the emphasis placed on the continued development of both psychosocial skills and academic skills, it's necessary that teachers have time to collaborate both with and about students. Elementary and middle school teachers have structured time within the school day dedicated to working with students on these skills. In addition, secondary teachers share a common conference period that they use at least once per week to collaborate with one another. Teachers at all levels are provided with substitute teachers once or twice during the school year so they have an extended period of time to work on larger projects with one another and with district personnel. Part of this time is always devoted to discussing students' academic progress and development.

While discussions about students are always grounded in an analysis of academic data, they may also include information about the students' psychosocial skills. If a student is having difficulties, the teachers want to be able to determine the root cause of that difficulty in order to help the student improve. School counselors, as well as special education professionals, are consulted and assist whenever needed.

Because transitions from elementary to middle school and then from middle school to high school can be particularly difficult for students, time is also provided for the teachers to visit ASPIRE classrooms on other campuses. Teachers need a clear understanding of both where their students are coming from and where they are going in order to appropriately scaffold learning experiences for them.

Assessment

In 2013, GCISD made the switch from traditional report cards to standards-based report cards for students in grades K–4. Groups of teachers at each grade level worked with district leaders to identify the most important standards to include on the report card. This change allowed elementary teachers to embrace more fully all of the promises held by personalized learning's focus on criterion-based assessment. Students and parents have a clear understanding of the learning targets and can better monitor progress toward each one. The standards are listed on the report card in the order in which they are taught, and for each standard in each subject, students receive either a blank (for standards which have not yet been taught) or a score of 1, 2, or 3 to correspond with the student's level of mastery. Once a student scores a 3 on a standard, the teacher is expected to extend the child's learning further on that concept. These extensions are communicated to parents through a comment section on the report card and are intended to convey a personalized learning plan for each child.

In addition to the typical standards-based report card, each ASPIRE elementary student is also evaluated using a supplemental report card that captures gifted and talented standards that are foci of the program. These include critical thinking, creative thinking, complexity, collaborative efforts, and social and emotional skills. Each of these skills is broken down into sub-skills, and students are scored from 1–4 on each one. This supplemental report card is included in Figure 9.1.

While all students complete the state-required tests that occur at the end of each school year, the program recognizes that for most of the students, these grade-level tests fail to capture the growth that occurs each year. To obtain more reliable data about the students' growth and development, the teachers also administer norm-based assessments, which provide a different type of information and contain higher ceilings. All second graders and all fifth graders in the district take a Cognitive Abilities Test (CogAT), which helps capture students' growth over time.

In addition, ASPIRE students complete additional achievement testing in math and reading three times per year. Students in grades 3–8 complete Scantron's Performance Series testing, which is computer adaptive and tests students on standards at all grade levels rather than just on the standards of the grade level in which they are currently enrolled. It also contains a growth measurement that captures whether or not each student has met their yearly expected growth target. In addition, students in grades 6–8 complete science testing and English language arts testing through Scantron. Parents and students receive written reports each time these tests are administered. In addition to containing the students' national percentile

206

Personalized Learning Examples

GRADING STANDARDS	
Exceeds expectations	4
Meets expectations	3
Approaching expectations	2
Below expectations	1

Gifted and Talented Standards	1NW	2NW	3NW	4NW
Critical Thinking				
Asks insightful, authentic questions and seeks answers				
Demonstrates evidence of high level reflection				
Shows perseverance when challenged				
Demonstrates integrity academically and individually				
Creative Thinking				
Brainstorms fluently and regularly to generate ideas				
Thinks flexibly; sees things in new and different ways				
Ideas are original and unique				
Elaborates on ideas to create a sophisticated product				
Takes risks in his/her thinking				
Complexity				
Uses the elements of Depth and Complexity to connect to learning				
Works at highest levels of Bloom's Taxonomy (synthesis and evaluation) regularly and with ease				
Views ideas through multiple perspectives				
Collaborative Effort				
Shows willingness to compromise				
Recognizes value in others' opinions in addition to his/her own				
Moves group toward completion of tasks and goals				
Seeks and accepts opportunities to lead				
Contributes ideas for group consideration				
Social and Emotional				
Demonstrates humility				
Uses failure as an opportunity to learn				
Shows self-confidence				
Demonstrates self-directed learning				

Parent signature

Figure 9.1 ASPIRE Academy Supplemental Report Card
Source: Taliaferro et al. (2019)

Application

rankings and growth measurements, these reports also include a list of the specific standards that the students need to work on. Students are taught to read the data contained in these reports and to set actionable learning goals for themselves based on that data.

In grades 7–11, students also take a yearly PSAT. Their scores are tracked over time by district personnel, shared with teachers each year, and discussed with students so that individual growth can be optimized.

Lindsay High School

Lindsay High School (LHS) is a rural public high school located in California's central valley. LHS enrolls approximately 1,036 students in grades 9–12 with a student demographic that is 93% Hispanic/Latinx, 87% free/reduced lunch program, and 34% English language learners. LHS is organized with a typical classroom structure and a 24:1 student to teacher ratio. The school is 1:1 with technology, and students are expected to always have their devices. The school district has provided community Wi-Fi to students at home as well as at school, with a goal of maintaining community-wide internet access 24/7 for all learners. The Lindsay Unified School District began the journey toward personalized learning in 2007 with a district-wide strategic plan that focused on becoming a model of competency-based learning. California education policy does not mandate identification and services for gifted students, but high ability learners participate in the LHS personalized learning model based on self-paced competency-based learning.

Learners at LHS spend their time divided between two learning environments, self-directed learning and facilitator-led instruction. Each learner has a playlist of academic work that guides their self-directed learning time. They are able to choose what they work on during self-directed learning time, and each learning objective includes multiple possible learning activities from which to choose. When LHS learners move to facilitator-led instruction, they still have a choice of assignments and spend learning time working in small groups or receiving one-on-one tutorials from the facilitator. High ability learners move at an accelerated pace through the competency-based learning system, and in their areas of strength and interest it is typical that they are one or more grade levels ahead of their cohort. They spend the facilitator-led learning time working

208

Personalized Learning Examples

in small groups on inquiry-based projects and receiving tutorials on advanced skills they encounter in the curriculum.

LHS uses Empower Learning technology for the delivery of content and criterion-based assessments. Learners access Empower both at school and outside of school as needed. Empower is a competency-based learning system, where students pre-assess and then spend time learning the skills on which they did not demonstrate mastery during the pre-assessment. They move through core curriculum content at a pace commensurate with their ability and motivation. Empower Learning maintains learning and achievement records for each learner, and teachers and parents/guardians also have access to see how the learner is progressing. LHS issues each learner a laptop, and learners use the laptop to access Empower both at school and beyond school. High ability learners are able to progress through learning sequences at their own pace with minimal waiting or repetition, and student achievement data in Empower provides a foundation for personalized learning planning for LHS learners.

Below are some specific personalized learning features employed by LHS.

- **Capacity Matrix**: LHS facilitators provide learners with a capacity matrix for each course. The capacity matrix is a pacing guide so that all learners know the typical pace of the course and use self-management skills to stay on pace or ahead of pace. This capacity matrix provides high ability students a clear and unencumbered path for acceleration.

- **Learning Playlists**: LHS uses learning playlists as a differentiation tool primarily employed during the individual learning time. The playlists provide a series of lessons that are targeted to each learner's specific abilities and aligned with the individual learner's personalized learning goals.

- **Individual Rotation Blended Learning Model**: In this blended learning model, learners rotate through stations on individual schedules established by the teacher or the Empower algorithms. Learners do not necessarily rotate to every station, but they rotate based on the rotation schedule in their learning playlist. In the rotation, the learner playlist may include direct instruction, intervention, small group seminar, or a group project. The playlist may also allow the student to work individually through learning progressions in the central learning lab.

209

Application

- **Block Schedule with Personalized Learning Time**: LHS uses an 85-minute block schedule with four rotations per day and a 20-minute homeroom period to start the day. On Wednesdays, the homeroom and first block are professional development time for the staff, and learners formally begin school during the second block. On Tuesdays and Thursdays, there are 85-minute blocks devoted to personalized learning time (PLT), where the learner is free to choose what to work on. During PLT, learners can schedule time with individual teachers to address specific problems or tutorial needs.

- **Acceleration**: High ability learners are able to complete two years of content in a single year by working on the courses simultaneously. For instance, a LHS learner may choose to complete levels 9 and 10 of high school English, simultaneously working on both levels of the aligned learning objectives (Common Core Standards for English Language Arts (Common Core State Standards Initiative, 2020)) at the same time. This simultaneous model means that the student spreads coursework for both levels across the entire year but masters each objective at both level 9 and level 10 simultaneously. In this model, acceleration is not so much working faster but rather learning and mastering each standard at a higher level at the normal pace.

Chicago International Charter School West Belden

Chicago International Charter School West Belden (West Belden) is a high performing charter school in Chicago, Illinois. West Belden serves approximately 500 students in grades K–8, employing personalized learning pedagogy with a diverse population of students that is 92% Hispanic/Latinx, 7% Black/African American, 96% free and deduced lunch eligible, and 40% English language learners. West Belden students score on average above the 70th percentile (US national percentile) on the Northwest Evaluation Association's Measures of Academic Progress (NWEA MAP) assessments in mathematics and reading. The school's core mission includes dedication to exceptional academic performance for typically underrepresented students in gifted/advanced academic programs. This mission includes six elements: academic excellence, social justice, ethics and integrity, optimism, literacy, and diversity.

West Belden operates in what appears to be a typical school building, but on the inside atypical school structures are the norm. West Belden uses multi-age classrooms, mastery-based progressions, and personalized pedagogy. West Belden is a 1:1 technology school, where elementary students in grades K–5 all use tablets and students in grades 6–8 use laptops. The primary technology platform used at West Belden is Google Apps for Education (GAFE). For the mathematics digital curriculum, West Belden uses Imagine Learning which allows for personalized mathematics education, IXL Math which allows student self-paced mastery of essential mathematics skills, and ST Math, which provides an online mathematics problem-solving curriculum. For the language arts digital curriculum, West Belden uses ThinkCERCA for personalized writing instruction, Lexia Learning for an online, personalized literacy learning program, and IXL Language Arts for self-paced mastery of essential language skills.

West Belden uses an individual rotation blended learning model to combine online learning with focused in-person interventions and seminars while emphasizing individual rotation schedules that are personalized based on student needs. At the center of the personalized learning model, West Belden uses Google Workspace for Education Fundamentals as a multifunction learning management system. To empower both face-to-face and remote learning, they also use Hāpara software which is compatible with Google Workspace for Education Fundamentals to enhance online learning.

As part of its personalized learning model, West Belden uses competency-based progressions so that students move at their own pace on a level matched to their ability and demonstrated achievement. Rather than pre-developed mastery assessments, West Belden teachers develop core content mastery tests for each unit and grade level. Students have significant amounts of choice when determining what they work on each day. Students complete online learning tasks that are accompanied by formative quizzes. When students are not mastering the content and skills, they continue through learning tasks until they are ready to request the mastery assessment provided by the teacher. Students' content and skills mastery is documented in their PLP.

Below are some specific personalized learning features employed by West Belden.

Application

- **PLPs**: Each student has a PLP that reflects a data-driven learner profile and serves as a starting point for teacher and student conferences, setting and tracking goals, content and skills mastery and student reflections. The PLP is supported through Google Workspace for Education Fundamentals and Google Docs web applications, and it reflects an achievement pathway consistent with capacities of students with high ability.

- **Above Grade-Level Pacing**: West Belden's personalized learning system supports students working at an accelerated pace on above-grade level content and objectives. Learning is not time based, and students can move as fast through the curriculum as their ability and motivation allow. When high ability students achieve above grade level, they are afforded additional choice and voice in the personalized learning with advanced curriculum.

- **Instructional Grouping**: Teachers use achievement data from NWEA, formative assessments, and digital curriculum programs to group students with similar ability for targeted differentiated learning. Students may be placed in engaging, advanced seminars or project-based learning with high-achieving peers. Groupings are flexible based on constant flow of data in order to elegantly match enrichment and acceleration aligned with students' immediate and long-term interests.

- **Default to Independent Learning Time**: The norm at West Belden is that when students are not working directly with a teacher or in a group, they are working independently based on their personalized learning plan and their progress through the self-paced, competency-based curriculum. Students are learning self-management skills on a daily basis while they are traversing the content curriculum.

- **Student Interest Surveys**: West Belden faculty constantly seek information about the students in multiple ways. One way they gather information is through student interest surveys. The student interest surveys are administered at the beginning of each year and then supplemented through teacher–student dialogue throughout the year. The information gathered in the student interest surveys is added to each learner profile and serves as a key component in the personalized learning process.

Summary

Personalized learning in gifted education can be created within a variety of different structures. For instance, existing programs can utilize personalized talent development plans, like Baltimore City Schools' ILPs, to personalize learning for gifted students without disrupting many existing structures. All four of the examples highlighted here used some type of PLP. The comprehensive school models of personalized learning at LHS and West Belden served high ability students who may not have been formally identified as gifted and talented. The structures of those programs served high ability students quite well regardless of formal designations as gifted students. The shift from time-based learning to mastery-based learning progressions enabled students to accelerate through the curriculum at a pace aligned to their ability and motivation. Technology is critical for personalized learning especially in models that employ digital content delivery and self-paced learning progressions.

Independently structured programs, like ASPIRE Academy, can also be created to focus entirely on personalizing learning for gifted students. The ASPIRE Academy actively facilitates acceleration, especially in mathematics and science. While all students experience some acceleration, ASPIRE also personalizes learning with additional acceleration experiences even on top of the systematic acceleration for all gifted students in the program. ASPIRE takes a more comprehensive approach to personalized learning through intentional teaching and mentoring associated with psychosocial skills, and social and emotional learning.

Across all examples we found student-centered philosophies and pedagogies. Students had a voice in the learning process, and they had choices across various points in the learning and assessment cycle. All educational systems want to develop self-directed students, and in some states (e.g. Texas) self-directed learning skills are a stated outcome of gifted education. All four of these programs were structured to support real, authentic self-directed learning that was developmentally appropriate at elementary grades as well as in high school. The examples of Baltimore City Public Schools and ASPIRE were specifically gifted programs delivered in a personalized learning model, and LHS and West Belden effectively provided gifted/high ability students differentiated learning pathways

Application

even in the absence of formal gifted education structures. Perhaps that captures the potential power of personalized learning. It removes barriers where barriers may traditionally exist (e.g. pacing and acceleration). It creates learning opportunities that are nuanced and personal in ways that fit students' ability and interest profiles. There are certainly common themes and elements across these four examples, but in the end, we suggest there are a myriad of ways to implement personalized learning that achieve the goals and recommended practices of high quality gifted education.

References

ADI. (2010). *The ADI instructional model.* Argument Driven Inquiry. www.argumentdriveninquiry.com/programs/adi-instructional-model

Baltimore City Public Schools. (2021). *City schools at a glance.* www.baltimorecityschools.org/district-overview

GCISD. (2017a). *LEAD 2021.* Grapevine-Colleyville Independent School District. www.gcisd.net/cms/one.aspx?pageId=187680

GCISD. (2017b). *LEAD 2.0.* Grapevine-Colleyville Independent School District. www.gcisd.net/our_district/lead_2_0

GCISD. (2017c). *LEAD 2.0 goals and pictures of success.* Grapevine-Colleyville Independent School District. www.gcisd.net/cms/One.aspx?portalId=96313&pageId=6489159

Lymer, R., & Jutras, D. (2020, November). Individualized learning plans: One district's answer to closing the gap in GT programming [Conference session]. National Association for Gifted Children, Orlando, FL.

Map, K. L., & Noonan, J. (2015). *Organizing for family and community engagement in the Baltimore City Public Schools.* Public Education Leadership Project at Harvard University. https://projects.iq.harvard.edu/files/pelp/files/pel074.pdf

Taliaferro, C., Mishoe, G., & Jones-Balsley, K. (November, 2019). Supporting the social-emotional growth of highly gifted middle school students. National Association for Gifted Children Annual Convention, Albuquerque, NM.

Tavernise, S. (2010, December 2). A mission to transform Baltimore's beaten schools. *The New York Times*. www.nytimes.com/2010/12/02/education/02baltimore.html?pagewanted=1&_r=2&hp

Texas Education Agency. (2020). *Restorative discipline practices in Texas*. https://tea.texas.gov/texas-schools/health-safety-discipline/restorative-discipline-practices-in-texas

Thorsborne, M., & Blood, P. (2013). *Implementing restorative practices in schools: A practical guide to transforming school communities*. Jessica Kingsley Publishers.

The Role of Technology in Personalized Learning

The paradigm of personalized learning emerged concurrently with conceptions of transformative learning technology. In the 1990s schools were learning to use technology in its most basic forms. Then, by the early 2000s, schools began using technology to learn. Technology moved from a production tool to a learning tool, primarily due to the growing ubiquity of internet access and the subsequent acceptance of instant access to information.

Most recently, educational technology is moving to the next phase, focusing on ways that technology transforms learning as a content delivery tool. This transformative phase represents a more radical shift from previous educational technology integrations because it seeks to change some fundamental structures of how schools operate (Amin, 2016). For instance, teachers were historically the primary mechanism for delivering information to students, but current technologies have moved the needle so that information delivery to students is now equally shared between teachers and technology. In some cases, information delivery is primarily achieved through technology. Technology is changing the role of the teacher (see Table 10.1) (Hepsiba et al., 2016).

The potential effects of technology in education have been debated for decades. Cuban (1986) argued that schools are deeply conservative institutions that have resisted change in the face of earlier technologies such as radio, film, and television, and contended that computer technologies would face similar fates in teaching and learning. As predicted, computers made their way into classrooms in the early 1980s and yielded essentially no impact on learning approaches or outcomes

DOI: 10.4324/9781003237136-13

The Role of Technology

Table 10.1 Transformative Technology Is Changing the Role of Teachers

From	*To*
transmitter of knowledge	facilitator of knowledge construction
controller of the learning sequence	creator of the learning environment
content expert	learning collaborator
expository work	interactive work
teacher-centered classrooms	student-centered classrooms
instructor	constructor, facilitator, and coach
presenter of information	mediator between students and information
lesson planner	problem-solver, designer, and resource coordinator
teaching to groups	personalizing learning

Source: Adapted from Hepsiba et al. (2016) and Lentell (2003)

through the 1990s. However, the arrival of internet technologies by the turn of the millennium amplified the potential for computer technologies to eventually defy what Cuban predicted and radically changed the nature of teaching and learning.

That revolution took its most radical form in hardware adoptions. Technology integration in classrooms evolved from a few bulky desktop machines scattered around the school to sleeker, more efficient tools such as laptops, notebook computers, tablets, and smartphones. Most contemporary research found that a few computers scattered around a building had little, if any, impact on teaching approaches or learning outcomes. Even when there were a few computers in each classroom, the effects were minimal, if any at all (Becker, 2000). Only when technology began to be available to each student, did changes began to appear (Warschauer, 2006). One-to-one (1:1) technology means that every student has a device with internet connectivity. The 1:1 initiative began in the 1990s, but 1:1 schools were few and far between. By 2019, slightly more than 50% of the public schools in the United States had achieved 1:1 status, with most of the other 50% reporting that they were gradually working toward 1:1. Complete and full-time technology access for all students may finally be the teaching and learning game changer that was anticipated when the first computers arrived in schools 40 years ago. Some evidence indicates that personalized learning approaches are more effective when 1:1 technology access

217

Application

exists with efficient and effective tech support established in the school infrastructure (Bingham et al., 2018).

How Does 1:1 Technology Impact Learning?

The most empirical examination of the impact of 1:1 technology comes from a recent meta-analysis and research synthesis which combined the research results published in 65 journal articles and 31 doctoral dissertations (Zheng et al., 2016). The Zheng et al. (2016) meta-analysis only included studies with clearly defined experimental and control groups and standardized testing outcomes. The meta-analysis revealed small positive effects across each of the subjects that had been studied (see Table 10.2). These effect sizes represent the increased amount of achievement observed on average for the 1:1 technology students compared to similar students not in 1:1 technology conditions.

For instance, in writing, the average effect size of .20 means that on average students in the 1:1 program scored 20% of a standard deviation higher than the comparison students. Thus, if the students not in the 1:1 program gained 40 points from the pre-testing to the post-testing with a standard deviation of 10 points, the students in the 1:1 program would have gained 42 points on average. Zheng et al. (2016) also observed that schools that had been implementing 1:1 technology longer seem to have achieved

Table 10.2 Average Effects of 1:1 Technology Programs on Student Achievement

Subject	Number of Effect Size Estimates	Average Effect Size	95% Confidence Interval Lower	Upper
English	19	.15	.03	.27
Reading	13	.12	−.01	.24
Writing	11	.20	.01	.39
Mathematics	21	.08	.00	.33
Science	3	.25	.02	.47
Total	67	.16	.09	.23

Source: Adapted from Zheng et al. (2016)

The Role of Technology

somewhat larger effects. Thus, we can conclude that 1:1 technology does have a small, but meaningful, positive achievement effect.

Beyond achievement effects, 1:1 technology yields some tangible differences in the classroom (Lawrence et al., 2018; Zheng et al., 2016).

- Students in 1:1 environments use technology more frequently than those in shared-technology environments with common uses including writing, editing, taking notes, searching for and organizing information, completing assignments at home and at school, and reading electronic textbooks.
- Students in 1:1 environments generally have more autonomy in the learning process compared to shared-technology environments.
- Students in 1:1 environments write more often and create longer texts than students in shared-technology environments.
- Students in 1:1 environments write in a greater variety of writing genres than students in shared-technology environments.
- Teachers in 1:1 environments use more student-centered instruction, personalized instruction, and inquiry learning models compared to teachers in shared-technology environments.
- Teachers and students in 1:1 environments report better teacher–student communications due to the 1:1 technology environment. Specifically, teachers and students reported enhanced communication through email, online collaboration tools, and other online tools.
- Teachers and students in 1:1 environments generally report very positive attitudes toward the impact of 1:1 devices on teaching and learning.
- School to home relationships seem to be improved when 1:1 environments are implemented. Parents report that they more actively monitor assignments, grades, and attendance because of the technology.

The arrival of 1:1 technology environments has had an impact on teaching and learning, and paved the way for further educational innovations. Gifted education models have remained relatively unchanged even as technology transitioned from a few computers scattered around a campus to 1:1 environments. The exception is Renzulli Learning (https://renzullilearning.com), where a technology system was developed to accompany the Schoolwide Enrichment Model (Renzulli & Reis, 2020) for providing gifted education services. Today the Renzulli Learning software is marketed as a personalized learning tool that supports high ability education. However, it remains to be seen how technology will push gifted education to new paradigms of high ability education.

Role of Technology in Personalized Learning

The US National Education Technology Plan 2017 defined personalized learning as:

> instruction in which the pace of learning and the instructional approach are optimized for the needs of each learner. Learning objectives, instructional approaches, and instructional content (and its sequencing) may all vary based on learner needs. In addition, learning activities are meaningful and relevant to learners, driven by their interests, and often self-initiated.
>
> (US Department of Education, 2017, p. 9)

Studies have found that students on average spend more time using information and communication technology in schools with a personalized learning focus than in schools without a personalized learning focus (Schmid & Petko, 2019). This pattern is consistent with previous research indicating that students experience more information and communication technology use in student-centered learning environments than in more traditional, teacher-centered learning environments (Wastiau et al., 2013). Moreover, most research on technology use indicates almost no meaningful relationship exists between the amount of time using technology and development of information and communication technology skills or depth of students' beliefs about the usefulness of those skills. However, Schmid and Petko (2019) found that not only did students in personalized learning schools (31 schools) spend more time using technology, but these students also demonstrated meaningful gains in technology skills, as well as beliefs about the importance of technology for work and learning. Schmid and Petko (2019) concluded that there seemed to be a technology use threshold that needed to be surpassed in order to yield skill development and attitude effects, and the personalized learning schools seemed to surpass that threshold.

Personalized learning approaches to gifted education may not *require* 1:1 technology infrastructure, but research data and practical knowledge gleaned from experienced educators indicate that 1:1 environments are *strongly advised*. The 1:1 technology infrastructure tends to yield more student-centered learning environments, more instructional collaborations between students and teachers, and slight achievement gains in general. There are four primary technology needs when applying personalized learning to gifted education. Those needs are captured by the following questions:

1. How might you utilize technology to develop and manage personalized learning plans that are data-rich, dynamic, and effective to inform instructional decisions and assessment?

2. How might you utilize technology for content delivery to support competency-based progressions, acceleration, and inquiry models of learning?

3. How might you utilize technology to enhance student collaboration with other students, with teachers, and with experts and mentors beyond the boundaries of the school?

4. How might you utilize technology to support student self-management as they learn in student-centered spaces, making decisions about learning content, time allocation, and self-directed high achievement?

Typically, there are four basic functions of technology that enable a personalized learning framework: record keeping, planning, instruction, and assessment (Reigeluth, 2014; Reigeluth et al., 2008, 2015). These four functions are fundamental to personalized learning, yet they are quite difficult to enact without the power of technology (see Figure 10.1). To implement a personalized learning approach for all students, or even just for gifted education program/services, schools must use technology to assist with these four elements of personalized learning (Lee et al., 2018).

Technology facilitates the record keeping that enables a personalized learning approach to gifted education. These records include student academic and non-academic data. Academic data may include measures of

Application

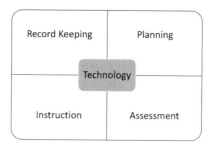

Figure 10.1 Four Functions of Technology in Personalized Learning
Note: In personalized learning, technology supports these four functions in a way that frees teachers' time so they can focus on the personalization of learning opportunities

cognitive ability, both general and domain specific, academic achievement data from standardized achievement tools, and curriculum-based assessments. Academic data should document areas where the student has been accelerated with both macro- and micro-acceleration methods. Non-academic data includes information about students' non-academic characteristics, interests, and career aspirations. The record keeping system should also document students' development of cross-curricular skills, such as collaboration, communication, creative thinking, critical thinking, and problem-solving, as well as self-management skills such as planning, organizing, and goal-setting.

The planning function of technology builds on the record keeping function to support just-in-time instructional support for gifted students in a personalized learning framework. Each student's personalized learning plan is the centerpiece of the planning function. The planning function of technology helps teachers utilize student data to look forward and to develop a sequence of problems, tasks, projects, inquiries, and opportunities. As students develop and mature, this planning function of technology should be shared between the teacher and the students. In other words, the students gradually take ownership of their learning plans with the guidance and support of the teacher and a documented sequence of learning targets (e.g. curriculum standards, gifted education program goals).

The instructional function of technology is to deliver content to students. This function may be accomplished through online asynchronous courses, instructional skills videos, and inquiry-based learning protocols. For

The Role of Technology

instance, in one of the schools we observed, students had access to online courses in each area of the core curriculum. These courses covered the basic curriculum, including all required learning objects (state curriculum). Students moved at their own pace, which was generally accelerated. In that school's approach, the online courses covered the foundational curriculum, while the teacher managed the more personalized inquiry-based learning projects that built on what students mastered in the online curriculum.

The assessment function of technology should seamlessly integrate with the instructional function. For instance, in one of the schools we studied, the online curriculum included technology-facilitated assessments. Students took quizzes and unit tests that were scored by the technology and that yielded both performance metrics (grades), as well as objective-by-objective feedback on which skills the students mastered fully, partially, or not at all. With the technology systems fully managing the delivery of instruction and assessment of core curriculum, the teacher was afforded time to focus on deeper learning and personalization through inquiry and interest-driven seminars based on students' personalized learning plans. Some of the gifted students at the school progressed through the core curriculum quite quickly and spent 80–90% of their time on the advanced, personalized learning.

Student Use of Technology in Personalized Learning

In addition to changing the role of teachers, technology also changes how students learn, especially in a personalized learning framework. When all students have devices with internet connectivity, the learning environment can demand more self-direction from students. Learning becomes more student-centered because of the technology. Schmid and Petko (2019) studied students' technology use in personalized learning schools in order to gain an understanding of how students typically use technology during personalized learning, and which types of technology use occur most frequently. Table 10.3 provides a summary of technology use for middle school and high school students engaged in personalized learning. Each of the technology uses are categorized into one of three categories: learning tasks, self-management, or collaboration.

Application

Table 10.3 Student Use of Technology in Personalized Learning Education

Type of Activity	Activity	Frequency
Learning tasks	Independent work using technology tools	Weekly
Self-management	Scheduling work – autonomous allotment of time	Weekly
Learning tasks	Searching for information	Weekly
Self-management	Making decisions about digital content to study	Weekly
Self-management	Dealing with difficult tasks by yourself	Weekly
Self-management	Following a daily or weekly schedule online	Weekly
Learning tasks	Working in the Learning Lab space	Monthly
Learning tasks	Working on an extended project	Monthly
Self-management	Self-checking solutions to student work	Monthly
Collaboration	Helping other students online	Monthly
Collaboration	Collaborating with a learning partner	Monthly
Collaboration	Collaborating online with a team of other students	Monthly
Learning tasks	Preparing a digital portfolio	Occasionally
Collaboration	Participating in online discussions	Occasionally
Self-management	Seeking help online from the instructor	Occasionally
Learning tasks	Maintaining an online journal/learning log	Occasionally

Source: Adapted from Schmid & Petko (2019)

As a gifted education program moves toward personalized learning pedagogy, decisions about technology ought to begin with thoughtfully constructed expectations about how the school envisions the technology supporting personalized learning. We encourage schools to maintain focus on the goals of gifted education and use technology to accomplish those goals. Technology is the tool, not the goal. In other words, how can gifted education programs use technology and personalized learning pedagogy to accomplish exceptional academic achievement, talent development, identity formation and career awareness, psychological strengths, and independence? Previous study of technology use in personalized learning points toward some potential applications in gifted education.

224

The Role of Technology

First, technology can enable students to make choices about the learning cycle. Through technology, they are able to choose what they learn, how they learn, and how they demonstrate what they have learned. In our study, we came across an Advanced Placement (AP) World History teacher who built his course around student choices in a 1:1 technology environment. The syllabus and weekly schedule for the course included topics of study, knowledge-building questions, and thought-provoking, open-ended questions. Using their technology resources, students independently searched for and utilized digital content about the topics and questions. They were expected to make judgments about the reliability of sources and to come to class prepared to engage in small-group activities, as well as whole class seminars about the topics and questions provided. Students' interests drove how they sought information and prepared for class. The small-group and whole-class discussions involved multiple perspectives and additional topics of interest that students encountered in their searches. This approach to learning productively deviates from traditional assigned readings in a teacher-led environment. Students were learning world history, building information literacy skills, and connecting topics of study to personal interest areas.

Second, technology introduces new and more efficient ways for students to receive and engage with relevant information. In our study, we observed a gifted and talented language arts program at a middle school that applied personalized learning to a blended learning model. Again, the learning environment involved 1:1 technology, and the teacher spent time having students develop their reading interest profiles. Using the learning management system of the school, the teacher was able to support student learning around the objectives of the curriculum while helping students to personalize their reading selections. For instance, the learning objective included understanding figurative language and how authors use figurative language to create layered meanings in texts. Through face-to-face and digital mini lessons, students learned about the concept of figurative language. Then they independently used their devices to search for texts (e.g. stories, poems, song lyrics) that illustrated uses of figurative language. The teacher also sent readings to students through the learning management system based on their reading preference profile. The technology supported both personalization and independence while students learned fundamental language arts content.

Application

Third, technology supports formative assessment so that teachers can make data-driven decisions for students' learning plans. We visited an elementary mathematics program that utilized personalized learning and 1:1 technology with a cluster-grouped gifted education model. The class included a cluster of seven identified gifted students with strengths in mathematics and 12 students who were generally in the average range for mathematics. Each week began with formative assessments that the teacher provided to students through the learning management system. The teacher maintained records of each student's progress on the math objectives and developed four tiers of weekly formative assessments. Two versions of the formative assessments were distributed to the typically average performers, and the teacher provided two versions of an advanced and highly-advanced formative assessment to the seven gifted education students. After students completed their weekly formative assessments, the teacher worked with students in small groups to design their weekly learning plans based on the data obtained in the formative assessments.

Fourth, technology allows multiple avenues for students to demonstrate what they have learned. The learning demands of the curriculum may be quite specific, but the possible ways to demonstrate mastery can involve broad student choice in most cases. Students can utilize technology to demonstrate what they know through mini documentaries, videos, digital concept maps, or participation in online small-group discussions. For instance, we observed a middle school science teacher who was using personalized learning with 1:1 technology in an advanced science course populated with identified gifted students. Most of the assessments in the course were student selected demonstrations of what they knew. The students actively explored apps and other software tools to develop technology-driven products to demonstrate what they had learned. The teacher also used online discussion boards and in-class, small-group Socratic seminars to assess student mastery of complex science concepts. The teacher commented that when students are making their own choices about demonstrating mastery, they have to apply metacognition and real understanding of what the learning objective demands. This student-centered learning involves shared and unique understandings of what is expected, and, as the teacher reminded us, students are learning from the moment they start deconstructing the objective until the final presentation of their chosen demonstration.

Lastly, students should become increasingly self-directed in their use of technology. Rather than specifying which technology students are expected

The Role of Technology

to use, have students make their own choices about which technology tools work best for them. With younger students, this independence might begin with an array of choices, but as students develop and become more self-sufficient, they should take on the responsibility of selecting appropriate technology resources. The student responsibility for technology choices also extends to technology choices for calendaring, planning, and organization so that they become increasingly independent learners capable of high achievement in personalized learning environments.

Merging Technology, Gifted Education, and Personalized Learning

As technology rapidly advanced, new conceptions of adaptive learning environments emerged. Adaptive learning environments stand in contrast to what we might think of as "factory models of education" or "one-size-fits-all education." Imagine the history of education as a constant rebalancing of efficiency and effectiveness. Perhaps the most effective model of learning was, and remains, one-on-one tutorials. One-on-one tutorials are the essence of personalized learning, and it was a common model among the aristocracy a few hundred years ago, before the rise of public education systems. It was quite effective but not very efficient in terms of human resources. By the late 19th century, the Industrial Revolution influenced a new model of public education based on the efficiency paradigm, the same paradigm that influenced manufacturing at the heart of the Industrial Revolution. History tells us that this model was somewhat the opposite of the tutorial model. It was highly efficient in terms of resources, but definitely less effective. Moreover, it was all but void of personalization.

The technologies emerging by the end of the 20th century moved our attention back to the balance between efficiency and effectiveness. Today, the innovation opportunity for educators occurs in new possibilities to merge efficiency and effectiveness so that we can create learning systems that are neither one nor the other, but rather a more nuanced balance of both. The resulting nuanced balance is conceptually captured by the concept of adaptive learning environments. Adaptive learning environments supported by technology present new opportunities for educators to

227

Application

deliver personalized learning more efficiently. A learning environment is considered adaptive if it:

- monitors the activity of students
- interprets student activity against the backdrop of domain-specific models
- infers student needs or requirements based on their learning activities
- adapts based on available knowledge of the student and the content (Paramythis & Loidl-Reisinger, 2003).

Personalized learning and adaptive learning are similar in that they both seek to create learning spaces that respond to the diverse needs of learners based on available data. Personalized learning seeks to reclaim the learning benefits of the tutorial model while maintaining the efficiencies of large-scale education systems, and only through sophisticated technology is that combination possible.

Gifted education shares similar aspirations with personalized learning and adaptive learning environments. For instance, the advanced academics model of gifted education (Peters & Borland, 2020; Peters et al., 2017) is fundamentally an adaptive learning environment using real-time data to adapt to the learning demands of students. The advanced academics model de-emphasizes formal identification and labeling, and instead focuses on ongoing use of data to adjust learning pace and complexity according to the needs of individual students as demonstrated by the data. The theoretical overlap of adaptive learning environments, personalized learning, and gifted education are extensive, and all three educational models are made possible by technology-rich learning systems that provide teachers real-time data so that gifted education evolves from a static curriculum to dynamic, personalized adaptations.

As gifted education embraces technology-driven, adaptive, and personalized learning, three expectations should be met. First, the technology should facilitate teachers' administrative and organizational work in a way that is efficient and saves the teacher time. The time saved by technology can be applied to developing and facilitating personalized learning opportunities. Second, the students should find the technology-driven learning to be engaging and motivating as they experience immersive and authentic learning tasks (Reigeluth, 2017). The technology should allow

The Role of Technology

students to engage with content that is richer and more complex than a static curriculum. Additionally, the technology should create opportunities for students to connect with other students locally or around the world who are interested in similar topics. Third, technology in gifted education can provide an infinite number of self-guided learning and tutorial opportunities for students at any time and in any place. What the student learns is no longer limited by what the teacher knows. The teacher's role is no longer as the fount of knowledge but rather the broker of learning opportunities. In many cases, the learning technologies are adaptive and personalized so that the learning tasks are responsive to students' performance patterns and mistake analyses.

The Shifting Role of the Teacher

Personalized learning is more than a set of teaching techniques and integrated technology. Personalized learning fundamentally changes the way technology is used in gifted and talented educational settings. Technology becomes a delivery mechanism for content, and the teacher is the facilitator of that delivery. This shift changes some structures and assumptions of the gifted education program and the classroom (Bingham et al., 2018). In other words, the move to technology-driven, student-centered education is no small shift for the teacher (Schmid & Petko, 2019).

For instance, a new skill for teachers in gifted education will be learning to develop personalized talent development plans. This task requires an understanding of talent development trajectories that can be personalized for each student. Teachers will need to know what knowledge and skills those trajectories typically include. A fifth-grade math teacher may be working with a student whose math trajectory includes eighth-grade math and introductory Mathematical Olympiad problem-solving. The teacher themselves may not be an expert in those math skills, but they need to know how to connect the student to the learning opportunities consistent with a gifted mathematics developmental trajectory. The teacher becomes more like a conductor of a learning orchestra. They guide and direct students toward learner-centered opportunities, and they coach and tutor them individually or in small groups based on targeted needs.

229

Application

At least one empirical study of personalized learning schools (Bingham et al., 2018) documented how teachers' work shifted with the move to personalized learning. They found that to be effective in personalized learning models, teachers need to be skilled in four specific areas. The teachers need to:

- tailor instruction to one or more of the following student characteristics: strengths, weaknesses, interests, and needs
- actively manage individual student data and the students' access to digital resources
- spend more time acting as tutors and coaches who facilitate learning rather than instructors and experts who deliver content
- redesign their classroom space to emphasize personalized learning rather than whole-group learning.

Challenges of Personalized Learning Implementation

Technology integration into educational environments has frequently met with resistance and apathy, and has revealed teacher skill gaps. As an additional challenge, technology use in personalized learning models may be more disruptive than other waves of technology integration. In some ways, personalized learning technology is a paradigm shift, taking teachers out of the role as primary content deliverers. Challenges associated with personalized learning and technology may include: (a) teachers' beliefs about the role of technology; (b) teachers' comfort with using the technology; (c) the quality of the technology being utilized to accomplish the tasks needed; and (d) teachers' classroom management skills while shifting away from teacher-centered instruction to learner-centered work.

Bingham et al. (2018) studied challenges schools face when implementing personalized learning. They identified the following technology-based challenges in a study of 28 schools that were beginning to implement personalized learning:

- The school infrastructure and available technology did not yet fully align with the needs of the teachers.
- Structural support for advanced technology use was not fully available.

The Role of Technology

- Multiple uses of digital content sometimes led to alignment problems or repetition.
- Teachers were not adequately prepared/trained for technology-based instruction.
- Ongoing professional development for personalized learning was insufficient.
- Teachers needed more clear technology use guidelines, definitions, and examples of best practices for using the technology.
- Personalized learning requires non-traditional approaches to student assessment.
- Parents may want to retain relics of traditional assessment (such as comparison to other students) rather than more personalized assessment based on individual growth.
- Schools sometimes failed to provide technology tools that were needed to sustain the approaches of personalized learning (e.g. easy access to dynamic student performance data).
- Without clear models of how to use personalized learning technologies, teachers often reverted to traditional teacher-centered approaches even if the technology was available.

Models of Blended Learning

The challenges presented by attempts to meaningfully integrate technology into education – particularly those challenges related to the shifting roles of teachers, and teacher and student access to appropriate technology tools – were amplified by the COVID-19 pandemic. As schools quickly shut their physical doors in March 2020, and students and teachers moved almost overnight to 100% remote instruction, educators and families were forced to embrace technology and to adapt to a new educational model. Teachers and school systems that previously were slow or resistant to integrating technology into everyday practice could simply no longer maintain their stance. Federal, state, and local governments, along with individual schools and the professionals who work within them, scrambled to ensure that students and their families had access to the devices, tools, and internet services that they needed in order to continue learning at home. In many

Application

cases, they also multiplied their efforts to ensure that teachers received training on best practices related to teaching with technology and had the tools that they needed to teach students remotely. While the impact of the digital divide on learning that exists among different populations of students and schools will likely not be fully understood for some time, efforts to eliminate that divide and to attenuate its negative effects have been at the forefront of educational efforts for more than a year.

At the time of writing of this book, our nation has largely experienced a full year and a few months of technology-based learning for students at all levels, from preschool through post-secondary education. In the 2020–2021 school year, only four states fully reopened schools for physical face-to-face learning, and the schools that did reopen largely offered remote options for families who did not feel secure in sending their children back into school buildings. The term "hybrid learning" became common at many of these schools, as teachers faced a new challenge of simultaneously providing instruction to students in person and remotely. As vaccinations for COVID-19 have become more widely available and the death toll has begun to subside, schools are now hoping for a return to some sense of normalcy. However, a recognition also exists that parts of technology-based instruction that became common elements of learning during the pandemic are now so entrenched in some school systems that they cannot disappear entirely. Blended learning models seem to offer the most promise of helping teachers and schools at all levels of technology integration effectively leverage the best parts of technology for personalized learning.

Several models of blended learning exist that can help schools and teachers achieve higher levels of personalization for gifted students. All of these models combine some online learning with some face-to-face instruction, with the expectation that both methods are utilized to personalize learning for particular students. While some of these models depend on students learning in a 1:1 technology environment, not all of them do. It is still possible to effectively implement blended learning where a limited number of devices exist. Not all models require the same physical spaces, either. While some can be implemented easily in existing, traditional classroom spaces, others may be better facilitated in a large learning area for greater numbers of students. Still, others simply require a safe space for small meetings. In this latter instance, most learning may occur online with teachers and students meeting in small groups at coffee shops or in libraries as needed.

The Role of Technology

Furthermore, both the amount of control that students are able to exercise over their own learning and the specific role of the teacher can be significantly increased, depending on the model adopted by the school. In some models, students control their learning during the online portion of class but not during the face-to-face portion. In others, students exercise control throughout most of the class. Likewise, depending on the model selected, the teacher may be primarily in charge of delivering face-to-face instruction or the teacher may be a facilitator and tutor, offering personalized assistance as students work through an online course developed by someone else.

Horn and Staker (2014) outline several types of blended learning that are well-suited for personalization, and recommend that as school personnel seek to adopt a new method, they first consider the physical resources they have (such as devices and physical space), what they want students to be able to control about their learning, and what they envision the role of the teacher being. Once those questions are clearly answered, they can select a model that is an appropriate match for their goals and needs. Specific models of blended learning that can work well in personalizing learning for gifted students and characteristics of those models are as follows:

- **Rotation Models**: Requiring that students rotate among different activities throughout the day, with some online and some face-to-face, rotation models of blended learning may occur in three different formats:
  - **Station Rotation**: Able to be implemented in existing classrooms with only enough devices for small groups of students, station rotations place teachers in charge of face-to-face instruction. Gifted students can control the pace and pathway of the online portion of their learning as they rotate through different stations in the classroom in small groups. These stations might include an online learning program that is installed on a small number of devices that remain in the classroom. This program enables individual students to move through the competency-based progressions at their own rate, small-group instruction with the teacher, and independent practice or group project work with traditional materials.
  - **Lab Rotation**: Similar in most characteristics to station rotations, lab rotations have students rotate out of their classroom and into a computer lab for part of their class time. They complete the

233

Application

online portion of their learning in the lab rather than on devices in the classroom. This model requires separate staff to monitor and offer assistance in the computer lab, but it frees up space and creates more flexibility in the classroom itself. It is also well-suited to schools that rely primarily on desktop computers rather than portable devices.

- **Individual Rotation**: Requiring that all students have their own device while they are at school, individual rotations have students working through individualized playlists throughout the day. The students' rotations among activities are not always physical ones but can instead involve them simply switching from one subject to the next on their device. Teachers serve as facilitators and tutors in this model, helping students individually as they work and offering enrichment and extensions as needed. Teachers may also pull students into small groups for face-to-face discussions and lessons. The physical space best suited for this model might be a large open area with small areas on the periphery for face-to-face small-group work. Students in this model can control both the path and the pace of most of their learning throughout the entire course

- **Flipped Classrooms**: In this model, students receive their basic instruction in an online format at home. When they return to school, they delve more deeply into that instruction by applying it. That application may involve completing practice problems, engaging in discussions, or creating projects, all with the support of their teacher. This model can be implemented in one large learning space, much as individual rotations are; however, teachers can also adopt this model within their existing classrooms. It envisions the teacher as a facilitator and tutor, and, depending on how the teacher implements it, can put students in control of much of their own learning throughout the entire course. Students must have their own devices at home in order to learn through this model

- **Flex Model**: Students learning under a flex model complete all of their learning online, but they do so in a physical school building with the help of a certified teacher who offers face-to-face tutoring to individuals or to small groups to support their online learning. While the physical teacher is the official teacher of record for this course, the online content itself may be purchased or created by someone else.

234

The Role of Technology

Originally used as an option for students seeking credit recovery, the model has been expanded as a way to offer advanced students more options for accessing advanced coursework. Students in this model can control the pace and path of their learning throughout the entire course. Like individual rotations, this method can be implemented in large spaces with flexible types of workspaces for small-group work and tutoring. Each student needs access to their own device at least while they are at school

- **A La Carte Model**: In this model, students who are otherwise learning in a traditional school setting may elect to take one or more classes completely online. For those classes, an online teacher is the official teacher of record for the students. A la carte models allow students – particularly those who are advanced – to take courses that their schools are not able to offer. Students may take these courses at home, or schools may arrange a period during the day in which students can work on them at school in any space where they can be safely supervised by a staff member. Students need access to a device to complete these courses, and the amount of control they have over their learning within them will vary depending on the structure of the individual courses. However, having access to these courses and the ability to choose to take them gives students a certain level of control over their learning that they might not otherwise have.

- **Enriched Virtual**: Students learning in an enriched virtual model meet face-to-face in school for part of the class and complete the rest of it online from home or another location of their choosing. For example, students may physically attend classes on Tuesdays and Thursdays, and complete assignments online on the other days of the week. Students learning via this model may have control over the pace and path of their learning, and they may also have control over whether or not to attend face-to-face meetings. Teachers may use face-to-face meetings to offer individualized or small-group instruction or to facilitate enrichment opportunities for students, depending on their needs.

While all these blended learning models require educators to reconceptualize what school and class time look like, and what role the teacher plays, they also all have the power to productively disrupt

Application

existing educational systems and make education for gifted students truly personalized for their own needs.

Clarifying the Role of Technology in Personalized Learning

Without a clear vision of what personalized learning will be for a school or for a gifted education program, even the best technology tools will be insufficient. Schools must begin with a clear conception of what personalized learning is, with an understanding of the role of teachers and students during personalized learning, and with an alignment of personalized learning to the goals of the school and/or program. That said, because technology tools are critical to the implementation of personalized learning, students should be expected to exercise personal agency and responsibility to engage in mastery learning and competency-based progressions, and blended learning models commonly implemented in personalized learning systems.

With key stakeholders aware of the shifts needed to make technology work for personalized learning, the technology must also work for those stakeholders. There are three broad roles that technology should play in support of personalized learning. First, technology supports automated, adaptive learning opportunities so that students engage in deep learning with appropriate levels of cognitive challenge. Second, technology supports resource curation and management in order to support student agency, competency-based learning, and a mix of blended learning models. Third, technology supports ethical and appropriate use of student data allowing for systematic and accurate personalization of learning opportunities (SRI International, 2018).

Technology for Adaptive Learning Opportunities

Adaptive learning technologies must include two features: (1) digital delivery of content and (2) capacity to use information about the learner's progress to adapt the delivery of content in response to the student's performance (Shute & Zapata-Rivera, 2012). In essence, adaptive learning technologies differentiate for each student based on how the student is performing. If the student demonstrates immediate proficiency, the adaptive system will rapidly progress the student toward more challenging learning. If the student struggles, the system will provide scaffolding opportunities to help the student reach mastery (Koedinger et al., 2013). Historically in gifted education, differentiated instruction is an expected norm, yet we find that truly responsive differentiation is relatively rare in most classrooms. Adaptive learning uses technology to accomplish what has typically been very difficult for teachers to accomplish alone even with excellent training and resources.

At this time, two common types of technology used to accomplish this task in personalized learning are cognitive tutors and adaptive competency-based learning systems. Cognitive tutor systems are designed to diagnose what students know and what they don't know while including some analysis of why those results have occurred. As students are learning and making mistakes, the cognitive tutor systems supply hints and tutorials based on the mistake patterns of students. While this accommodation seems like common sense to most educators, this type of individual diagnosis is near impossible for a middle school math teacher who teaches 125 students every day with minimal time to plan and assess.

Competency-based learning systems are similar but are more content-driven and less diagnostic than cognitive tutors. Competency-based learning systems do typically yield detailed reports that teachers can use to diagnose student problems and design interventions. While this type of learning technology may seem new to classroom learning, this type of adaptive technology has been used for years in video game designs and online learning apps (e.g. Duolingo). Adaptive learning technology does not eliminate the need for the teacher, but it does shift the role of the teacher. Adaptive learning technology allows teachers to emerge as enrichment specialists as they take students' learning beyond the digital limits of technology. Examples of these technology tools are presented in Table 10.4.

Technology for Resource Curation and Management

There is a vast world of resources available to support personalized learning. In some cases, students are tasked with self-direction and autonomy in selecting their technology tools. However, there are many

Application

Table 10.4 Examples of Technology Tools to Support Personalized Learning

Adaptive Learning Opportunities	• Carnegie Learning MATHia www.carnegielearning.com/solutions/math/mathia • DreamBox Learning http://dreambox.com • Expert Electronic Coach (E² Coach) https://ai.umich.edu/software-applications/ecoach • Khan Academy www.khanacademy.org • Achieve 3000 www.achieve3000.com • Read 180® www.hmhco.com/programs/read-180-universal#overview • IXL www.ixl.com/ • Membean https://membean.com/
Resource Curation and Management	• Gooru Learning https://gooru.org/ • eSpark Learning www.esparklearning.com • Education Elements https://www.edelements.com • Agilix Buzz https://agilix.com/buzz-learning-delivery-platform • ClassLink www.classlink.com/
Ethical and Appropriate Use of Student Data	• Illuminate Education https://illuminateed.com • eScholar www.escholar.com • Edugence www.edugence.com/

benefits to systematically vetting and curating digital tools and curriculum. The technology that supports curating and managing educational tools are open-content systems or platforms that can be integrated with either free or purchased resources. These systems typically operate with a unified

The Role of Technology

log-in and delivery interface that students can access at school, at home, or other remote locations. There are two types of technology systems that can fill this purpose for schools. First, *content curation systems* vet and search for resources to help students and they are generally adaptive, meaning they store information about the student's searches and performances to suggest vetted learning tools. Second, *learning resource platforms* provide centralized access to customized content providers. Some of these platforms work directly with schools to set up personalized learning systems tailored to the school's preferences.

Technology for Ethical and Appropriate Use of Student Data

Personalizing and adapting learning requires systematic collection and use of student data to match learning opportunities with student characteristics. Data that may be collected and used for personalized learning may come from diagnostic assessments, adaptive learning system assessments, state testing, district testing, and profiles of student interests and career pathways. Student data are never static and need systematic technologies to keep them updated so that instructional decisions are made using accurate and timely data. Student data technology systems typically use a type of dashboard design that allows teachers and administrators to easily access and use data on a daily and weekly basis as they work with students. Ideally, the student data technology can interface with the adaptive learning technology so that part of each student's dashboard reflects the most recent work on the adaptive learning curriculum. Many of these systems also have capacity for parent/guardian access so parents can monitor their student's academic progress and talent development.

Summary

Personalized learning approaches to gifted education begin with a conceptual framework for providing advanced content and exceptional talent development within the parameters of personalized learning theory. Technology is critical for personalized learning, and technology decisions and support ought to be carefully considered. Historically, technology initiatives in school systems have faced resistance and challenges, and personalized learning technologies may be no exception. Personalized learning is more than simple technology integration; it is a disruptive technology that shifts the role of teachers and students. However, these shifts apply technology to accomplish what has historically been quite difficult to achieve in gifted education – widespread and systematic differentiation and seamless acceleration opportunities for students. In personalized learning in gifted education, the role of the teacher shifts from content provision to learning orchestration. The gifted education teacher becomes a specialist at accessing advanced learning opportunities matched to students interests and pathways. The technology of personalized learning allows students to progress toward significant expertise and achievement along talent development trajectories. In other words, personalized learning combined with appropriate and supported technology has the potential to remove the ceiling so that students who begin with exceptional potential can progress toward exceptional outcomes.

References

Amin, J. N. (2016). Redefining the role of teachers in the digital era. *The International Journal of Indian Psychology, 3*(3), 40–45.

Becker, H. J. (2000). Findings from the teaching, learning, and computing survey. *Education Policy Analysis Archives, 8*(51), 1–31. https://doi.org/10.14507/epaa.v8n51.2000

Bingham, A. J., Pane, J. F., Steiner, E. D., Hamilton, L. S. (2018). Ahead of the curve: Implementation challenges in personalized learning school models. *Educational Policy, 32*(3), 454–489. https://doi.org/10.1177/0895904816637688

Cuban, L. (1986). *Teachers and machines: The classroom use of technology since 1920*. Teachers College Press.

Hepsiba, N., Subhashini, A., Raju, M. V. R., & Prasada Rao, V. F. W. (2016). Changing role of teachers in the present society. *International Research Journal of Engineering, IT, & Scientific Research, 2*(9), 67–72.

Horn, M. B., & Staker, H. (2014). *Blended: Using disruptive innovation to improve schools*. Jossey-Bass.

Koedinger, K. R., Booth, J. L., & Klahr, D. (2013). Instructional complexity and the science to constrain it. *Science, 342*(6161), 935–937. https://doi.org/10.1126/science.1238056

Lawrence, A. C., Al-Bataineh, A. T., & Hatch, D. (2018). Educator perspectives on the instructional effects of one-to-one computing implementation. *Contemporary Educational Technology, 9*(2), 206–224. https://doi.org/10.30935/cet.414950

Lee, D., Huh, Y., Lin, C., & Reigeluth, C. M (2018). Technology functions for personalized learning in learner-centered schools. *Educational Technology Research and Development, 66*, 1269–1302. https://doi.org/10.1007/s11423-018-9615-9

Lentell, H. (2003). The importance of the tutor in open and distance learning. In A. Tait & R. Mills (Eds.), *Rethinking learner support in distance education: Change and continuity in an international context* (pp. 64–76). Routledge.

Paramythis, A., & Loidl-Reisinger, S. (2003). Adaptive learning environments and e-learning standards. Second European Conference on e-Learning, Vol. 1, No. 2003 (pp. 369–379).

Peters, S. J., & Borland, J. H. (2020). Advanced academics: A model for gifted education without gifted students. In T. L. Cross & P. Olszewski-Kubilius (Eds.), *Conceptual frameworks for giftedness and talent development: Enduring Theories and Comprehensive Models in Gifted Education* (pp. 289–316). Prufrock Press.

Peters, S. J., Erstad, H., Matthews, M. S. (2017). Advanced academics: A response to intervention perspective on gifted education. In J. A. Plucker, A. N. Rinn, & M. C. Makel (Eds.), *From giftedness to gifted education: Reflecting theory in practice* (pp. 267–282). Prufrock Press.

Reigeluth, C. M. (2014). The learner-centered paradigm of education: Roles for technology. *Educational Technology, 54*(3), 18–21.

Reigeluth, C. M. (2017). Designing technology for the learner-centered paradigm of education. In C. M. Reigeluth, B. J. Beatty, & R. D. Myers (Eds.), *Instructional-design theories and models, volume IV: The learner-centered paradigm of education* (pp. 287–316). Routledge.

Reigeluth, C. M., Aslan, S., Chen, Z., Dutta, P., Huh, Y., Lee, D., et al. (2015). Personalized Integrated Educational System technology functions for the learner-centered paradigm of education. *Journal of Educational*

Computing Research, 53(3), 459–496. https://doi.org/10.1177/0735633115603998

Reigeluth, C. M., Watson, W. R., Watson, S. L., Dutta, P., Chen, Z., & Powell, N. D. P. (2008). Roles for technology in the information-age paradigm of education: Learning management systems. *Educational Technology, 48*(6), 32–39.

Renzulli, J. S., & Reis, S. M. (2020). The three-ring conception of giftedness and the schoolwide enrichment model: A talent development approach for all students. In T. L. Cross & P. Olszewski-Kubilius (Eds.), *Conceptual frameworks for giftedness and talent development: Enduring theories and comprehensive models in gifted education* (pp. 145–180). Prufrock Press.

Schmid, R., & Petko, D. (2019). Does the use of educational technology in personalized learning environments correlate with self-reported digital skills and beliefs of secondary-school students? *Computers & Education, 136*, 75–86. https://doi.org/10.1016/j.compedu.2019.03.006

Shute, V. J., & Zapata-Rivera, D. (2012). Adaptive educational systems. In P. Durlach & A. M. Lesgold (Eds.), *Adaptive technologies for training and education* (pp. 7–27). Cambridge University Press.

SRI International. (2018). *Using technology to personalize learning in K-12 schools.* www.sri.com/publication/using-technology-to-personalize-learning-in-k-12-schools/

US Department of Education. (2017). *Reimagining the role of technology in education: 2017 National Education Technology Plan update.* US Department of Education, Office of Educational Technology. https://tech.ed.gov/files/2017/01/NETP17.pdf

Warschauer, M. (2006). *Laptops and literacy: Learning in the wireless classroom.* Teachers College Press.

Wastiau, P., Blamire, R., Kearney, C., Quittre, V., Van de Gaer, E., & Monseur, C. (2013). The use of ICT in education. A survey of schools in Europe. *European Journal of Education, 48*(1), 11–27. https://doi.org/10.1111/ejed.12020

Zheng, B., Warschauer, M., Lin, C. H., & Chang, C. (2016). Learning in one-to-one laptop environments: A meta-analysis and research synthesis. *Review of Educational Research, 86*(4), 1052–1084. https://doi.org/10.3102/0034654316628645

Implementation of and Teacher Support for Personalized Learning

Personalized learning is an appealing approach to education in a world that is continually becoming more personalized. Imagine asking parents if they want their child's school to use a generic, traditional approach to educating their child or a personalized approach that accounts for their child's traits, interests, strengths, and eventual career pathway. It is likely that most parents would want the personalized approach. For their part, schools can implement personalized learning on a spectrum from a little bit of personalization to moderate amounts of personalization to full-blown, deep personalization of learning. As we have noted throughout this book, personalized learning is a disruptive innovation – it fundamentally changes some features of educational structures. This shift from typical, traditional education to personalized education is not simple. The transition from typical to personalized learning in gifted education requires planning, collaboration, training, and support structures.

Why Adopt Personalized Learning for Gifted Education?

Disruptive change is no walk in the park. When deciding to move from typical gifted education to gifted education implemented through personalized learning models, we recommend that schools convey a clear message to all of their stakeholders about why this change is desired. Generally, the primary reason schools move from typical to personalized learning is to benefit the students affected. Personalized learning in gifted

Application

education should accomplish efficiently the goals of gifted education more effectively than the existing structure of the gifted education program in a school.

The goals of gifted education may vary somewhat from school to school, but the delivery of gifted education should always be goal-directed. The goals of gifted education should clearly focus on the students, and the goals should not be confused with strategies. For instance, a group of teachers recently told us their goal was to differentiate instruction. Differentiation is a strategy to accomplish a goal; it is not a goal itself. Similarly, a few administrators told us that their goal was to comply fully with their state policies and guidelines. That is not a student-centered goal; complying with policies in a public school is a matter of professional ethics. A great first step in the move toward personalized learning in gifted education is to collectively – as a school or school district – become clear on the goals of the gifted education program and services that have been agreed on.

Passow (1986) recommended seven general goals for gifted education based on the cognitive characteristics of students recognized for high ability or high academic potential:

1. Students will understand themselves, humanity, and the world around them in order to flourish as citizens, parents, and participants in an ethical, fulfilling life.

2. Students will build a rigorous academic foundation that supports specialized competencies in areas of strengths and interests.

3. Students will foster curiosity, imagination, and a love of learning reflected in self-direction and independence.

4. Students will develop intellectual character and strong personal identities, and value their unique traits and their responsibilities to their communities and society at large.

5. Students will think critically and creatively as they wrestle to solve contemporary and persistent problems.

6. Students will appreciate diverse cultures from around the world and across the ages to magnify the dignity of all humanity and the progress of justice and equality.

7. Students will develop the psychosocial skills associated with success and achievement commensurate with high ability and exceptional potential.

Iterations of these goals have influenced gifted education for more than six decades, and they provide a good starting point for a school to have crucial conversations about gifted education goals. The goal statements may be broad like the Passow (1986) goals above, but they should be translated into specific, measurable student outcomes. For each goal, all stakeholders of the gifted education program (administrators, teachers, parents, and students) should know the goals and the process of measuring students' progress related to each goal. Passow (1986) stated that these goals would generally apply to all students, but there were qualitative differences in how students with exceptional ability would meet these goals, and those differences should be apparent in the measurable outcomes.

Only when the goals are clear can the school engage the question of whether personalized learning allows the school to more effectively meet the goals than the existing gifted education approach. When implemented with fidelity, personalized learning can become an effective vehicle for accomplishing these goals. Personalized learning supports self-understanding, identity development, self-direction, and independence. Mastery learning/learning progressions support acceleration and opportunities for advanced achievement and specialization. Inquiry models within a personalized learning framework support critical thinking, creative thinking, and problem-solving.

At its core, all gifted education should be dedicated to exceptional student achievement. The primary reason gifted education exists is the ineffectiveness of typical educational structures to support exceptional achievement. The reason schools should consider adopting personalized learning in gifted education should fundamentally come back to the facilitation of exceptional student achievement for a broad and diverse selection of students who demonstrate potential for exceptional student achievement.

Variations of Personalized Gifted Education

When school officials consider adopting a personalized learning framework for gifted education, it is critical that they understand the structural requirements of personalized learning and how gifted education fits within their larger school system. Some facets of personalized learning yield minimal disruption to the school systems, but others can introduce more intense disruptions. For instance, developing personalized talent development plans for students in the gifted education program is minimally disruptive. In contrast, placing all students in gifted education in competency-based progressions is quite a deviation from typical school structures, thus it can be significantly disruptive.

Total School Personalized Learning

The most obvious way to implement personalized learning is to have all students and staff in the school engaged in personalized learning. In this scenario, the school devotes all resources and training, and infrastructure to personalized learning. All students have personalized learning plans and learn through competency-based progressions. In this model, gifted education is the specialized attention to matching the personalized learning to the high cognitive ability of students. Teachers overseeing gifted education would facilitate acceleration, differentiation of inquiry-based learning, and mentorship opportunities. Personalized learning plans for gifted students would specifically include the measurable student outcomes derived from the gifted education goals. While the learning tasks may be differentiated, the daily structures and schedules of gifted students would be very similar to those of general education students. Since all students engage in personalized learning, the matching of advanced content to students' readiness and capacity is easily facilitated.

Personalized Learning in Gifted Education in Traditional Schools

In this implementation model, the gifted education program in a school or school district shifts to a personalized learning model while the general education programs remain in typical, traditional structures. This implementation model requires significant attention to the merging of two different learning structures. The traditional, general education model may still operate with teacher-centered instruction and time-based learning schedules, implementing a relatively uniform curriculum sequence. Students in the gifted education program, however, would experience personalized learning for some or all of their learning.

A school-within-a-school model is one option in this scenario. The gifted students would experience personalized learning for the core curriculum but also participate in traditional models of learning for elective courses. The gifted education program could fully implement personalized learning plans, competency-based learning progressions, inquiry learning, and mentorship opportunities within the core curricula. Students could still make personalized schedules as they become self-directed in their use of learning time. Continuous progress acceleration could still be easily achieved in this school-within-a-school model, and students might work alone or in interest-based teams on inquiry learning projects.

One drawback to this model is that it would be difficult to locate the gifted students in the same classrooms as the general education students who are learning through a traditional model. This difficulty reflects the altered roles of both teachers and students in personalized learning compared to traditional teacher-centered classroom structures. It would be asking a great deal of a teacher to perform in both teacher roles and simultaneously manage some students who are self-paced and independent, and others who are working within whole-class learning processes and structures. This version of the model would require a strong technology platform to deliver formative assessments and customized learning in response to the assessments. While it is possible to implement both personalized and traditional learning in the same classroom, it is more difficult and potentially less effective than offering separate personalized learning classrooms.

Phasing in Personalized Learning in Gifted Education

Another option for schools wanting to start personalized learning in gifted education is a phase-in model that begins with the least disruptive elements. The phase-in approach allows a school to move gradually from traditional structures to student-centered personalized learning structures. Personalized learning plans are a good place to begin. Creating and using personalized learning plans, which begin with data-driven student profiles and are aligned to gifted education goals and measurable student outcomes, establishes a foundation for adding the other elements of personalized learning. Using criterion-referenced assessments and student self-assessment techniques is a good addition as a next step. Defining and using ways that students have voice and choice in learning and assessment design can be added without much disruption. Many schools already implement inquiry models, but making those models truly student-centered and personalized is a vital part of aligning them with the principles of personalized learning. The most difficult element to introduce in the phase-in model is likely to

Application

be competency-based progressions and accelerated learning pathways that are technology-driven. However, phasing in one component at a time over a period of three or four years should create a foundation that is ripe and ready for more disruptive facets of personalized learning.

Implementing Personalized Learning

Bray and McClaskey (2016) have studied implementation of personalized learning in multiple school settings. Through observations and interviews with teachers and administrators, they developed a three-stage model that characterizes how school environments transition from typical structures and roles to personalized learning structures and roles (see Table 11.1).

McClaskey (2021b) described four phases through which schools should progress when implementing personalized learning. These four phases apply to schoolwide implementation and also to gifted and talented personalized learning implementation.

1. *Phase 1: Build a Common Language*
    Schools spend time learning about personalized learning, including core components of personalized learning for gifted education. This learning should foster a collective understanding of technical terms (e.g. competency-based progression) and the shifting roles of teachers and learners.

2. *Phase 2: Develop a Shared Vision and Beliefs*
    Schools develop a shared vision of how personalized learning will operate within the gifted and talented program. This shared vision should include core beliefs about teaching, learning, high ability/ potential, and the talent development process. The shared vision and beliefs process should involve all stakeholders, including parents and students within the school community.

3. *Phase 3: Implement Personalized Learning*
    Schools develop a strategic plan that describes the implementation process and timeline. The plan should clearly define roles for teachers, administrators, and support staff. The timeline should allow for adequate professional learning and preparation.

Implementation and Teacher Support

Table 11.1 Bray and McClaskey's (2013) Stages of Personalized Learning Environments

Stage 1 *Teacher-Centered*	*Stage 2* *Learner-Centered*	*Stage 3* *Learner-Driven*
The teacher...	*The learner...*	*The learner...*
understands how each learner learns based on learner profile and data	updates the learner profile, with guidance from the teacher, by recognizing how learning changes	monitors and adjusts the learner profile as they learn with the teacher as a partner in learning
makes instructional decisions on methods and materials based on diverse learners' learner profiles to create a CLS	identifies learning strategies and skills with the teacher to create action steps for learning goals in the PLP	is an expert learner with agency who applies innovative strategies and skills to redesign and achieve learning goals in the PLP
refers to the CLS to redesign learning environments by changing the physical layout of the classroom	co-designs the learning environment with multiple learning zones with the teacher	expands the learning environment in and outside of school to include the local and global community
universally designs instructional methods and materials, and guides learners to establish learning goals in PLPs	decides, with the teacher, how they access information, engage with content, and express what they know using the learning goals in the PLP	self-directs how, when, and where they achieve, monitor, and adjust learning goals in the PLP
revises lessons and projects to encourage learner voice and choice	transforms, alongside the teacher, lessons and projects to include learner voice and choice	designs challenging learning experiences based on interests, aspirations, passions, and talents

(continued)

Application

Table 11.1 (Cont.)

Stage 1 Teacher-Centered	Stage 2 Learner-Centered	Stage 3 Learner-Driven
designs activities to include tools and strategies that effectively instruct and encourage all learners in the classroom	acquires, with the teacher, skills to choose and uses the appropriate tools and strategies to access information, engage with content, and express what they know and understand	independently applies tools and strategies so they can explore deeper and more challenging experiences that extend learning and thinking
is introduced to competency-based learning. Learning may be part of a standards-driven, time-based grade level system	demonstrates mastery of learning standards that may or may not be in a grade-level system transitioning to a competency-based system	learns at their own pace and demonstrates mastery with evidence of learning in a competency-based system
suggests after-school and extracurricular activities to learners based on the learning goals of the PLP. This could also be carried out by a counselor	works together with the teacher to determine ELOs based on college, career, personal, and citizenship goals in the PLP	self-selects ELO based on college, career, personal, and citizenship goals, as well as their interests, aspirations, passion, and purpose
uses or adapts existing formative and summative assessment strategies and leads learner conferences with parents	contributes to design of peer and self-assessment strategies, reflects on learning, and leads conferences with parents, teachers, and peers	designs assessments and showcases evidence of learning through exhibitions that involve parents, peers, teachers, and community

Note: CLS, class learning snapshot; ELO, extended learning opportunity; PLP, personalized learning plan
Source: Based on Bray & McClaskey (2016) and McClaskey (2021a)

Implementation includes identifying, acquiring, and mastering technology tools that will be key components of the personalized learning gifted education program.

4. *Phase 4: Sustain Personalized Learning*
   Schools plan for sustainability of the education program. This plan should include technology support and upgrade schedules, ongoing professional learning for teachers and administrators, and onboarding processes for new staff members. Sustainability plans should also include processes for program evaluation grounded in data collection and analyses so that the program operates in a paradigm of continuous improvement.

Prepare for Radical Change

The shift from traditional school to personalized learning is a radical change, and thinking of this shift in any other way is ill-advised. Radical change is manageable, though, when all stakeholders know what to expect. Moving from traditional school to personalized learning changes the role of teachers and students, reconceptualizes fundamental elements of the learning cycle, such as time and space, and replaces stable curriculum structures with dynamic and customized learning pathways. Some teachers might describe this shift as taking most of what they know about teaching and throwing it out the window.

Embracing radical change and implementing personalized learning requires changes on two levels: district policy and classroom operation. When the New Jersey Department of Education launched personalized learning initiatives, they identified six major obstacles to be addressed (Hanover Research, 2014):

- **Teacher Buy-In**: Teachers must believe that the shift to personalized learning will yield substantial benefits for the students. The New Jersey program evaluation found that teachers who lacked complete buy-in did not implement the personalized learning programs as robustly as expected, did not attend as many trainings, and were more likely to revert back to teacher-centered instruction.

Application

- **Scheduling**: Schools that were the most successful made accommodations to schedules to allow teachers extra planning time and extra training time to support the personalized learning initiatives. Some teachers noted time as the most valuable resource needed for successful implementation.

- **Access to Technology**: Adequate and always available technology is necessary for successful personalized learning. Schools with 1:1 technology are better prepared for personalized learning than schools with shared technology. Technology goes beyond the devices, though. Schools that are most successful make thoughtful decisions about software and digital content, and have robust infrastructures for technology training and support.

- **Implementation Consistency**: Consistency of implementation is linked to teacher buy-in. Successful schools develop processes and tools to ensure fidelity of implementation. Personalized learning is not an "every now and then" learning approach. Administrative supervision and clear expectations for implementation yield more consistent personalized learning.

- **Physical Space in the School Building**: Personalized learning requires flexible use of space. Students need spaces where they work alone with their devices and spaces where they work in groups on inquiry projects and problem-solving. Successful personalized learning schools develop creative spaces in which student-driven learning can flourish.

- **Parental Involvement**: Successful personalized learning schools pro-actively educate and involve parents so that parents embrace and support the shift from traditional school to personalized learning.

The radical change to personalized learning in gifted education may include personnel decisions as well. Most teachers' formal training and experiences are not aligned with the expectations of orchestrating learning in a personalized, learner-driven classroom. School leadership should provide clear and accurate information on what is expected for the role of teacher in personalized learning in gifted education. Teachers will need to embrace a radically altered role and demonstrate a commitment to the training necessary to be successful as a personalized learning facilitator with gifted and talented students.

Supporting Teachers to Implement Personalized Learning

Teachers are the most critical component in the successful implementation of personalized learning in gifted education. In a recent study of teachers' perceptions of implementing personalized learning (Dinkins, 2017), teachers indicated that even though they had training, they still felt underprepared because personalized learning is a paradigm shift. Making the move to personalized learning is not like other new initiatives the teachers had experienced. Teachers indicated that even starting small was challenging because shifting from teacher-directed to student-directed learning is a radical shift in thinking. Students in many cases were not ready for the shift in expectations either, which sometimes led to challenges managing student behavior in the early phases of implementation.

Teachers in the Dinkins (2017) study described time as one of the most important resources necessary for implementing personalized learning. During the first two years of implementation at the school, teachers were given extra planning time during the day. The extra time helped teachers with planning and record keeping. In year three of implementation, the extra time was removed, and teachers described difficulty managing the personalized learning without the time they had in years one and two. One aspect the teachers described as beneficial was participation in a cohort of other schools launching personalized learning at the same time. The schools had cohort meetings and mentors who were externally funded to organize and run the meetings, which included training, sharing of ideas, and general encouragement and support for the implementation.

When describing the challenges to implementation, teachers mentioned two challenges in particular – student behavior and lack of support from the district. It is possible that students are strongly conditioned for teacher-centered education and the radical shift to learner-centered education illuminates students' lack of self-management and self-discipline skills. As schools prepare to implement personalized learning, even with high ability learners, teachers should plan for challenges in the transition to student self-managed learning. Teachers in the Dinkins (2017) study also described lack of district support as a challenge. They felt strong support from campus leadership but indifference from district leadership. For instance, in some cases they felt like some district mandates contradicted the principles of

Application

personalized learning, but they were forced to adhere to the mandates. This finding should be a caution to districts that want to implement personalized learning gifted education programs. Strong support and willingness to accommodate the demands of personalized learning in terms of district-level mandates is necessary for effective implementation.

Robyn Howton is an English teacher and department chair at Mount Pleasant High School in Wilmington, Delaware, where she has been actively involved in personalized learning initiatives. She offered advice on how to turn the classroom into an effective personalized learning environment (Howton, 2021). The advice she shares comes from four years of training, research, and trial and error. She remarked that making these changes was not easy, but seeing students learn at deeper and more meaningful levels was absolutely worth it. Some of the lessons Howton (2021) described are:

- Accept that some things are going to fail. This may include technology failures, content delivery failures, blended learning failures, or assessment failures. Regardless, see failure as essential in the journey toward success. Learn from it but do not let it define you as a teacher.

- Collaborate and work with others on this journey. Sometimes, especially when working with older students, teachers may find students to be collaborators in the learning process. Personalized learning is fundamentally a collaborative learning environment where teachers and students can learn together, and the traditional hierarchies are less prevailing.

- Avoid technology envy. Use the technology you have. Too many teachers hold back until they have the perfect technology, and months or years pass before they realize there is no such thing as perfect technology. When personalized learning is done best, the technology, whatever it is, is a mere backdrop for the engaging learning spaces.

- Release some control and let students make more choices. This is always easier to say than to do. As Howton (2021) noted, where she once required all students to write an essay, now she has opened up to student choice and students show what they learned with websites, infographics, scripts and videos, and an occasional well-crafted essay.

- Embrace innovative ways for students to receive content. A necessary paradigm shift in personalized learning is that the teacher no longer has to be the chief deliverer of content. While this may initially seem

Implementation and Teacher Support

scary for teachers, it can become quite liberating. Use blended learning models, videos, seminars, and screencasts. Sometimes challenge the students to find the content and bring what they found to the group discussion.

- Assess more authentically. Assessment should focus on learning and progress, not grading and sorting. Teach students to self-assess and expect them to do it. Most assessments should be formative so that the data inform the next steps. When learning is personalized, students are assessed at different times, on different content, in different ways.

As Howton (2021) describes the journey to becoming a personalized learning teacher, she notes that her classroom is vastly different than it was when she began implementing personalized learning. Perhaps the best advice to support teachers is to embrace the journey and know that personalized learning classrooms are going to look vastly different than traditional classrooms. The good news is other teachers have taken this journey and left a trail of wisdom for the next group to follow.

The International Society for Technology in Education (ISTE) is a great resource for teachers and school leaders in the journey toward personalized learning. ISTE provides standards for teachers and standards for students that reflect adaptive, technology-driven learning. The seven standards for teachers include the categories of learner, leader, citizen, collaborator, designer, facilitator, and analyst. Those standards can be found at www.iste.org, Similarly, ISTE has created student standards that can be applied across all grade levels and content areas in the following seven categories: empowered learner, digital citizen, knowledge constructor, innovative designer, computational thinker, creative communicator, and global collaborator. Those standards can also be found at www.iste.org. The ISTE standards have been widely used by schools in their journey toward personalized learning.

Growing Personalized Learning in Gifted Education

The Institute for Personalized Learning (2015) (www.institute4pl.org) has worked with schools to implement personalized learning. Their model (described below) includes four areas to consider when implementing personalized learning, and regardless as to whether the personalized

255

Application

learning includes all students or just the gifted and talented program, these four areas are a good framework for implementation.

Core Components

The core work of launching personalized learning includes three components:

- learner profiles
- customized learning paths
- proficiency-based progress.

Start with these three components. The learner profiles should provide rich data about each student entering the personalized learning system. The data are critical as they lead to the development of customized learning pathways, also known as personalized learning plans. The big shift in thinking at the core component level is adopting proficiency-based progress to replace typical time-based learning. Proficiency-based progress is a core structure to support accelerated learning pathways for students in gifted education.

Learning and Teaching

Surrounding the three core components are 13 learning and teaching practices to support the personalization of learning. These 13 practices are a framework for what teachers need to know and be able to do as they facilitate personalized learning in gifted education. They are:

- personal learning goals
- timely actionable feedback
- conferring and conferencing
- learner voice
- learner choice
- learning readiness-based groups
- culture and life relevance
- assessment as evidence of learning

Implementation and Teacher Support

- deeper learning through application
- standards-guided learning
- multiple instructional methods/modes
- customized responsive instruction
- curiosity-driven learning.

As schools plan for implementation, they should study and define all 13 elements. Discuss them, learn how they work in general, and determine how they will work with your gifted and talented student population. Implementing these elements in addition to the three core components truly transforms student learning from a standardized model to a personalized model. All 13 of these elements can be implemented across grade levels and disciplines, and will support learning with advanced content, complex thinking, and conceptual understanding – hallmarks of gifted education.

Relationships and Roles

The implementation of personalized learning in gifted education introduces new roles and relationships between both educators and learners. These new roles are fundamental to the shift from traditional, standardized education to learner-centered personalized education. Teachers need to be trained on how to understand and perform their new roles in personalized learning. Gifted and talented students will also need to learn their new roles. The new roles are defined by the following elements:

- co-designers of learning
- shared commitment to success
- learner independence
- learner agency
- learner as a resource
- engaged families
- connected communities
- co-designers of assessment
- learning coach.

257

Application

The implementation process has to address the new roles of both teachers and learners, but it should also address the role of families and the educational infrastructure (e.g. administrators and counselors). A school implementing personalized learning in gifted education should study all nine of these relationships and roles, and clearly define them for all stakeholders to see and understand. Again, these elements should be integrated into a well-defined professional learning plan. For instance, teachers may need initial and ongoing training on their role as learning coaches. Both teachers and students may need seminars in how to co-design learning and assessment. The idea of teachers and learners in professional development side by side may be new, but it is indicative of this paradigm-shifting approach to personalized learning.

Structures and Policies

Interestingly, the Institute for Personalized Learning (2015) believes that addressing structures and policies should be formally implemented after the other three areas (i.e. core components, learning and teaching, and relationships and roles). Based on their experience and research, districts that begin with structure and policy are less successful than those that begin with the core components and address structures and policies last, after the ground-level changes have begun. The Institute for Personalized Learning (2015) identifies ten structures and policies that should be considered, understood, and addressed at this fourth phase of implementation:

- integrated data ecosystem
- recognition of anytime, anywhere learning
- interdependent teams
- supportive educator systems
- learning aligned technology
- learner-centered staffing
- learning-based continuums
- proficiency-based assessment system
- flexible learning spaces
- flexible time and pace.

The Institute for Personalized Learning (2015) found that only when schools are actively implementing personalized learning and they begin to bump up against challenges or hinderances associated with existing structures and policies are they truly prepared to modify those structures and policies. In some cases where schools try to start with structures and policies, the change seems to stifle the essential changes in teaching and learning. It is a fascinating lesson that could benefit schools seeking to implement personalized learning in gifted education.

Organizing for Change

Moving from typical gifted education to personalized learning in gifted education is a significant change. It is bigger and more radical than changing curriculum materials or changing instructional models. The move to personalized learning shakes up some basic structures and assumptions held by most educational systems. For this reason, we suggest schools approach the move to personalized learning in gifted education through an established model of change. Kotter's (1996) model of change is among the most widely recognized change models in the field of change management (Pollack & Pollack, 2015). Kotter's model has successfully been applied as an approach to educational change specifically (Borrego & Henderson, 2014; Kange et al., 2020).

Kotter's (1996) change model includes eight steps applied sequentially to achieve systematic improvement (see Figure 11.1).

In the first phase, the leaders of change intentionally create a sense of urgency. This involves developing a bold aspirational change statement that compels others of the need to act with urgency. For a school wanting to change to personalized learning in gifted education, the opportunity statement may describe how gifted students would benefit from a personalized learning approach to gifted education. The team would provide details of the vision, such as fluid acceleration and daily encounters with appropriately challenging content adapted to students' interests and career pathways. It would also describe how students will embrace advanced talent development trajectories leading to exceptional achievement, and social and emotional flourishing.

In the second phase, leaders of change build a guiding coalition. The leaders begin to build a team of supporters who believe in the importance

Application

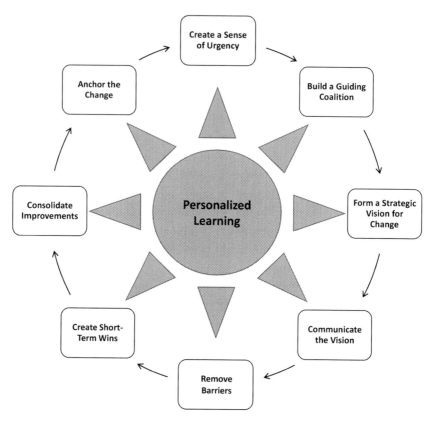

Figure 11.1 Applying Kotter's (1996) Model of Change to Implement Personalized Learning

Note: Adapted from Kotter's (1996) model of change. This model begins by creating a sense of urgency and concludes by intentionally anchoring the change. The Kotter model of change is widely used in business and industry around the world and has been used previously to guide educational change. Schools could apply the model to the implementation of personalized learning gifted education

of the vision for aspirational change. Think of this process as a grassroots movement where team members join from within the organization because they believe in the purpose of the change, even if the change requires significant transformation. The guiding coalition begins to coordinate the effort and communicate to others the vision and process for change. For instance, a team of teachers and administrators working in the school could form the guiding coalition to move toward personalized learning in gifted education. They would work on a shared vision that is increasingly compelling to stakeholders, such as parents and district leadership.

The third phase is the forming of a strategic vision and initiatives. The leadership team and guiding coalition describe in detail how the future will look different from the past, and most importantly, they communicate that such a future can indeed become a reality through the strategic plan and specific initiatives linked to the vision for personalized learning in gifted education. This is the phase where the team has to give specific actions and steps that will logically lead to the desired outcomes. A clearly presented strategic plan with specific actions and timelines is recommended. The team should describe exactly how the school or the district will transition from the current state of the gifted education program to personalized learning in gifted education.

The fourth phase requires enlisting a volunteer army that supports the vision and the process of the change. Think of this phase as the point at which the project is transformed into a movement. The size of the change army will reflect its momentum and urgency. When changing to personalized learning in gifted education, this change army should include teachers, students, parents, administrators, counselors, and curriculum leaders. The army needs diverse voices in unified support of the change.

In the fifth phase, the team begins to enable action by first identifying and then removing barriers. Barriers are often systems that inherently stabilize the existing system to resist change. Sometimes the barriers are policies or hierarchies of the system. Sometimes they are people or groups of people who seek to cling to the traditional way of gifted education. This is not a quick and simple phase of the process. Sometimes there are barriers that no one even knows exist until they are encountered. Recognizing barriers to change is essential to progress effectively.

The sixth phase calls for generating short-term wins. Significant change is often a long and slow process where the pain is noticed more than the gains. A strong leadership team needs to recognize, collect, and communicate gradual progress toward the transformed vision. Kange et al. (2020) found that members of the change army in their study repeatedly mentioned the value of celebrating incremental progress, and short-term wins. Just reflecting on the personalized learning implementation processes described above indicates the complexity of this transition to personalized learning in gifted education. Leaders of change in school systems must intentionally recognize and celebrate the progress. For this movement toward personalized learning in gifted education, firstly we recommend

Application

focused celebration of student achievement in the new learning system. Secondly, celebrate the progress of teachers who are shifting the nature of their work into roles and responsibilities that were not part of their professional training or experience. That calls for celebration along the way.

Phase seven asks the leadership team to sustain acceleration. Sustain acceleration of the changes. Build on early successes. The leaders of the change movement are building increasing credibility with short-term wins. They should use that credibility to push harder toward the vision. With the acceleration of change, they need to continue to circle back to phase seven and celebrate as many wins as possible until the vision for an amazing, personalized learning gifted education program becomes a reality. Change is stressful and difficult, especially in the later phases of change. Slowing down can break the momentum of the changes. The leadership team must keep the focus on the vision of how great this new approach will be for gifted and talented students.

The final, eighth phase of the change process is anchoring, or finalizing, the changes. Previous research on implementation of personalized learning includes many examples where the teachers and students revert back to traditional, teacher-centered modes of learning. The new program requires vigilant monitoring and attention until the new processes, behaviors, and roles are solidly in place. The leadership team must keep the focus on the students and student outcomes. The teachers need continued support and acknowledgement for their work transforming to personalized learning gifted education.

Research (Klempin & Karp, 2018; Pollack & Pollack, 2015) and common sense tell us that theoretically modeled change is superior to random and hopeful change. We recommend the Kotter (1996) model as it has been widely used in business and industry as well as in education. The move toward personalized learning gifted education will be smoother and more effective by applying a model of change (such as the eight steps put forward by Kotter (1996)).

Rethinking What Is Possible for Gifted Learners

The point of this book is to help school systems provide great opportunities for gifted and talented learners. Gifted education is the practice of recognizing potential and providing educational opportunity to transform that potential into exceptional student outcomes. Personalized learning departs from traditional educational structures that have characterized schools and gifted education programs for close to 100 years. Personalized learning also reflects what has already happened with personalized business and commerce. As life itself becomes ever more personalized, it is time we asked how too will education become more personalized? More specifically, for us, how can we make gifted education more personalized so that students thrive, achieve, and love the process of learning along the way?

Join us in rethinking what is possible for gifted learners. How can we remove all the learning ceilings that are mere remnants of the factory model system of education? How can we make engagement, as opposed to waiting, the universal experience of school for gifted students? How can we take achievement to the next level so that gifted students have opportunities to perform at world-class levels in their areas of strength and interest? The time has come for us to acknowledge that we can do better for students in gifted education programs. We can do better by focusing on developing talent that represents a diversity of ideas, backgrounds, and opportunities. Let us make gifted education a great liberator rather than a segregator. Personalized learning gifted education affords remarkable potential to restore joy to learning and to teaching. The short history we have of personalized learning is only a rough draft beginning of what is possible. Gifted education can bring its history of innovation in teaching and learning to this arena and broadly achieve the mission of connecting diverse learners to opportunities leading to exceptional outcomes.

References

Borrego, M., & Henderson, C. (2014). Increasing the use of evidence-based teaching in STEM higher education: A comparison of eight change strategies. *Journal of Engineering Education*, 103(2), 220–252. https://doi.org/10.1002/jee.20040

Bray, B., & McClaskey, K. (2016). How to personalize learning: A practical guide for getting started and going deeper. Corwin.

Dinkins, T. M. (2017). Teachers' perceptions of implementing personalized learning in urban elementary school classrooms (Publication No.

10277178) [Doctoral dissertation, Cardinal Stritch University]. ProQuest Dissertations & Theses Global.

Hanover Research. (2014, March). Best practices in personalized learning implementation. www.hanoverresearch.com/media/Best-Practices-in-Personalized-Learning-Implementation.pdf

Howton, R. (2021, September 24). Turn your classroom into a personalized learning environment. International Society for Technology in Education. www.iste.org/explore/Personalized-learning/Turn-your-classroom-into-a-personalized-learning-environment

Institute for Personalized Learning. (2015). Our model. https://institute4pl.org/index.php/our-model/

Kang, S. P., Chen, Y., Svihla, V., Gallup, A., Ferris, K., & Datye, A. K. (2020). Guiding change in higher education: An emergent, iterative application of Kotter's change model. *Studies in Higher Education*, 1–20. https://doi.org/10.1080/03075079.2020.1741540

Klempin, S., & Karp, M. M. (2018). Leadership for transformative change: Lessons from technology-mediated reform in broad-access colleges. *The Journal of Higher Education*, 89(1), 81–105. https://doi.org/10.1080/00221546.2017.1341754

Kotter, J. P. (1996). *Leading change*. Harvard Business School Press.

McClaskey, K. (2021a). *Stages of personalized learning environments, version 5*. Make learning personal. http://kathleenmcclaskey.com/stages-of-personalized-learning-enviroments/

McClaskey, K. (2021b). *Make learning personal for every learner!* Make learning personal. http://kathleenmcclaskey.com/services/

Passow, H. A. (1986). Curriculum for the gifted and talented at the secondary level. *Gifted Child Quarterly*, 30(4), 186–191. https://doi.org/10.1177/001698628603000409

Pollack, J., & Pollack R. (2015). Using Kotter's eight stage process to manage an organisational change program: Presentation and practice. *Systemic Practice and Action Research*, 28, 51–66. https://doi.org/10.1007/s11213-014-9317-0

Printed in the United States
by Baker & Taylor Publisher Services